The Mythopoeic Code
of Tolkien

CRITICAL EXPLORATIONS IN SCIENCE FICTION AND FANTASY
(a series edited by Donald E. Palumbo and C.W. Sullivan III)
Earlier Works: www.mcfarlandpub.com

55 *Gender and the Quest in British Science Fiction Television: An Analysis of* Doctor Who, Blake's 7, Red Dwarf *and* Torchwood (Tom Powers, 2016)

56 *Saving the World Through Science Fiction: James Gunn, Writer, Teacher and Scholar* (Michael R. Page, 2017)

57 *Wells Meets Deleuze: The Scientific Romances Reconsidered* (Michael Starr, 2017)

58 *Science Fiction and Futurism: Their Terms and Ideas* (Ace G. Pilkington, 2017)

59 *Science Fiction in Classic Rock: Musical Explorations of Space, Technology and the Imagination, 1967–1982* (Robert McParland, 2017)

60 *Patricia A. McKillip and the Art of Fantasy World-Building* (Audrey Isabel Taylor, 2017)

61 *The Fabulous Journeys of Alice and Pinocchio: Exploring Their Parallel Worlds* (Laura Tosi with Peter Hunt, 2018)

62 *A* Dune *Companion: Characters, Places and Terms in Frank Herbert's Original Six Novels* (Donald E. Palumbo, 2018)

63 *Fantasy Literature and Christianity: A Study of the Mistborn, Coldfire, Fionavar Tapestry and Chronicles of Thomas Covenant Series* (Weronika Łaszkiewicz, 2018)

64 *The British Comic Invasion: Alan Moore, Warren Ellis, Grant Morrison and the Evolution of the American Style* (Jochen Ecke, 2019)

65 *The Archive Incarnate: The Embodiment and Transmission of Knowledge in Science Fiction* (Joseph Hurtgen, 2018)

66 *Women's Space: Essays on Female Characters in the 21st Century Science Fiction Western* (ed. Melanie A. Marotta, 2019)

67 *"Hailing frequencies open": Communication in* Star Trek: The Next Generation (Thomas D. Parham III, 2019)

68 *The Global Vampire: Essays on the Undead in Popular Culture Around the World* (ed. Cait Coker, 2019)

69 *Philip K. Dick: Essays of the Here and Now* (ed. David Sandner, 2019)

70 *Michael Bishop and the Persistence of Wonder: A Critical Study of the Writings* (Joe Sanders, 2020)

71 *Caitlín R. Kiernan: A Critical Study of Her Dark Fiction* (James Goho, 2020)

72 *In* Frankenstein's *Wake: Mary Shelley, Morality and Science Fiction* (Alison Bedford, 2020)

73 *The Fortean Influence on Science Fiction: Charles Fort and the Evolution of the Genre* (Tanner F. Boyle, 2020)

74 *Arab and Muslim Science Fiction* (Hosan Elzembely and Emad El-Din Aysha, 2020)

75 *The Mythopoeic Code of Tolkien: A Christian Platonic Reading of the Legendarium* (Jyrki Korpua, 2021)

76 *The Truth of Monsters: Coming of Age with Fantastic Media* (Ildikó Limpár, 2021)

The Mythopoeic Code of Tolkien
A Christian Platonic Reading of the Legendarium

JYRKI KORPUA

CRITICAL EXPLORATIONS IN
SCIENCE FICTION AND FANTASY, 75
Series Editors Donald E. Palumbo *and* C.W. Sullivan III

McFarland & Company, Inc., Publishers
Jefferson, North Carolina

This book has undergone peer review.

ISBN (print) 978-1-4766-7288-5
ISBN (ebook) 978-1-4766-4361-8

LIBRARY OF CONGRESS AND BRITISH LIBRARY
CATALOGUING DATA ARE AVAILABLE

Library of Congress Control Number 2021021179

© 2021 Jyrki Korpua. All rights reserved

No part of this book may be reproduced or transmitted in any form or by any means, electronic or mechanical, including photocopying or recording, or by any information storage and retrieval system, without permission in writing from the publisher.

Front cover image © Cesare Andrea Ferrari/Shutterstock

Printed in the United States of America

*McFarland & Company, Inc., Publishers
Box 611, Jefferson, North Carolina 28640
www.mcfarlandpub.com*

Table of Contents

Acknowledgments — vii
Introduction — 1

1. Construction of Mythology — 13
    On Constructive Mythopoeics — 17
    A Fictional Mythology Dedicated to England — 20
    Speculative Historical Epic — 22
    Myth and Genre — 36

2. Creation and Existence — 57
    The Song of Ainur: Christian Platonic Creation Myth in *The Silmarillion* — 57
    Cosmology and the Chain of Being — 78
    Tolkien's Christian Platonic Mythopoeics — 90
    Concerning Sidney and Coleridge — 94
    The Philosophy of Afterlife — 101
    The Inklings and the Power of Words — 109

3. Fall and Struggle — 117
    Long Defeat — 117
    Mythopoeic Allegories — 122
    Mythic and Biblical Heroes — 135
    The Fall: Númenor as an Atlantis Myth — 149
    The Struggle: The One Ring and the Ring Motif — 154

Conclusion — 164
Notes — 167
Works Consulted — 175
Index — 185

Acknowledgments

This book has been in development for great number of years. I finished my first academic essay on Tolkien's fiction in the year 1999, when I had just changed my main subject of studies from general history to comparative literature at the University of Oulu, Finland. At the same university in 2002, I conducted my bachelor's thesis on Plato's Atlantis myth and Tolkien's Númenor, and in 2005, my master's thesis on Christian Platonic and other mythological elements in J.R.R. Tolkien's *The Silmarillion*. Ten years later, in 2015, I finalized my doctoral dissertation, *Constructive Mythopoetics in J.R.R. Tolkien's Legendarium* (Acta Universitatis Ouluensis). After that, I published several articles and book chapters either on Tolkien's fiction or on topics related to Tolkien's fantasy. Of course, even before that, I had been a keen Tolkien reader since the 1980s, when I first borrowed *The Lord of the Rings* from the public library and later got the book as a Christmas present from my parents.

Because of this quite long personal history, portions of this material and reasonings—in a different shape—have appeared in other works and presentation over the years as it was developing. I have presented altogether eleven annual seminar papers on Tolkien's fiction at the Finfar seminar, organized by FINFAR—the Finnish Society for Fantasy and Science Fiction Research—and three presentations on Tolkien at ICFA—the International Conference for the Fantastic in the Arts. Important presentations for this book also include "Christian Platonic Elements in J.R.R. Tolkien's *Legendarium*" at the 2011 3rd Conference on Middle-earth, in Westford, Massachusetts, organized by Jan Howard Finder, and "J.R.R. Tolkien's Mythopoeia and the Familiarisation of Myth" at the 2012 Return

Acknowledgments

of the Ring conference, University of Loughborough, England, organized by the Tolkien Society. The material in all these presentations and all my previous essays or academic works was part of the research for this book, and I am grateful to their audiences for any comments regarding them. As the project is based in part to my doctoral dissertation, I would like to thank the University of Oulu and Acta Universitatis Ouluensis series for permission to republish that material.

For critical assessments, suggestions, comments, and assistance, I would like to thank Klaus Brax, Dimitra Fimi, Edward James, Kuisma Korhonen, Pekka Kuusisto, and all my research colleagues from the Finfar society, especially Irma Hirsjärvi, Aino-Kaisa Koistinen, Kaisa Kortekallio, Urpo Kovala, Cheryl Morgan, Merja Polvinen, Liisa Rantalaiho, Hanna-Riikka Roine, Markku Soikkeli, Sanna Tapionkaski, Jani Ylönen, Tanja Välisalo, and Päivi Väätänen. I also thank emerita and emeritus researchers whose work on Tolkien studies I appreciate a lot, some of which I have had the honor of meeting, including (again) Dimitra Fimi, Verlyn Flieger, Tom Shippey, Elizabeth Whittingham, and Mark J.P. Wolf. Also, thanks to Guy Gavriel Kay for an interesting discussion on *The Silmarillion* at a Florida pool party in 2009.

Many thanks for the reading of the manuscript to language consultants Andrew Pattison and Nikola Pantchev, Layla Milholen at McFarland, and all the anonymous peer reviewers and editors during the last years.

Wholehearted thanks to my parents, Jaakko and Raija Korpua, my brother Jarkko Korpua and his family, and a long list of friends who have always been interested on discussions in literature, movies, television, roleplaying, or just sheer enthusiastic academic banter.

My deepest gratitude goes to my dear wife Tarja Longi-Korpua, who has been the main listener of all my theories and readings, but who also during this long period of writing had to put up with all my nuisances and mannerisms. Sincere acknowledgments go to my children Kreeta-Leena and Kaius, who are both interested in fantastic in its many modes. Thank you all. *Kiitos*.

Introduction

J.R.R. Tolkien (John Ronald Reuel Tolkien, 1892–1973) is the most influential fantasy writer of all time. He is the author of the seminal epic fantasy, *The Lord of the Rings* (three volumes, 1954–55). It is not an exaggeration to say that Tolkien's fiction has changed our imagination. His mythographic[1] fiction touches the reader's deep yearning for feelings of wonder and magic. Many have been interested in Tolkien's stories and the vastness of his sub-created fantasy world Arda—the Middle-earth and its surroundings. The scale of his created world alone separates Tolkien from most other fantasy writers. The amount of background work and the level of details that you can feel when reading Tolkien's fiction mesmerizes us, the readers.

This book is an attempt to unravel how Tolkien constructed his literary works from one specific viewpoint—a Christian Platonic reading of Tolkien's fiction. The main thesis of this book is that there are elements of Platonism, Neoplatonism, and Christian Platonism observable in Tolkien's fiction. In other words: Tolkien used Platonic ideas to create his fantasy world. To understand how he used these elements in his fiction, we must first get an understanding of what Platonism, Neoplatonism and Christian Platonism are. *Platonic*, meaning Plato's own texts and his followers' philosophy, and *Christian Platonic*, meaning a concordant combination of Platonic and later Christian traditions, are used in this study in some cases as separate terms but mainly understood as a solid tradition that regarded Platonic and Neoplatonic philosophy as the best instrument for understanding Christian theology. The term *Neoplatonists*, which is of modern origin, denotes a group of thinkers, beginning (usually) with Plotinus, who, as James A. Coulter (1976: 1) states, did not

Introduction

consider themselves "*Neo*platonists," but Platonists "pure and simple, faithful to the fundamental doctrines of their Master." For centuries in Western culture, these ideologies were inseparable since for centuries Platonic thinkers were also Christians and they were influenced by Christian theology.

The formation of Neoplatonism, the so-called New Platonism, is usually credited to the Hellenistic philosopher Plotinus, who lived in Roman Egypt in the 3rd century CE and based his metaphysical writings mainly on the teachings of Plato. But in a way, Neoplatonism developed right after Plato died in Athens circa 347 BCE, since everyone who studied Plato's writings afterward, in fact, created a new interpretation of Plato's thoughts. For these reasons, Platonism, Neoplatonism and later Christian Platonism have been interpreted in many ways by scholars throughout the Western history of philosophy. When concerning a Christian Platonic reading of Tolkien's fiction, Plotinus' Neoplatonism is quite interesting. Plotinus' interpretation of Plato's philosophy is essentially a type of idealistic monism where God, the ultimate being of infinite consciousness, is "The One." As Plotinus writes in *The Enneads* (I 1): "The One is all; it is universal power, of infinite extent and infinite in potency, a god to great that all his parts are infinite." Similarly, in Tolkien's fantasy world, God is represented by Eru, The One, and that is also a notion that most Christian Platonic philosophers share, for example the ancient thinkers Augustine of Hippo and Origen of Alexandria, or Marsilio Ficino in the Renaissance period.

The influence of Platonic and Christian Platonic elements in Tolkien's fiction is understandable if we ponder the development of Tolkien's thought and theory. First, Plato was the central Greek philosopher for early Christian thinkers. Roman Catholic theology followed, for the most part, the theology of early Church Fathers, most of all Augustine, who was greatly influenced by Plato's philosophy and later Neoplatonic logic and reasoning of Plotinus. Secondly, Tolkien in his turn, was a devout Roman Catholic who diligently followed Catholic beliefs and practices, where Christianity was influenced by central elements of

Introduction

Platonism and this transformed Christian theology. Plato's theory of forms assimilates the Christian understanding of Heaven as a "perfect place," of which the physical level of existence is a mere imitation, or a reflection. Thus, the cosmology in Christian Platonism appears in two levels: as an *ideal*, spiritual plane of existence, and as a *real*, physical plane.

By reading Tolkien's fiction as a depiction of "ideal and real," from the vision of creation to the process of realization, this work illuminates a part of Tolkien's aesthetics and mythology that previous studies have unnecessarily overlooked. The purpose is to create a reading of Tolkien's fiction—his myths and legends—that will unveil the magic Tolkien used to build his fantasy. As such, the book is aimed toward an audience generally interested in Tolkien's fiction and not solely other Tolkien scholars and literary researchers. Although some of the concepts used here, such as Christian Platonism, might seem unfamiliar concepts for some readers, the following sections will explain these more thoroughly.

Tolkien's texts are undoubtedly prime examples of mythopoeic vision in literary history. Mythopoeic in this case meaning creative myth-making, or "productive of myth" (Nagy 2003: 239). Tolkien used the term "mythopoeia" in his poem of the same name ("Mythopoeia" 1931), and the term has later been applied to various works of fantasy fiction whose authors have integrated mythological themes and archetypes. As this study implies a Platonic and Christian Platonic reading to Tolkien's text, it is interesting that "Mythopoeia" is quite Platonic in its essential tone (see also Weinreich 2008).

Tolkien was a writer and a scholar, a professor of language and literature at Oxford University and co-founder of the literary association "The Inklings," of which, for example, fantasy writers C.S. Lewis and Charles Williams were also members. Tolkien is in many ways the father of modern fantasy, and his *The Lord of the Rings* is the most influential work in the genre. *The Oxford Companion to English Literature* (2000: 352) calls Tolkien "the greatest influence within the fantasy genre." His position in the genre of fantasy literature is central. As Mark J.P. Wolf (2012: 5) discusses, Tolkien's fiction

Introduction

has a strong influence over "fantasy novels, fantasy art, role-playing games, and video games of the adventure genre, and collectively an effect on the culture in general." Also, the so-called "post–Tolkien fantasy" has relied heavily on the Tolkienisque kind of myth-making (see Attebery 2014).

The collection of Tolkien's fantasy texts is exceptional; it shows a coherence on levels of language, myth, and inter- and intratextual[2] background, even throughout the various texts and fragments of his fiction. From the cosmogonical creation myth of the posthumously published *The Silmarillion*, to the fairy-story lightness of *The Hobbit*, or the quest fantasy of *The Lord of the Rings*, Tolkien's fiction has its beginnings in the mythopoeic logics of his theory of creative writing or myth-making that is—as I see it—altogether Platonic. Tolkien is the *sub-creator*; he is creating myths and building his own world.[3] For Tolkien, God is the primary creator, but the author is the sub-creator of his own creation. This is consistent in Tolkien's fantasy fiction, even though while creating his fiction, Tolkien is "pretending" to be a translator of mythical pseudo-historian documents.

In this book, my reading is first oriented by my previous studies on general theology, most importantly on the links between the history of Western philosophy and early Christian theology. Secondly, my literary approach is mostly influenced by both Northrop Frye's constructive theory of literature and Benjamin Harshav's theory of constructive poetics. This study discusses the creative methods of speculative historical epic and the dichotomies of beginning and end, good and evil, mortality and immortality, spiritual and physical and visibility and invisibility, and how these elements are manifesting in Tolkien's mythopoeic vision. The structure of Tolkien's mythopoeics is illuminated through the grand concepts of Creation, Existence, Fall, and Struggle.

The structure of the reading follows the inner timeline of Tolkien's fictive world and mythology. Starting from the creation of the world, the study moves into the long fall and struggle and to the end of the world. The beginning of the book discusses how Tolkien addresses the concept of creation, both in his fantasy fiction and in

Introduction

his theoretical essay "On Fairy-Stories." After that, Tolkien's implementation of his theory of creation is explored, first on the ontological level of his own created fantasy world, and secondly on the poetic level of stories within this fantastic world.

Tolkien's poetics can be seen as functioning coherently as a closed fictional and mythological world, but it could also be seen as a collection of literary works clearly influenced by other literary works, myths, allegories and cultural phenomena, such as, for example, the Bible, the Finnish national epic the *Kalevala*, or old Scandinavian and Germanic mythology. Accordingly, this study illuminates the different levels of Tolkien's mythopoeics. The focus moves from the cosmogonical creation myth, which is altogether Platonic, to the logics of Tolkien's creative work and to examples of Tolkien's mythopoeics, such as his use of the Atlantis myth and the Ring motif, both derived from Plato's dialogues. The focus of the work is on Tolkien's own texts, but the study also illuminates other relevant contextual references. Some of the texts from Tolkien's contemporaries are addressed as such; and some other contextual elements—most importantly the literary tradition—is discussed, as far as is relevant for the study.

The central focus in the beginning of the book is on Tolkien's aesthetics and Tolkien's creative method: the sub-creation. Tolkien, in "On Fairy-Stories" (1939), describes this method in terms of the author's independent invention, inheritance and diffusion, and by the concept of imagination (Tolkien 1983: 121, 138–139). Tolkien's aesthetics are discussed in the continuum of the Platonic tradition, in such creative theories as Sir Philip Sidney's *The Defence of Poesie* (1595)[4] and Samuel Taylor Coleridge's literary theory described in *Biographia Literaria* (1817).

The method used for researching Tolkien's mythopoeics in this study is *constructive*. The focus is on the "big picture" of Tolkien's fiction. As Lubomir Doležel (1998: ix) points out, literature needs a "theory of poiesis which demonstrates the invention of new stories in and through new texts." Therefore, constructive poetics is used here as a theory of poiesis and as a method to organize inter- and

Introduction

intratextual references to Tolkien's texts. This method, introduced by literary theorist Benjamin Harshav (originally Hrushovski), implies that a work of literature invites the reader to evoke or project a network of interrelated constructs. The work of literature is not just a narrative, but a text which projects a fictional world or an internal field of reference, which in this study is referred to as intratextuality, creating meaning through the evocation of frames of references such as scenes, characters, or ideas. In this study, the theory of constructive poetics accommodates the detecting and researching of mythopoeics and Christian Platonic elements in Tolkien's fiction.

Using methods of constructive poetics also necessitates the question of *historical poetics* in Tolkien's fiction, meaning simply the historical significance of Tolkien's fiction and the inner built "historiality" on it. The study discusses Tolkien's creative methods in comparison with the genre of the historical novel, since Tolkien's intratextual references—references between his own texts—create an illusion of fictional older eras. Even Plato in his dialogues used this kind of "stories inside stories" structure; for example, the Atlantis myth in *Timaeus* and the Ring of Gyges in *The Republic*, which are analyzed later in this book. The so-called fictional and factual history, the tools authors of the historical novel use, become interesting in Tolkien's fiction because the mythology's seemingly factual sources are created by the author.[5] The study also explores the archaistic language[6] employed in Tolkien's fiction and the usage of intratextual fictionality in the background stories, myths and legends that form the credibile and coherent basis for Tolkien's texts.

As most readers know, the basis of Tolkien's fantasy fiction is in three separate works: *The Hobbit: Or, There and Back Again* (1937, 2nd revised edition in 1951), *The Lord of the Rings* (1954–55, six books, originally published in three parts), and *The Silmarillion* (1977, posthumously published). *The Hobbit* is a fantasy book and a children's book, essentially about an episodic adventure to win back a treasure stolen by an evil dragon, written in a fairy-tale style and in the spirit of medieval *roman d'aventures*. *The Hobbit* is not so much an epic quest, but a lighter adventure. *The Lord of the Rings* is

Introduction

perhaps the most popular quest-tale, resembling medieval *chansons de geste*, stories about heroic deeds, but it is also central epic fantasy of the 20th century.[7] Compared to *The Hobbit*, *The Lord of the Rings* is more a quest, than an adventure. The grand narrative of *The Lord of the Rings* addresses themes such as world domination, apocalyptic visions, the battle between Good and Evil (and the poor individuals caught up in this battle), heroism, and both success and failure. In *The Lord of the Rings*, the basic task and quest is to destroy the evil "One Ring," which in the wrong hands could bring about the destruction of all Middle-earth.

Thirdly, the posthumously published *The Silmarillion* is a collection of Tolkien's works edited by his son Christopher Tolkien (1924–2020). The mythologically oriented stories of *The Silmarillion* form the backbone of the cosmogony and cosmology in Tolkien's fiction. Of course, we must acknowledge the problematic status of *The Silmarillion*. The book was published four years after J.R.R. Tolkien died, and is structurally fragmentary when compared to books published in Tolkien's lifetime. For some readers, it is the most important book, describing Tolkien's mythology which illuminates the grand scale of his fantasy fiction. For other readers, it is mostly unreadable, unattractive and should not have been published in its unfinalized form. Still, to study Tolkien's mythopoeic fantasy fiction in totality, *The Silmarillion* and other posthumous works must be taken into consideration. Mark J.P. Wolf also discusses the question of canonicity regarding this kind of posthumous work. Concerning *The Silmarillion*, Wolf comments (2012: 274) that because Tolkien attempted to have a version of *The Silmarillion* published during his lifetime, he must have considered much of it complete and ready to go.

This book attempts to create a reading of Tolkien's fiction which shows how Tolkien used mythopoeics, i.e., invented and used myths, to create a fictional literary history, and how Christian Platonic aesthetics are central to understanding Tolkien's methods and the overarching storyline. Or, to use Northrop Frye's words, how Tolkien "displaced" myths.[8] In this study this is seen as constructive myth-making. The word "constructive" is used to refer to the artistic

Introduction

purpose behind the creation of Tolkien's highly original and complex literary works, and while it is of course usually used in different contexts,[9] the major philosophical starting point is that Tolkien is deliberately creating—constructing—a new "mythology": a new fictional literary collection of legends.

As central elements of Tolkien's poetics, the study illuminates the Christian Platonic concepts of Creation and Existence and Fall and Struggle. These elements of Tolkien's fiction are read through dichotomies of Beginning/End, Good/Evil, Mortality/Immortality, Physical/Spiritual, and Visibility/Invisibility. Along with these dichotomies and juxtapositions, selected central fantastic elements and functions are discussed. These textual elements include the Song of Ainur as a method of Creation within the fantasy world, the Atlantis-like island kingdom of Númenor as a mythopoeic example of fall from greatness, and The Great Ring as a centrally functioning magical artifact in *The Lord of the Rings*.

Tolkien's mythopoeic fantasy fiction is a vast, diverse, and complex creative work. Tolkien's objective was to create a fictional literary history using mythopoeic aesthetics and re-imagining of myths. In a way, he succeeded in this with *The Hobbit* and *The Lord of the Rings*, and his vision was finished posthumously with *The Silmarillion* and *The History of Middle-earth*-series (1983–96). Tolkien's fantasy fiction is a crucial example of a 20th-century transformation of pre-modern myths and modern text. Similarly, the mythopoeics of Tolkien's fiction could be seen as a modernization of pre-modern myths.

Tolkien creates a fictional mythology dedicated to England, England being—of course—a real, actual place compared to the "unreal," fictional world of Middle-earth. Tolkien invents a coherent "other" world Arda, the Middle-earth and its surroundings, for readers in a real existing plane. As a creator of a literary fantasy world built on myths, Tolkien is a mythographer. Tolkien in this role as a mythographer of the English language has of course been noted by many scholars, for example researchers in the 1960s and '70s, such as Northrop Frye and Lin Carter, or scholars in late–20th-century

Introduction

or 21st-century studies. For example, Verlyn Flieger (2005a: ix) sees Tolkien as part of a long tradition of mythmakers in English literature, such as Edmund Spenser, John Milton, and William Blake. In the collection *Tolkien's Modern Middle Ages*, Tolkien is seen as a continuum of the Victorian tradition of literary medievalists, and of a long list of earlier writers and composers such as James Macpherson, Mary Shelley, Alfred Lord Tennyson, Walter Scott, William Morris and the pre–Raphaelites, and Richard Wagner (Chance & Siewers 2005: 2–3). Tom Shippey sees Tolkien's fiction in comparison with, for example, such classical works of the English language as *Beowulf*, *Pearl*, and *Sir Gawain and the Green Knight* (Shippey 2003: 5).

On the one hand, Frye finds traditional similarities between Tolkien and the Victorian fantasy of William Morris, Lewis Carroll and George MacDonald (Frye 1976: 4, 42–43), but on the other hand, also finds similarities on the level of language (archaistic and "invented") between Tolkien and the historical novels of Walter Scott and modernist novels of James Joyce (Frye 1976: 110). Flieger, too, sees similarities between Tolkien's and Joyce's mythmaking, although they are using myths in a different mode (Flieger 2005a: ix–x). This perhaps unsuspected resemblance between Tolkien and classical modernism on the level of mythopoeics is also seen by Jed Esty, who compares Tolkien with the canonical writer T.S. Eliot, a writer who also used myths in his writings (Esty 2004: 121–123). In his study, Esty writes that 20th century modern English literature is concentrated on the "antipositivist and antihumanist philosophical turn" (2004: 3) flowing from the central authorities and critics of modern society: Marx, Nietzsche, Darwin, and Freud. Of course, all these authorities and events could have influenced Tolkien's writings. Tolkien himself wrote in the foreword to the second edition of *The Lord of the Rings* that "[an] author cannot of course remain wholly unaffected by his experience, but the ways in which a story-germ uses the soil of experience are extremely complex" (Tolkien 1995: xvii).

Although no one can be fully untouched by the surrounding era, in a way Tolkien's texts turn against the so-called modern directions of literature. Tolkien indeed is not only looking to the past, but also

Introduction

to the "Neo-Paganist future." In his article about Tolkien's connections with the *Beowulf* poet, Tom Shippey (2007: 8) suggests that "Tolkien might not be looking back into the pit of heathenism, but in 1936 [the publication date of Tolkien's essay 'Beowulf: The Monster and the Critics'] he could well be looking forward into it." Shippey sees that, at this point, Tolkien correctly foresaw the future, since England in the 21st century is in many ways a "post–Christian" country (Shippey 2007: 8). Shippey's point is valid since Tolkien's texts are concerned with both the problems of modernization and secularization. In a way, the criticism of modernization and secularization is the major starting point of Tolkien's mythopoeics. He wanted to look back to "our" mythical past.

As a 20th-century English writer, Tolkien turned his attention and affection toward a much older literary history and tried to integrate pre-modern myths and legends for the contemporary audience. Tolkien's texts reflect myths and stories from many different periods of history, for example ancient, medieval and renaissance literature, but familiarize these materials by using "modern" literary tools, such as modern English, and by choosing approachable protagonists: the hobbits in *The Hobbit* and *The Lord of the Rings*—characters to whom apparently the reader can relate.[10] Tolkien's texts could be seen as functioning in pre-modern, but also modern, or, as some researchers suggest, even postmodern modes of fiction. This postmodernism is clearly in reference to a periodization of "post," or after, modern, rather than what is usually addressed as the genre of postmodernism.

Researchers Jane Chance and Alfred Siewers (2005: 4) see that Tolkien's fantastic works create a system of mythology for Middle-earth that can be recognized as modernist but also as "a critique through medievalism of modern that again is ultimately postmodernist." In *Tolkien's Modern Middle Ages*, both Verlyn Flieger (2005b: 25) and Gergely Nagy (2005: 29–30), in their separate articles, see clear postmodernistic tones in Tolkien's fiction, although Flieger notes that Tolkien's "postmodernism," e.g., stories inside stories and metatextual references in *The Lord of the Rings*, are technically "not so innovative," since they were used by the *Beowulf* 1,200

Introduction

years ago (Flieger 2005b: 25).[11] Of course, for later modern and postmodern fiction, Tolkien's texts have been influential, for example, as lodestars of high fantasy and modern fantasy. *The Lord of the Rings*, one of the most popular books in history with more than 150 million copies sold (Moore 2019), can be seen not only as a major genre-defining work, but also as a work that evades the canonized genre definitions. It can be seen as a fantasy novel, for some as fitting within the children's or young adult's genre, or alternatively, as a major English mythological work and a re-imagining of pre-modern (fictional) stories and legends.

As we all know, Tolkien's literary works have been widely studied. A recapitulative article "Scholarly Studies of J.R.R. Tolkien and His Works (in English)" (2000), written by Michael D.C. Drout, Hilary Wynne and Melissa Higgins, and the *Tolkien Encyclopedia: Scholarship and Critical Assessment* (2006), edited by Drout, indicate hundreds of individual studies on Tolkien's fiction written in English. The past four decades have seen a flood of well-written contributions to the field of study which is nowadays called either Tolkien studies or Tolkien scholarship. The mythological background of Tolkien's fiction has been studied on many occasions, such as by Tom Shippey in his *The Road to Middle-earth: How J.R.R. Tolkien Created a New Mythology* (1982) and *J.R.R. Tolkien: Author of the Century* (2000); and Verlyn Flieger in her *Splintered Light: Logos and Language in Tolkien's World* (1983), *A Question of Time: J.R.R. Tolkien's Road to Faerie* (1988), and *Interrupted Music: The Making of Tolkien's Mythology* (2005).

I therefore acknowledge the viral and versatile continuum of Tolkien studies. My study contributes by addressing the totality of Tolkien's mythopoeics in a new way, from a Christian Platonic point of view. This book introduces original ideas and concepts including, the idea of three planes of existence in Tolkien's fantasy world: ideal world/upper spiritual level; the changeable world/lower spiritual level; and the "interspace," associated with the invisible and shadows, and their elucidation via Platonic philosophy. The work also addresses the importance of Owen Barfield's Neoplatonism

Introduction

for Tolkien's thought, e.g., Barfield as an intermediary between Coleridge and Tolkien in terms of theorizing the imaginary and fantastic. This study provides a new reading of the blurred lines between allegory, symbol, and myth in Tolkien's fiction, using Platonic thought as the catalyst. It explores the notion of Tolkien's mythopoeics as an effective combination of intertextual and intratextual elements, and finally, it explains and analyzes several Platonic motifs and ideas in Tolkien's fiction that shed new light on scenes, plotlines, and characters (Fimi 2015).[12]

The primary materials examined here include Tolkien's *The Hobbit: Or, There and Back Again*, *The Lord of the Rings*, *The Silmarillion* and *The History of Middle-earth*, the last being a twelve-volume series that J.R.R. Tolkien's son Christopher edited from his father's previously unpublished materials, which Mark J.P. Wolf sees "as perhaps the most extensive 'Making of' documentation in literature" (Wolf 2012: 224).

1

Construction of Mythology

> *In the beginning Eru, the One, who in the Elvish tongue is named Ilúvatar, made the Ainur of his thought; and they made a great Music before him. In this Music the World was begun; for Ilúvatar made visible the song of the Ainur, and they beheld it as a light in the darkness.*—Tolkien 1999: 15

The great inner story of Tolkien's fantasy world begins with music—the Music of the Ainur—played by the Ainur,[13] the divine spirits, made from the creator's thoughts, and executing (at first, it seems) the creator's exact wishes. The timeline of Tolkien's fantasy world reaches from the beginning of his "cosmos" to its destruction—from start to finish, although this is not exactly evident in his central fictional works. The main popular works, *The Hobbit* and *The Lord of the Rings*, portray only a tiny temporal segment of Tolkien's fantasy fiction. As Gergely Nagy notes, on the story level *The Lord of the Rings* spans a few years, but *The Silmarillion* thousands (Nagy 2003: 243), and then again, *The Silmarillion* is only a small part of the wider timeline.

The following chart shows that the timeline of Tolkien's world is linear and, in a way Biblical, and follows the logics of Christian Platonic cosmology typical of the Roman Catholic worldview. It begins with the creation of the world and ends with its destruction, and hints at an apocalyptic future where everything will be healed and once again unmarred. The image reflects my research logic in this study: Starting from the creation of the world and chronologically moving on to the long fall and struggle.

In my reading of Tolkien's fiction, the structure follows the given order: (1) Creation; (2) Building the World; (3) The Fall; (4) The

The Mythopoeic Code of Tolkien

Struggle; and (5) The End. Thus, it is a coherent cosmological account that starts with the creation of the world and ends with an apocalyptic vision of the end of the world. In the timeline, at first, the active inhabitants of the fictional world are immortal beings: the creator god Eru Ilúvatar and his offspring, the Ainur.

Chart 1: The Timeline of Tolkien's Fantasy World

Era	Theme	Active Inhabitants	Source (in Tolkien's fiction)
Creation	"Arda Unmarred" and The Song of Ainur	Eru Ilúvatar and Ainur (Valar/Maiar)	"Ainulindalë"
Building the World	The first great cosmological battles between Good and Evil	Ainur (Valar/Maiar)	"Valaquenta" and the beginning of "Quenta Silmarillion"
The Fall	"Arda Marred"	Ainur (Valar/Maiar) Elves	"Quenta Silmarillion," "Akallabêth"
The Struggle	"Arda Marred" and "The Long Defeat"	Elves Men (Hobbits)	*The Lord of the Rings* (*The Hobbit*)
The End	The Second Music and "Arda Healed"	All	*The History of Middle-earth* (selected parts)

As the timeline progresses, the activity of these immortal beings diminishes. A similar structure can be seen in the Judeo-Christian Bible, where in the Old Testament (as Christians call it), God is active and Creation is described in detail. In the Christian New Testament, God's activity is seen through the incarnation of Christ and through the results of Christ's preaching, doings, and most importantly for the context of Christian theology, Christ's death and resurrection. Similarly, in Tolkien's fantasy world, the immortal but created Elves[14] first take an active role in *The Silmarillion*, but in the later timespan of *The Hobbit* and *The Lord of the Rings*, the activity moves from the race of Elves to the race of Men (and to the Hobbits). After the storyline of *The Lord of the Rings* comes the Time of Men, which is in a

1. Construction of Mythology

way a reference to the more realistic ages that follow the cosmological battle between Sauron and the Free Peoples of Middle-earth. In the end of this cosmological account, Tolkien describes that Melkor will once again find his way back to Arda, the created world, and the Great End will begin (Tolkien 2002a: 282). There shall be "the Last Battle" (Tolkien 2002e: 76), after which all corruption and evil deeds will be addressed and Arda will be healed (Tolkien 2002c: 333).[15]

The timeline, especially its beginning and ending, is written in the style of older mythological works, such as the *Iliad* and the *Kalevala*. As a writer Tolkien always had "a flair for verse," as John Hunter put it (2005: 67), and there is strong evidence in the fragments of *The History of Middle-earth*, and in works published in Tolkien's lifetime, that Tolkien appreciated reading and writing poems, verse, and lyrical works. In Tolkien's fiction, there is a vast quantity of both songs and poems: a variety of poems and songs of the Hobbits, Elves, and the Riders of Rohan, and in *The Silmarillion*, the allusions to poems and songs of Valar, Elves, and Men.[16]

Tolkien himself, as a medievalist and a professor of medieval literature, edited and published Old and Middle English poems, and wrote many individual works on the subject. Tolkien's fantasy fiction indeed began in verse form. In 1914, as a student at Oxford, Tolkien wrote "The Voyage of Eärendel," a fairy-tale poem, the beginning of Tolkien's fictional mythology (Flieger 2003a: 26). The same original story, re-written in prose later, operates as one of the major parts of *The Silmarillion* as well.

The long, almost 60-year span of the writing of Tolkien's fantasy began with a poem, and the fictional creation of Tolkien's fantasy world begins with music. Bradford Lee Eden (2003: 183) discusses that as a medievalist, Tolkien understood the importance of music as a material for creation in mythologies. Eden points out that Boethius' treatise *De instituione musica* divides music into three types in order of priority and importance: "the music of the universe, human music (vocal), and instrumental music" (Eden 2003: 184). In Tolkien's world, Ainur (with Eru) created the celestial music, the music of the universe, and I would argue that perhaps poetical texts, too, could be seen as a sort of "vocal music," since in the pre-modern period poems were sang and recited. For Tolkien, writing was a form of creating—even on the universal and religious scale. In his poem "Mythopoeia," Tolkien writes "we make still by the law in which we're made" (Tolkien 1988: 87).

Tolkien wanted to create legends ranging from the large and cosmogonic, to the level of romantic fairy-story, and that his basic passion was for myths and heroic legend on the brink of fairy-tale and history (Tolkien 1999: x–xi). His vision is evident, since Tolkien's fiction functions on the level of myth, heroic legend, fictional "historicism," and fairy-tale. In Northrop Frye's theory of fictional modes, which he introduces in his study *Anatomy of Criticism*, Frye claims that fictions may be classified into five different categories based on the hero's "power of action": (1) myth; (2) romance, legend or folktale; (3) high mimetic mode of most epic and tragedy; (4) low mimetic mode of most comedy and realistic fiction; and (5) ironic mode (Frye 1967: 33–34).[17] Tolkien's fantasy writing functions separately in all of these fictional modes but also, on occasion, combines them. Tolkien's center works function in different genres and modes. *The Hobbit: Or, There and Back Again* is written on the simplest form of fairy-story, or a story for children or younger audiences. *The Hobbit*'s literary tone is a tone of romantic fairy-story, and it is still mainly considered to be a children's book. Then again, Tolkien's poetics and some aspects of Tolkien's mythical high fantasy overlap with *The Hobbit*: some scenes, elements and references link it to the other major texts of his fiction.

The Hobbit, originally a separate work compared to the other writings concerning Middle-earth, is a troublesome text for many scholars,[18] as *The Hobbit* has a different tone compared to both the fantasy epic *The Lord of the Rings* and the more biblical textuality of *The Silmarillion*. At the time of its publishing, *The Hobbit* was a comparable success as a children's story, but Tolkien's higher fame as the "Godfather of Fantasy" was secured with the publication of *The Lord of the Rings*.[19] When Tolkien started to write *The Lord of the Rings*, he began it at as a sequel to *The Hobbit*, at his publisher's wishes.

1. Construction of Mythology

Tolkien's tone in the beginning of *The Lord of the Rings* is quite similar to the tone in *The Hobbit*, but changes as the story grows and moves toward the literary tone of *The Silmarillion* (Carpenter 1977: 226).

It is now possible to see that Tolkien ranged his fiction from the mimetically "lower" fairy-story of *The Hobbit* to the higher myth of *The Lord of the Rings*, and still higher to the cosmogonical and cosmological mythology of *The Silmarillion*, where myth and fictional history are vital. *The Silmarillion* begins with a Platonic cosmogonical myth, the Music of the Ainur, and slowly moves on to the History of Elves. Tolkien has declared that, in his own vision, the "legendarium[20] ends with a vision of the end of the world..." (1999: xvii). Tolkien thought that the timeline of the World would be chronological and complete: ranging from the cosmogonical beginning to an inevitable end.

Tolkien's aesthetic purpose was to create a mythology that he could dedicate to England, because there was, as Tolkien put it, Greek, Germanic, Scandinavian and Finnish mythology, but nothing English (Tolkien 1999: x–xi). Verlyn Flieger discussed that Tolkien meant that "it would embody what he saw as the English (not British) heritage, and would incorporate into a fictive legendarium elements from myth and history that fostered a sense of specifically English identity, as *Kalevala* had done for the Finns" (Flieger 2004: 44). As Flieger and Whittingham have noted, Tolkien's generation was familiar with the mythologies of Greece and Rome, but Tolkien's passion for myth was not directed by the so-called "Southern myth," but rather by the so-called "Northern Myth" of German, Scandinavian and Finnish origins (Flieger 2005a: 27–37, Whittingham 2008: 37–38). Tolkien's re-imagining and creation of myths, therefore, is a complex conception that functions, knowingly or unknowingly, in cooperation with these references.

On Constructive Mythopoeics

Tolkien (1981: 147) wrote in his letter to Milton Waldman in 1951 that the tales in *The Silmarillion* are "'new,' and not directly deriving from other myths and legends, but they must inevitably contain a large measure of ancient wide-spread motives and elements." Although Tolkien's tales are "new," they are fictively constructed myths, and this construction is affected by re-imagining older myths and legends, and by forming new ones and creating new mythographic connections. This construction is both an aesthetic measure—an attempt to make the text coherent and stable—but also a structural tactic. Tolkien's use of mythopoeics is creative and the formed fantasy fiction is at the same time both extremely complex but also comprehensible for the reader. How is this double action possible?

Tolkien's mythopoeic style is a creative method which adroitly uses literary mediums such as inter- and intratextuality as tools of world-making. Inter- and intratextual references create plausibility, coherence, and a type of realism in the text, and function as familiar elements. The reader believes in the world because it is, in many ways, coherent and almost believable. Familiar elements within the text make them readable for contemporary audiences and create an illusion of secondary creation. Familiar elements in the fiction are, for example, the use of English language, the use of Hobbits as protagonists, or the use of familiar flora and fauna: plants and animals.

Tolkien's mythopoeics is formed on inter- and intratextual references and diverse mythic elements. Here, the terms of inter- and intratextuality are used, which of course can be understood semantically in different ways. Benjamin Harshav's theory of constructive poetics is used here to organize the inter- and intratextual materials of Tolkien's fantasy fiction, although this study is not an attempt to simply create a theoretically focused reading. Harshav introduced the theory of constructive poetics, collected in *Explorations in Poetics* (2007), to create a systematic theory of literature—or a "grammar" of literature—that did not necessitate heavy terminology or a bibliography. His approach does not assume that the work of literature is a text with fixed structures and meaning, but a text that invites the reader to project a network of interrelated constructs. In Harshav's view, a work of literature is not just a narrative, as studies

1. Construction of Mythology

in narratology claim, but something which projects a fictional world or internal field of reference. Harshav sees that texts convey meaning through the evocation of "frames of reference." Language in literature is bi-directional: it relates the internal to the external and vice versa.

The fictional world in J.R.R. Tolkien's *The Lord of the Rings* or *The Silmarillion* could form its own intratextual "field of reference" composed of many small elements, such as, for example, the character of Frodo Baggins, the fictional time of the Third Age of Middle-earth, the "long expected party" at the beginning or *The Lord of the Rings*, or the dragons in *The Silmarillion*. Also, intertextual references are any references outside of a given text: for example, the real world in time and space, history, a philosophy, ideologies, views on human nature, or other texts. A literary text may either refer directly to or invoke these references. As Harshav (2007: 23) argues, this category includes not only such obvious external referents as names of places and streets, historical events and dates, or actual historical figures, but also various statements about human nature, society, technology, national character, psychology, religion, etc. In this way, the theory can be applied when analyzing literary texts of any genre: they all have their own referents and types of referencing.

Traditionally, these types of links that bind literary works in succession were examined under the heading *influence*. However, after the late 20th century, this concept has been questioned and displaced by the concept of *intertextuality* (Doležel 1998: 199–200).[21] In my reading, intertextuality and constructive myth-making are mostly inseparable in the Christian Platonic mythopoeics of Tolkien's fiction. Basically, intertextuality can be understood as a textual connection between text A and text B (see Godard 1993: 568–569). These kinds of textual relations have been an object of much research in the last century. Many relations can be interpreted as relevant for the researcher, such as cultural intertextuality or interculturality, and interdiscursivity, which is a focus of thinkers such as Michel Foucault, Michel Pêcheux, and Gérard Genette (see Genette 1979: 81–83).

The Mythopoeic Code of Tolkien

Tolkien himself wrote that he was not interested in influences (or intertextualities) of his text. On the contrary—quoting famous translator Sir George Dasent's words—Tolkien wrote that "[w]e must be satisfied with the soup that is set before us, and not desire to see the bones of the ox out of which it has been boiled" (1983: 7). Still, illuminating the sources, influences and strategies of Tolkien's world-building is interesting. Because of that, the next section will focus on Tolkien's own Christian Platonic reasoning behind fantasy fiction. Why did he create such an ingenious fictitious mythology for a fictive fantasy world? When constructing his fantasy fiction, and giving plausibility to it, Tolkien uses creative methods that are common to the genre of the historical novel (on the concept of the genre, see Lukács 1962). Tolkien creates a plausible fictional background for his work, in much the same way as Umberto Eco does in his novel *The Name of Rose* (*Il nome della rosa*, 1980), or Sir Walter Scott in many of his classical historical novels. The section discusses how Tolkien poses as a translator of historical texts, creating his own mythology and history for his fantasy world, as well as how he creates fictional materials as his source materials for these translations. This all is used in a way that is balanced with Tolkien's Christian Platonic vision of the author as sub-creator of his fictive world.

A Fictional Mythology Dedicated to England

Tolkien indicates the motivation for his mythopoeic vision in a letter to a publisher Milton Waldman, in 1951. Tolkien writes about the myths, the material he has been looking for, and the lack of a truly English Mythology:

> I am not "learned"—in the manners of myth and fairy-story, however, for in such things (as far as known to me) I have always been seeking material, things of certain tone and air, and not simple knowledge. Also—and here I hope I shall not sound absurd—*I was from early days grieved by the poverty of my own beloved country: it had no stories of its own* (bound up with its tongue and soil), not of the quality that I sought, and found (as an ingredient) in legends of other lands. There was Greek, and Celtic, and

1. Construction of Mythology

Romance, Germanic, Scandinavian, and Finnish (which greatly affected me); but *nothing English*, save impoverished chap-book stuff [Tolkien 1981: 144. Emphasis mine].

Tolkien continues his statement by declaring that the Arthurian culturally mixed mythology was not appropriate enough. It had been affected by the Christian religion too much and did not accord with what Tolkien sought, since it was imperfectly naturalized, too fantastical, incoherent, and repetitive, and it also included clear allusions to Christian religion (Tolkien 1981: 144).

Tolkien objected to views that his mythopoeia allegorizes Christian religion or his own faith. He also objected to calling the Arthurian legendarium an "English" mythology, although this objection did not stop Tolkien from writing a long (but unfinished) poem about King Arthur, *The Fall of Arthur*, that was published posthumously in 2013.

Tolkien's aim was to dedicate a mythology to England, his own country. In many Tolkien studies Tolkien's intention is referred to as a desire to create "a mythology for England," as Humphrey Carpenter calls it in Tolkien's authorized biography (1977: 89). Scholars have later pointed out that what Carpenter calls "a mythology for England," however well known, is a misnomer. A more precise phrasing would be then a mythology "dedicated to England."

Tolkien's mythopoeic purpose is to create a coherent mythology. Tolkien uses many different modes of literature to succeed in this purpose. Then again, we might ask what the reasons for making such a fantasy world are, and what motivates the different parts of Tolkien's fiction?

Verlyn Flieger examines the aspects that drove Tolkien and finds: his literary inclinations, his bent toward myth and fairy-tale, and many biographical influences, such as the impact of the World War I on him and his friends (Flieger 2002: 15). Flieger explains that for Tolkien "[m]yths embody the quest of meaning in an otherwise random universe" (Flieger 2002: 11). Tolkien drew from the myths that he knew, particularly from the Scandinavian, German, and Finnish mythologies. Tolkien's aim was "to create a secondary world, a world with its own myths, languages, beings, and history" (Whittingham 2008: 35). This process of creating took a long time to carry out. Tolkien began his work by placing various myths and tales in the context of the framework. Whittingham (2008: 35) writes that Tolkien later "revised, started anew, dropped one framework for another, turned from one interest to another, and his stories grew and evolved." The evolution was long and painful, and the intratextual frame of reference—and the whole textual body of the fiction—is vast, complex and in many major parts unfinished, as can be seen from Tolkien's posthumously published *The History of Middle-earth* series. When Tolkien died in 1973, he had created what Flieger characterizes as "a body of overlapping, competing, endlessly revised, and often incomplete texts, the outcome of more than half a lifetime's worth of invention" (Flieger 2002: 15).

Speculative Historical Epic

> This book is largely concerned with Hobbits, and from its pages a reader may discover much of their character and a little of their history. Further information will also be found in the selection from the Red Book of Westmarch that has already been published, under the title of The Hobbit. The story was derived from the earlier chapters of the Red Book, composed by Bilbo himself, the first Hobbit to become famous in the world at large, and called by him There and Back Again, since they told of his journey into the East and his return: an adventure which later involved all the Hobbits in the great events of that Age that are here related [Tolkien 2008: 25].

The prologue of *The Lord of the Rings* starts with the above quotation in which Tolkien formulates the fictional background of his fiction. Tolkien's fantasy fiction is a work of coherently build mythopoeics. Tolkien is a mythographer of contemporary language for contemporary readers and he is using many literary tools in his pursuit to do so. Tolkien's interesting intratextual references, most importantly the Red Book of Westmarch, create a sense of coherence and fictional historicism for the fantasy world of Middle-earth.

Thus, Tolkien writes that *The Lord of the Rings* is based on the

1. Construction of Mythology

Red Book of Westmarch, which is a non-existing, fictional book. The Red Book of Westmarch is an etymological reference to the so-called Four Ancient Books of Wales—*The Red Book of Hergest*, *The Black Book of Carmarthen*, *The Book of Aneirin*, and *The Book of Taliesin*, plus a fifth, *The White Book of Rhydderch* (Flieger 2005a: 56). *The Red Book of Hergest* and *The White Book of Rhydderch* are also the main manuscript sources of modern English-language translations of Welsh tales, *The Mabinogion* (or *The Mabinogi*).[22]

Shippey (2003: 117) discusses that Tolkien pretended to be a translator, and as time went on, Tolkien "felt obliged to stress the autonomy of Middle-earth—the fact that he was only translating analogously." Tolkien feigned not only to translate textual material, but also create a whole manuscript tradition behind his own text. Tolkien pretended to be a translator, and because of that, all the inconsistencies between for example *The Hobbit* and *The Lord of the Rings* can be explained by different background materials.

In one aspect, Tolkien pretends to be a translator, but his creative method is far more complex than that assumption shows. But this claim of authenticity is an interesting one. Tolkien gives his fantasy fiction a credible background, credible of course only inside his fictional world. These intratextualities create a feeling of a plausible, coherent secondary creation. In *The Encyclopedia of Science Fiction*, John Clute says that Tolkien's "is the most detailed of all invented fictional worlds, perhaps rivaled only by Austin Tappan Wright's *Islandia*" (Clute 1979: 609).

The Lord of the Rings and *The Hobbit* are based on "the Red Book of Westmarch." *The Hobbit*, or "earlier selections from the Red Book," as he calls it, Tolkien describes to be written by Bilbo Baggins (Tolkien 2002f: 29), and the later parts of "the Red Book" were written by Bilbo, Frodo Baggins, Sam Gamgee and their descendants, as declared in the preface of *The Lord of the Rings* in an account of the history of this fictive "Great Book." After the War of the Ring, the book—originally Bilbo Baggins' private diary but now included records by Hobbit members of the Fellowship of the Ring—was preserved by Fairbairns as a valuable historical relic. Tolkien even recollects the history of the actual book, how the original Red Book did not survive the years to come, but many copies of the first volume was crafted and kept safe. Tolkien writes that "[t]he most important copy ... was kept at Great Smials.... It is an exact copy in all details of the Thain's Book in Minas Tirith" (Tolkien 2008: 40). This history of authentic copies and their whereabouts resembles marvelous histories of sacred books, such as the *Bible*.

In a preface of *The Hobbit*, Tolkien also describes his translation work. Tolkien (1975: 11) starts the text with an explanation of why he uses modern English to tell the tale: "This is a story of long ago. At that time the languages and letters were quite different from ours of today. English is used to represent the languages."

Dependence on translations has been of course a fundamental part of Western culture altogether, since the *Bible*, the single most important book for European culture for more than a thousand years, has long been known to most readers in translations, and the same has been also the case with Platonic philosophy. Northrop Frye argues that Christian scholarship has been from the beginning dependent on translation—for example "Septuagint" Greek translation of the Old Testament, and St. Jerome's "Vulgate" Latin translation (Frye 2006: 21). Yet, as Frye points out, "everyone concerned with language is aware of the extent to which reading a translation is settling for the second best" (Frye 2006: 22). For Tolkien as a philologist, the concept of many different versions and translations of his own fiction is easily understandable feature since most medieval texts are known to readers of this day also as different versions and different translations. Tolkien's purpose is to create a credible background for his texts.

The Silmarillion, as Christopher Tolkien describes, "is a compilation, a compendious narrative, made long afterwards from sources of great diversity (poems, and annals, and oral tales) that had survived in agelong tradition; and this conception has indeed its parallel in the actual history of the book, for a great deal of earlier prose and poetry does underlie it, and it is to some extent a compendium in fact and not only in theory" (Tolkien 1999: vi).

1. Construction of Mythology

The same tone of coherent fictional background functions in all parts of Tolkien's fantasy. Tolkien describes that the fictional Elven folklore described in *The Silmarillion* is based on the preserved works of fictional character called Ælfwine of England, whom Tolkien describes as meeting Elves on the island of Tol Eressëa on his sea voyages. Ælfwine translated Elven folklore into Old English, and later Tolkien translated these into modern English:

> The tales are feigned to be translated from the preserved works of Ælfwine of England (c.900 A.D.), called by the Elves Eriol, who being blown west from Ireland eventually came upon the "Straight Road" and found Tol Eressëa the Lonely Isle. He bought back copies and translations of many works. I do not trouble you with the Anglo-Saxon forms [Tolkien 2002e: 5].[23]

Of *The Silmarillion*, according to Tolkien, the first part "Ainulindalë" was originally "written by Rúmil of Túna and was told to Ælfwine in Eressëa (as he records) by Pengoloð the Sage" (Tolkien 2002e: 8). Then again, from *The History of Middle-earth*, the Elven mythic and cosmogonical tale "Of the Beginning of Time and its Reckoning" is "drawn from the work of Quennar Onótimo," who wrote also "Annals of Aman & Beleriand," "Counting of Years" and "Tale of Years" (Tolkien 2002e: 50). Thus, in his speculatively fictive way, Tolkien is only a translator of these earlier Elven tales.

In his fantasy fiction, Tolkien is—most interestingly—also writing a fictional history of languages. For example, Tolkien writes that "according to Elvish historians the Elven-folk, by themselves called the Quendi, and Elven-speech were originally one" (Tolkien 2002f: 29). Later the Elves were scattered and their languages changed. Tolkien writes that, at some point, Ælfwine the Mariner asked Pengoloð the Wise of Gondolin why the tongues of the Elves changed and were sundered (Tolkien 2002f: 395). There is also a straight evolution of languages in Tolkien's fictional historism. This happens with the other languages in Tolkien's cosmology too. Tolkien writes that at the time of the Red Book the language had gone through an evolution, and cites changes in the names for the days of the week have changed (Tolkien 2002f: 12).

The Mythopoeic Code of Tolkien

Tolkien's texts and intratext are interesting on their diversity. The terms text, intertext, intratext, or discourse and dialogue have of course been widely discussed in comparative literature over the last centuries. Mikhail Bakhtin, a Russian philosopher and a literary critic in the 20th century, for example, used the term dialogue in many different, but related senses, some of which are also relevant for the research on Tolkien's fantasy fiction, and speculative fiction in general.

Bakhtin, a theorist of historical poetics, uses the term *heteroglossia*, basically meaning differentiated speech. Bakhtin's heteroglossia takes two general forms: first, "social languages" within a single language; and second, "different languages within the same culture." Within the novel, these forms of heteroglossia appear as, first, characters' dialogue and inner speech; second, the various kinds of "speech genre" which exist within, say, English at a given moment, the languages of a profession, class, literary school, newspaper, and so on; and third, texts which reproduce a culture's various dialects and languages (see Vice 1997: 18–19). This kind of heteroglossia can be seen in Tolkien's fiction as a created literary effect. In the text, the "speech genre" differs depending on the speaker: for example, the Hobbits in *The Lord of the Rings* use a different English language than, for example, the Riders of Rohan.

One perfect example of this kind of heteroglossia in Tolkien's fiction is the Council of Elrond in *The Lord of the Rings*. There, in a thirty-pages-long chapter, the free peoples of Middle-earth get to share their views on the forthcoming War of the Ring, and all the participants seem to be using different discourses, speech genres and even various languages. First, Elrond represents the Elves and opens the dialogue. Then, in the narrative, some passages of dialogue are skipped, but the next important part of the discussion is given to Glóin, who represents the Dwarves, and whose speech is filled with gallant wordings and almost mythical (or even biblical) discourse. For example, when he shouts "Moria! Moria! Wonder of the Northern world! Too deep we delved there, and woke the nameless fear" (Tolkien 2008: 307). After Glóin's speech Elrond once

1. Construction of Mythology

again addresses the audience, but his account of the old days is interrupted by simplistic observations and comments from Frodo and by more appropriate comments from Boromir, a man from the South, who comes from the land of Gondor and speaks in a different way than the Men of the North. After Elrond, Boromir gets his moment to speak and shares his views on the threat of Sauron. Boromir's discourse is proud, nostalgic, and old-fashioned compared to Frodo's discourse. In the discussion, Galdor, representing the Elves of the Havens, and Glorfindel, representing the Elves of Rivendell, get their opportunity to ask questions and Aragorn, Bilbo and Gandalf speak in turn. Gandalf's speech at the end of Council is most interesting. Although Tolkien's text is in many ways a diegetic narrative, Gandalf's speech on some levels ends up being a mimetic representation of earlier events and discussions. Gandalf mimics both Radagast's and Saruman's discourse, he recalls what he read earlier from a scroll that the human hero Isildur wrote thousands of years ago, and even goes on to quote from the inscription of the One Ring, written in the Black Speech of Mordor: "Ash nazg durbatulûk, ash nazg gimbatul, ash nazg thrakatulûk agh burzum-ishi krimpatul" (Tolkien 2008: 322). The quoted language itself, and Gandalf's voice uttering it, is described as "menacing, powerful and harsh as stone" (Tolkien 2008: 323).

This example evidence that there are heteroglossic discourses functioning in Tolkien's fiction. Bakhtin says that once heteroglossia enters the novel, it does not represent simply a neutral series of different languages; these languages are bound to conflict at least with the author's language, with each other, and with any surrounding languages which may not necessarily appear in the text. If they appear in a character's mouth, they become "another's speech in another's language," expressing the author's intentions but in a refracted way. Heteroglossia is thus a double-voiced discourse, as it "serves two speakers at the same time and expresses simultaneously two different intentions: the direct intention of the character who is speaking and the refracted intention of the author" (Vice 1997: 18–19).

Paul de Man has criticized Bakhtin's use of the terms. De Man

The Mythopoeic Code of Tolkien

writes that Bakhtin's vision of the novel clearly belongs to what Northrop Frye calls the low-mimetic modes: it is on the ideological level prosaic, anti-romance, anti-epical, and anti-mythical; its multivoicedness, or heteroglossia, postulates distinct and antagonistic class structures as well as crossing of social barriers (De Man 1989: 108). De Man's approach in turn has been criticized by Mathew Roberts, who sees that the fundamental difference between Bakhtin and de Man lies in their respective conceptions of the self or subject (1989: 115–116). Roberts summarizes that whereas de Man sees the classical trivium of grammar, rhetoric, and logic as riven within by the middle term, and thus disarticulated from "the knowledge of the world in general," Bakhtin sees "the world in general" obtruding on this classical epistemology from without, as an open totality of singular event-contexts, at once concretizing its abstract potentiality and radically denying its abstract unity (Roberts 1989: 134).

It is true that Bakhtin's notion of the novel is quite limited. For Bakhtin, epic is another literary genre which concords negatively with the novel (Vice 1997: 78). Tolkien's "novels," which he himself called heroic romances *(1981: 414)*, are closely connected to epic and high fantasy as genres. In fact, on his preface to *The Children of Húrin*, Christopher Tolkien calls the tale a "heroic-fairy-romance" (Tolkien 2007: 10), a genre definition suitable for many of Tolkien's works. Nevertheless, Bakhtin's terms of heteroglossia can be useful for researching Tolkien's fantasy fiction. In the fictitious tone of Bakhtinian heteroglossia, basically meaning differentiated speech, Tolkien writes in different styles depending on the surrounding milieu. For example, Shippey has pointed out that the language and the names of the Rohirrim in the second part of *The Lord of the Rings* are derived from both old Gothic language and old-English (Shippey 2003:15, 114–116, 122–123). Tolkien's fantasy fiction is protean and mythographic.

Tolkien's mythopoeic work could be compared with the works of such mythographers as Brothers Grimm and Elias Lönnrot or to the fake works made by Thomas Chatterton (1752–1770) and Scottish poet James Macpherson (1736–1796). Thomas Chatterton

1. Construction of Mythology

(1752–1770) was an English poet who wrote his pseudo-medieval poetry under the pseudonym of an imaginary 15th-century monk Thomas Rowley. The most famous of these fake transcripts is posthumously published *History and Antiquities of Bristol* (1789). Then again, Macpherson's collection *Poems of Ossian* (or: *The Works of Ossian*, 1765) is one the greatest works of fictional archaism in the Western literature. Originally, in the 18th century, Macpherson's pseudo–3rd-century poetry, which Macpherson claimed was authentic, was by the critics such as Samuel Johnson declared as forgery.[24]

Malcolm Laing in his 1805 preface for *The Poems of Ossian* writes about the authenticity of poetry, based on ideas originating from his dissertation on Macpherson's poetry. Laing argues that "our modern Ossian has acquired the rank of a classical poet," and that this should not be the case:

> In Ossian there are some hundred similes and poetical images, which must either be original, or derived from imitation. If the poems are authentic, they must be original; and their casual coincidence with other poetry can possess only such a vague resemblance.... If the poems, however, are not authentick, these similes and poetical images must be derived from the classicks, scriptures, and modern poetry, with which the author's mind was previously impregnated, and, however artfully disguised, they may be traced distinctly to their source [Laing 1974: v–vii].

Thus, for Laing, and many other contemporary critics, Macpherson's re-imagining of older eras of literary history and claims of authenticity of the text were unpardonable.

Tolkien's work has not received such a "stigma," because Tolkien of course never declared his texts seriously and critically authentic—and because the sources he is "translating," such as sources from Hobbit or Elven folklore, are all understood as fictional—but then again Tolkien's speculative fiction has often been criticized, especially by literally realistically orientated critics because of its fantastic and unreal content. Even though, as Richard Mathews writes, Tolkien "emphasizes that fantasy is not avoidance of the actual but a means of more complete understanding" (Mathews 2002: 57).

The Mythopoeic Code of Tolkien

Tolkien's fiction is therefore not intentionally escapism, but on the contrary quite the opposite.

As Verlyn Flieger discusses, Tolkien wanted to find a middle ground between these different types of mythographers. He wanted to find his way in between "frauds" such as Chatterton and Macpherson and scholars such as Grimms and Lönnrot. Tolkien wanted to be "neither scientist nor fraud" (Flieger 2004: 50).

Tom Shippey sees that similar results that Tolkien did with his fiction was achieved also by other philologist-creators. Lönnrot's the *Kalevala* is "now viewed with suspicion by scholars, because Lönnrot, like Walter Scott with his *Border Ballads*, did not just collect and transcribe, but he wrote, rewrote and interpolated, so that you cannot tell what is by him and what is 'authentic.'" Shippey remarks that "similar accusations of interference and meddling have been made about the Grimms and their Fairy-Tales" (Shippey 2001: xxxiv).[25]

The differences and similarities of fiction and fact have of course been considerations of literary theory and criticism literally from the beginning of theoretical orientation. In the *Poetics* Aristotle discusses the difference between fact and fiction—of history and poetry. Aristotle sees that "it is not the function of the poet to narrate events that have actually happened, but rather, events such as might occur and have the capability of occurring in accordance with the laws of probability and necessity" (*Poetics* IX 1). Aristotle sees that the works of historians of his time, such as Herodotus, do not differ from poets in their writing of prose or verse. The difference, Aristotle sees, lies in "the fact that the historian narrates events that have actually happened, whereas the poet writes about things as they might possibly occur" (*Poetics* IX 2). In the light of this study, this notion makes the writing of fiction inherently *speculative*—it is a writing of things "that might occur."

For Aristotle, this view makes poetry more philosophical, and hence, more significant than history. For Aristotle, poetry is more concerned with the universal, and history more with the individual (*Poetics* IX 2–3). In the *Republic*, Plato discusses that poetry, in one way, is imitation. In his famous allegory, Plato gives a general

1. Construction of Mythology

definition of this *imitation*. Plato writes that whenever several individuals have a common name, we assume that there is one corresponding idea or form. For instance, Plato explains, there are many beds and tables in the world, but there are only two ideas or forms of such furniture: the idea of a bed, and the idea of a table. The maker of either of them makes a bed or he makes a bed in accordance with the idea, but no artificer makes the idea itself (Plato: *Republic* X 595c–596c).

Plato goes on to explain how an artist, in his example a painter, depicting a table or a bed, is only a second-hand imitator of the workman, who then again, is still an imitator of the original idea of a table or bed, created by God—or the original maker of the idea. For Plato, there are thus three levels of "makers" on this occasion: first the original maker of the idea of table or bed, then secondly, the craftsman or carpenter who made the "physical" table or bed, and then thirdly, the "imitator," the painter who tries to paint a picture of the "physical" table or bed (*Republic* X 596e–598e). For Plato, the second and third maker could be designated "as the imitator of that which the other makes" (*Republic* X 597e).

Plato declares that "the tragic poet is an imitator, he too is thrice removed from the king and from the truth: and so are all other imitators" (*Republic* X 597e). Then again, Plato contradicts this in *Ion*, saying that poets are inspired by divine frenzy, and that they speak the truth, which without the influence of gods they could not otherwise master (*Ion* 553d–554e).

Aristotle also discusses imitation and truth in his *Poetics*, in a possible answer to Plato's claims, seeing the poet as "an imitator" who is "imitating human actions" (IX 4). But then again, Aristotle sees imaginative truth in poetry. Poetry is not history; it is not fact, but fiction, but this does not make it "unreal," but more "philosophical." One might say, more speculative.

Tolkien's mythopoeic fiction is also compared to the work of the makers of historical novel, such as Walter Scott. Richard Maxwell has pointed out that in the 19th-century criticism it was commonplace to declare that Scottish novelist Walter Scott's *Waverley*

The Mythopoeic Code of Tolkien

(1814) introduced historical fiction to the world. Maxwell sees that one famous 20th-century work has helped perpetuate this somewhat dubious idea, and that is Georg Lukács' *The Historical Novel*, a study which begins by denying that there is a meaningful connection between the "so called historical fiction" of the 17th century and the historical novel as it arose just after the fall of Napoleon (Maxwell 2009: 2–3).

This is exactly the point Lukács makes (1962: 15). His Marxist vision of historical novel sees the historical novel arising at the beginning of the 19th century at about the time of Napoleon's collapse. He writes that novels with historical themes are to be found in the seventeenth and eighteenth centuries, too, and, should one feel inclined, one can treat medieval adaptations of classical history or myth as "precursors" of the historical novel, but one will find nothing there that sheds any real light on the phenomenon of the historical novel. Lukács sees that the so-called historical novels of the 17th century are historical only as regard their purely external choice of theme and costume (Lukács 1962: 15).

Lukács points out that writers of the 18th century, such as Swift, Voltaire and Diderot, set their satirical novels in a "never and nowhere," which "nevertheless faithfully reflects the essential characteristics of contemporary England and France" (Lukács 1962: 16). One can say the same on Tolkien too, as it will be discussed later on: Tolkien's *The Lord of the Rings* is set in a secondary world, but for example the milieu of The Shire reflects that of 18th or 19th century pre-industrial England.

Lukács sees that soon after Lessing, in the Sturm and Drang, the problem of the artistic mastery of history already appears as a conscious one. For Lukács, Goethe's *Götz von Berlichingen* not only ushers in a new flowering of historical drama, but it has a direct and powerful influence on the rise of the historical novel in the work of Scott (Lukács 1962: 18). Scott's historical novel could be seen as the direct continuation of the great realistic social novel of the 18th century (Lukács 1962: 30). Lukács sees that Scott both continues and extends Goethe's tendency towards historic (Lukács 1962: 55). This

1. Construction of Mythology

kind of a "hero's journey" is simply a tendency for a character of a historical novel to first live a heroic life, and after that, return to simple everyday life. This tendency, common also in the fairy-stories, is easily seen in Tolkien's *The Hobbit*, and in some extension also in *The Lord of the Rings*.[26]

Maxwell writes about the chronological frame of historical novels, seeing that no matter how detailed a chronology becomes, it will always have empty spaces. There is a difference between attitude towards those blanks by both historians and writers of fiction: a historian might find such empty spaces rather alluring, but a writer would find them as an opportunity for fictional interpolations (Maxwell 2002: 19). One might say that many parts of Tolkien's fantasy fiction unpublished in his time were attempts to fill the empty blanks of Tolkien's chronological framework for *The Lord of the Rings*, and attempts to make the chronological framework of *The Silmarillion* more functional.

Therefore, Tolkien uses some methods that are common in the genre of historical novel in his fantasy. Tolkien creates a plausible fictional background for his work, which creates a sense of familiarization in the fictional universe. This also facilitates credibility for the secondary world: the fictional fantasy world, which the reader accepts as a coherent environment in the texts.

In Tolkien's fiction, this speculative illusion is created with quasi-historiality of the fantasy world that is altogether coherent. The critical focus there is the "illusion" or fantasy created through literature, the difficulty of keeping up the illusion, and the possible breaking of the illusion. Thus, there is a simple juxtaposing of both historical knowledge and the reader's (re)assumption, and the illusion created by a literary work of art.

Many of the classical historical novels can, at the one hand, be seen as functioning at the same time in the context of the contemporary writing period, and on the other hand trying to form the illusion of an older era—the period the text is referring to. Umberto Eco, for example, points out that famous adventurous historical novel *The Three Musketeers* (*Les Trois Mousquetaires*, 1844) by Alexandre

The Mythopoeic Code of Tolkien

Dumas, père, is basically a classist novel. Its background is in classical and medieval literature, but it deals with characters familiar to us. Eco calls them "superuomo di massa," supermen of the masses. Eco sees that Athos equals mythical Greek hero Achilleus, Porthos equals hero Ajax, and Aramis equals biblical character of Joseph (see Eco 1978). As characters, they are like "displaced" mythical heroes.

When discussing his own best-selling historical novel, *The Name of the Rose*, Umberto Eco differentiates three models of historical novels. (1) In the first, the past is a fairy-story-like construction, a scenery where there appears to be a free zone for imagination to work. The fictional world is quite distant from our known (realistic) world. Clearly, this model can be seen at work in Tolkien's fiction as well. (2) In the second, there is an illusion of the past, which is populated with familiar historical characters, but the main part of the fiction is on adventure. The psychology of the main characters has little to do with a real era, which the novel tries to cover. This model is not employed in Tolkien's fiction. Although Tolkien is building "an illusion of the past," it is only realistic inside his created world. (3) And thirdly, there is the so-called "real historical novel," as Eco describes it, where the characters and elements of plot are fictional, but from these elements a truthful image of past and historical era is drawn, even more real than in theoretical history books. Eco (1985: 74–75) writes that with the *Name of Rose* in this sense, he wanted to write a historical novel. Tolkien's fiction of course cannot have this kind of historicity, since the image of past and historical era that it is portraying, is fantastic. It is the same kind of magical fantastical past that Plato uses in his dialogues. For example, when in Plato's *Timaeus*, Critias, one of the characters, tells a story of Atlantis that Solon heard in Egypt "long-ago." This fantastic, mythical story of Atlantis is later continued in another dialogue, *Critias*.

In Tolkien's fantasy, the main tool that creates the authenticity and feeling of "older era" is the archaistic language. For Frye, Tolkien's "special languages" and textual archaism are closely related to symbolic visual emblems. Frye sees that the invented languages of Tolkien come at the end of a long tradition, including the synthetic

1. Construction of Mythology

Gothic of *Ivanhoe* and the "yea-verily-and-forsooth lingo" in which William Morris wrote his later prose romances and translations. Frye discusses though that the synthetic languages, "however absurd they often sound," do seem to belong to romantic decorum: Frye raises also two very different contemporary examples of Nigerian story of *The Palm-Wine Drinkard* (1952) and Anthony Burgess' *A Clockwork Orange* (1962). For Frye, the special language can have even dream-like quality, as he sees in Lady Gregory's brutal "drivel" in Joyce's *Ulysses* (Frye 1976: 110).

One of Tolkien's intentions, perhaps crucial, was to activate pre-modern myths for contemporary readers. Tolkien's intratextual references create an illusion of older eras. In his theory of the historical novel, Hans Vilmar Geppert (1976) calls this an "Illusion der unmittelbaren Darstellung," kind of direct depiction, a coherent image. Likewise, in Tolkien's works, there is no factual history behind the stories, but an invented history, credible inside his fantasy fiction.

The situation becomes complex when Tolkien refers to his own created fantasy fiction (then only unpublished works) in *The Lord of the Rings* and *The Hobbit*. *The Lord of the Rings* for example is full of intratextual references to "old stories" or legends, of which some were later published posthumously in *The Silmarillion* or in *The History of the Middle-earth* series: for example the story of Tinúviel (or Beren and Lúthien), which is recounted by Aragorn as a "tale of the old days," during the scene still called Strider by the narrator, in *The Lord of the Rings*, when the Hobbit character Sam Gamgee wants to hear an old story (Tolkien 2008: 249).

Tolkien wrote many versions of the stories that form his fantasy world, and the stories can be found published in many forms. A good example is the tale of the tragic hero Túrin Turambar. Tolkien first started writing on the subject in 1917, in the story then titled "Turambar and the Foalóke." One version of the story was published in *The Silmarillion* in 1977, under the title "Of Túrin Turambar." Other different versions have been published in *The Unfinished Tales, The Book of Lost Tales part II* and finally in most complete form in the posthumous text *The Children of Húrin* (2007). The title refers to the main characters Túrin and his sister Lalaith, also known as Urwen, who are children of Húrin, yet another epic hero in Tolkien's fiction.

There are also intratextual stories and myths used in other parts of Tolkien's fiction. For example, Elves at first in *The Lord of the Rings* function as folklore for the Hobbits. Sam Gamgee, for example, "recalls old tales of elf-ships sailing west from the Grey Havens, leaving the folk of Middle-earth" (Gasque 2000: 5). The evil kingdom of Mordor is also described more as a nightmarish story for the Hobbits, a name which they knew only in legends of dark past or as "a shadow on the borders of old stories" (Tolkien 2008: 80).

Myth and Genre

In the beginning of *The Lord of the Rings*, it is stated that the era which the book describes, The Third Age of Middle-earth, is now long past and shape of lands is changed (Tolkien 2008: 27). Tolkien's *The Lord of the Rings* is situated in a mythical era, "long past," but Tolkien claims that the world is the same as the reader's real, factual world. Tolkien's fiction therefore is not originally based on "another world," even though Middle-earth is in our concept—a fantasy world. According to Tolkien, the Hobbits used to live—and still live—in the "North-West of the Old World," precisely in "England" (real or non-real). But as Tolkien's fiction makes contextual external references to "our world," it is still mythical. Maybe the era of "long past" that Tolkien is describing has something to do with the *epiphanic*, unhistorical time that Nothrop Frye is referring to, and where Frye sees the archetypal imaginary of our mythic literature emerging from (see Frye 1951). Therefore, the next section will focus on myth and genre. What is constructed or re-imagined myth, and how is it used in Tolkien's fiction? What is the genre, or what are the genres, of Tolkien's literary works? This section focuses on these questions.

Tolkien's fantasy fiction is situated in an era that is "long past,"

1. Construction of Mythology

a mythic prehistory of "our world." In *The Great Code. The Bible and Literature*, Northrop Frye discusses on Giambattista Vico's three ages in the cycle of history: a mythical age (or age of gods), a heroic age (or age of an aristocracy), and an age of the people. Vico himself was an Italian Christian Platonic philosopher in the Age of Enlightenment, who was affected by both Plato's philosophy and Christianity (DuBois 2001). According to Vico, after these periods comes a *ricorso* (a return), and the whole process starts all over again. Each of these ages produces "its own kind of language," which Vico calls the poetic, the heroic (or noble), and the vulgar. Frye's names for these different types of languages are hieroglyphic, the hieratic and the demotic (Frye 2006: 23).

Frye explains that the era before Plato was hieroglyphic, and with "Plato we enter a different phase of language, one that is 'hieratic,' partly in the sense of being produced by an intellectual elite" (Frye 2006: 25). As an example of "a Viconian ricorso in literature," Frye sees the rise of the European culture in the early Christian period after the destruction of the Roman Empire (Frye 2006: 30).

This kind of temporal trichotomy could be seen in Tolkien's fiction. The early part of *The Silmarillion*, the cosmogonical "Ainulindalë" and cosmological accounts of "Valaquenta" refer to an age of "gods": an era when the creator Eru and his offspring the Ainur create the World, and when Ainur enter the created World. Even Tolkien's style of writing is mythic and poetic, in a Biblical way: "Then the voices of the Ainur, like unto harps and lutes, and pipes and trumpets, and viols and organs, and like unto countless choirs singing with words, began to fashion the theme of Ilúvatar to a great music..."(Tolkien 1999: 3–4).

After that, in *The Silmarillion*, and in the parts of Tolkien's fiction situated in the same era, such as *The Children of Húrin*, the focus moves from the divine Ainur to Elves and Men: towards more familiar characters of elven and human heroes (and anti-heroes). The cycle in the history of Middle-earth is heroic, and the writing more hieratic, as can be seen from the following scene when Túrin Turambar climbs to meet the dragon Glaurung in a battle:

The Mythopoeic Code of Tolkien

> Then he summoned to him all his will, and all his hatred of the Dragon and his Master [Melkor/Morgoth], and it seemed to him that suddenly he found a strength of heart and of body that he had not know before; and he climbed the cliff, from stone to stone, and root to root, until he seized at last a slender tree that grew a little beneath the lip of the chasm, and though its top was blasted it still held fast by its roots. And even as he steadied himself in the fork of its boughts, the midmost parts of the Dragon came above him, and he swayed down with their weight almost upon his head, ere Glaurung could heave them up. Pale and wrinkled was their underside, and all dank with a grey slime, to which clung all manner of dropping filth; and it stank of death. Then [Túrin] Turambar drew the Black Sword of Beleg and stabbed upwards with all the might of his arm, and of his hate, and the deadly blade, long and greedy, went into the belly even to its hilts [Tolkien 2007: 237].

In *The Lord of the Rings*, the heroic age coincides and impacts with the age of people: that is, the age of the Hobbits, and of (more or less) un-heroic humans. This is also the point that Saruman makes in his monologue in *The Fellowship of the Ring*, when he tries to assure Gandalf that their future as Istari, the Wizards (also known as "The Wise") would be to rule the coming non-heroic time of Men:

> The Elder Days are gone. The Middle Days are passing. The Younger Days are beginning. The time of the Elves is over, but our time is at hand: the world of Men, which We must rule. But we must have power, power to order all things as we will, for that good which only the Wise can see [Tolkien 2008: 328].

The Hobbit, with its different literary tone is, of course, written more in the vulgar or demotic language. A good example of this vulgar speech is the language used by the trolls, Bert, Tom, and William (Bill). Despite their vulgar appearance and behavior, Trolls are also quite strange characters for the milieu, since they speak with "modern" cockney accents:

> "Mutton yesterday, mutton today, and blimey, if it don't look like mutton again tomorrer," said one of the trolls.
> "Never a blinking bit of manflesh have we had for long enough," said a second. "What the 'ell William was a-thinkin' of to bring us into these parts at all, beats me—and the drink runnin' short, what's more," he said jogging the elbow of William, who was taking a pull at his jug.

1. Construction of Mythology

> William choked. "Shut yer mouth!" he said as soon as he could. "Yer can't expect folk to stop here for ever just to be eat by you and Bert. You've e ta village and a half between yer, since we came down from the mountains." [Tolkien 1975: 39].

Then again, we can say that all these fictional ages of Middle-earth, and different tones of language of Tolkien's fiction are mythical in some sense: Tolkien's fantasy fiction is in all of its parts closely related to a fictional mythology, and could be seen as operating in many ways on the level of basic myths.

In fact, J.R.R. Tolkien's fiction is primarily fantasy deriving from the world of myths. Tolkien's creative method uses myths, activates them, modernizes them, and familiarizes them. Different myths, such as Platonic myth or Northern myths, form wide range of external references for Tolkien's fiction. Of course, myths are at the center of Tolkien's constructive poetics. Myths are also one of the focus areas of contemporary literary theory. Scholes & Kellogg point out the great difference between the epic storyteller's traditional story (*mythos*, in ancient Greece), and fact, truth or entertainment:

> The epic story-teller is telling a traditional story. The primary impulse which moves him is not a historical one, nor a creative one, it is re-creative. He is retelling a traditional story, and therefore his primary allegiance is not to fact, not to truth, not to entertainment, but to mythos itself—the story is preserved in the tradition which the epic story-teller is re-creating. The word mythos meant precisely this in ancient Greece: a traditional story [Scholes & Kellogg 1966: 12].

So, as Scholes & Kellogg see, mythic storyteller is re-creating the story: likewise, as Tolkien pretends to be a translator or a re-teller of stories. Tolkien is re-creating myths. Myth is also one of the main concepts in Tolkien's "On Fairy-Stories." In his letter to publisher Milton Waldman, Tolkien (1983: 144) describes that his basic passion from the beginning was for myth and fairy-story but not clear allegory.

As stated, Tolkien is trying to follow the footsteps of mythographers of folk tales, such as Grimm brothers, Elias Lönnrot and John Francis Campbell. Tolkien is following his literary "instinctive bent towards myth and fairy-tale," his "search for cultural identity" and "literary ambition" (Flieger 2005a: 6–7, 11–12, see also Whittingham 2008: 35).

The concept of myth is complex and of course has been a matter of discussion for the last centuries. For Frye, myth—in its literary context—means: "first of all mythos, plot or narrative," and in general, the "sequential ordering of words" (Frye 2006: 49). Frye therefore objects the contemporary meaning of myth as something "not really true," since for Frye, mythical means the opposite of "not really true": "it means being charged with a special seriousness and importance." Frye's examples include sacred stories that illustrate a "specific social concern." Frye sees that after the rise of metonymical language, stories have been used as "concrete illustrations of abstract arguments," which is close to the role of Platonic myths (Frye 2006: 50–51).

Joseph Pearce sees myth as a tool for Tolkien's personal theological belief and for his literary creative methods. Pearce writes that one result of Tolkien's Christianity was his development of the philosophy of myth that underpins his sub-creation. Pearce states humorously that Tolkien is "a misunderstood man because he is a mythunderstood man." Pearce sees that for Tolkien, myth was not a leap from reality but a leap into reality. For most modern critics, a myth is merely another word for a lie or a legend, but intrinsically not true. Like for Frye, myth had for Tolkien also the opposite meaning. It was the only way that certain transcendent truths could be expressed in intelligible form (Pearce 1999: xiii–xiv).

What then is the type of myth that Tolkien uses in his literary works? The simplest way of answering the question is to focus on the genre and themes upon which Tolkien's books are constructed. By these tools, Tolkien's fantasy fiction is a collection of classical myths re-written for contemporary readers. Tolkien is rediscovering the pre-modern myth and writing a new mythology, or re-writing mythology. His myth is therefore a re-written myth in a 20th-century genre-fantasy, a genre which in the opinion of many researchers owes its sheer existence—in contemporary magnitude—to Tolkien's fiction.

1. Construction of Mythology

When *The Lord of the Rings* was published in 1954–55 it was compared in gentle criticism to much older and fundamentally classic works of literature, such as Edmund Spenser's *The Faerie Queene* (1590), John Milton's *Paradise Lost* (1667), or Dante's *Divine Comedy* (1308–21).When *The Silmarillion*, with its old fashioned almost biblical language, was published posthumously in 1977 it was compared to classical works such as Homer's the *Iliad* and the *Odyssey*, or "The Book of Chronicles" of the *Bible*. Of these, Homer's the *Odyssey* has also been seen as a "pre–Platonic" work of literature by Seth Benardete on his study *The Bow and the Lyre: A Platonic Reading of the Odyssey* in 1997. And the *Bible* is of course the most important book for Christian audiences.

As these comparisons show, for contemporary critics it was hard to see Tolkien as a modern writer. Debbie Sly writes that Tolkien's mythological cosmology is fundamentally medieval, although touched by 20th-century's cataclysms (Sly 2000: 109). Then again, 21st century's criticism, like Richard Mathews' *Fantasy: The Liberation of Imagination* (2002), sees that Tolkien's *The Lord of the Rings* "breathed new life into fantasy" (Mathews 2002: 54) and thus vitalized, modernized and re-created the genre.

Richard C. West (1970: 9–10) sees Tolkien in a long continuity of classic adventure novel or fantastical novel writers such as Walter Scott, Robert Louis Stevenson, Rudyard Kipling, George MacDonald, and Lord Dunsany. West calls Tolkien and his contemporaries T.H. White and C.S. Lewis "medieval authors." West writes that Tolkien's *The Lord of the Rings* can be categorized as a novel, but its fantastic nature fits ill into the traditional idea of the novel as a "reflection of real life." Therefore, West calls *The Lord of the Rings* "the twentieth-century romance" (West 1970: 9–10). Harold Bloom combines the genres of romance and fantasy fiction, calling *The Lord of the Rings* a "fantasy-romance" (Bloom 2000: 1). That is exactly the point Tolkien himself makes. Tolkien writes (1981: 414) in a letter to Peter Szabo Szentmihaly that *The Lord of the Rings* is not a novel, but a heroic romance, representing much older and a very different type of literature. We might say that it is written in a completely different genre than a modern English novel. To stress the difference, on his preface of *The Children of Húrin*, Christopher Tolkien calls the tale "a heroic fairy romance" (Tolkien 2007: 10). A genre definition suitable for many of Tolkien's so-called novels.

Tom Shippey has pointed out that Tolkien was a "philologist before he was a mythologist, and a mythologist, at least in intention, before he ever became a writer of fantasy fiction" (Shippey 2001: xvi). But after his philological and mythological ambitions, Tolkien is of course a writer of fantasy fiction. Shippey sees Tolkien as a Chrétien de Troyes of the 20th century: "Chrétien, in the twelfth century, did not invent the Arthurian romance, which must have existed in some form before his time, but he showed what could be done with it...." Tolkien, in the same way, "did not invent heroic fantasy, but he showed what could be done with it; he established a genre whose durability we cannot estimate" (Shippey 2001: xviii–xix). There was a vivid tradition of epic and heroic fantasy before Tolkien, English and Irish writers such as E.R. Eddison or Lord Dunsany, and also the American tradition of pulp-writers from magazines such as *Weird Tales* or *Unknown* (Shippey 2001: xxiv). Genre-defining works such as Eddison's *The Worm Ouroboros* (1922), Lord Dunsany's *The King of the Elfland's Daughter* (1924), or even Robert E. Howard's Conan-series (1932–36) were familiar for some readers of Tolkien's fiction. Lin Carter, for example, sees William Morris' Lord Dunsany's, and E.R. Eddison's heroic fantasy romance resembling Tolkien's fiction in many ways (Carter 1969: 134–151).

Frye sees Tolkien's traditional background deriving from the genre of romance. Frye postulates the tradition from Sydney's *Arcadia* (and similar works), and sees the genre continuing after the development of novel as "Gothic" stories, such as Matthew Gregory Lewis' *The Monk* (1796), and its Victorian successors. For the successors, Frye sees William Morris as the most interesting figure of this tradition, mostly for his encyclopedic approach to romance, which Frye calls "his ambition to collect every major story in literature and retell or translate it." Frye implicates Tolkien in the same "rise of genre fiction" of the 1950s as science fiction, writing that "In

1. Construction of Mythology

the twentieth-century romance got a new lease of fashion—with the success of Tolkien and the rise of what is generally called science fiction" (Frye 1976: 4).

William Morris, an English 19th-century artist and writer, medievalist and translator of ancient and pre-modern texts, was in many ways a traditional predecessor for Tolkien.[27] Morris' intention was to bring back the beauty of the Middle Ages, drawing from old French poetry and romance, and from Northern Sagas. Morris "wanted to make his contemporaries appreciate the Northern Sagas," and as an artist (designer and illustrator) he "revived old patterns as well as made new ones, largely under the influence of the old" (Cole 1948: xiii). The same can be said of Tolkien, who certainly wanted his contemporaries to appreciate his re-imagining of old myth. And certainly, in his literature, Tolkien revived many of the older stories, but at the same time made them into something completely new and different.

Morris' work as a reteller or translator of literature was of course familiar to Tolkien, who on some occasions explained his gratitude for this earlier mythographer. In his letter to his wife-to-be Edith Bratt (later Edith Tolkien) as early as in the year 1914, Tolkien writes (1981: 7) that his ambition at the time was to write a short story in a fashion of William Morris' romances with a bit of poetry in between. The story, on which Tolkien is referring in a letter as "a very great" "and most tragic" story, as Carpenter states in his notes to his edition to *The Letters of J.R.R. Tolkien*, is "The Story of Kullervo," the *Kalevala*-based story on a hero Kullervo's tragic life, a story that was published for the first time in August 2015. Although the story acts as one of the foundation stones for Tolkien's mythopoeic fiction, the story itself is based on the *Kalevala* and is not part of Tolkien's own mythology. Kullervo's story proved to be the starting point for Tolkien's tragedy of Túrin Turambar in *The Silmarillion* (Carpenter 1981: 434), and that cycle was published as a complete version in *The Children of Húrin*.

Tolkien's sympathies for Morris' fiction are seen again much later in the year 1960, when in a letter to Professor L.W. Forster

The Mythopoeic Code of Tolkien

Tolkien (1981: 303) illuminates that he personally thinks that the war-scenes in *The Lord of the Rings* are not affected directly by the World Wars. Tolkien argues that although the scenes in *The Lord of the Rings* on The Dead Marches and the approaches to the Morannon owe something as a level of landscape to Northern France after the Battle of Somme, but they owe more to William Morris and his Huns and Romans, as in *The House of the Wolfings* or *The Roots of the Mountains*. Tolkien declares his passion for Morris' fiction and the genre of romance by calling *The Lord of the Rings* a romance, as declared earlier.

Thus, what are the genres of Tolkien's fantasy fiction? Shippey points out that *The Lord of the Rings* in a way created its own genre, a genre or sub-genre of heroic fantasy trilogy, totally unknown before, but one that has now become extremely popular. Shippey (2001: 221) asks, is *The Lord of the Rings* still a novel, or is it a romance or an epic? At this point, it is only meaningful to say that Shippey sees *The Lord of the Rings* as romance, but as a romance "which is in continuous negotiation with, and which follows many of the conventions of, the traditional bourgeois novel" (Shippey 2001: 223). Tolkien's fiction uses different genres and modes of literature as a purpose to form and create a feeling of vastness: the whole, large Tolkien's fantasy world, his invented mythology; with many different operative fields of references.

Raymond H. Thompson studies the similarities and differences of romance and contemporary fantasy and sees many similarities that can be seen represented in Tolkien's fiction. Thompson sees that proving the hero's values is important in both the "modern" fantasy—as Thompson calls the genre—and medieval romance. The "danger inherent in the ambitious pursuit of power" is the subject of both *The Lord of the Rings* and T.H. White's *The Once and Future King* (1958), as well as of the medieval romances of Alexander and the 14th-century English alliterative *Awntyrs off Arthure* (Thompson 1982: 213).

As for the genre of Tolkien's fiction, it could be said that it is variable. As mentioned earlier in the introduction, all three books which

1. Construction of Mythology

form the basis of Tolkien's fantasy fiction functions in different genres and modes. *The Hobbit*'s literary tone is a tone of romantic fairy-story, and it is still mainly considered a children's book. *The Lord of the Rings* is an epic-romance and epic-fantasy or a heroic-fantasy. *The Silmarillion*, in my opinion, is a mythological heroic-epic of the highest form.

Then again, it is surprising and quite peculiar to find out that when Tolkien was writing a sequel for *The Lord of the Rings*, the unfinished "The New Shadow" that has been published in *The History of Middle-earth*, he was writing in yet another genre: a genre, which Christopher Tolkien calls a thriller. From the short published fragment we can as well say that it has not the level of excitement, suspense or tension usually found in the genre of thriller, but it is definitely not written in the same mode as *The Lord of the Rings*. "The New Shadow" was not published in Tolkien's lifetime, and it was never meant to be published. Christopher Tolkien quotes his father saying that "There would be no tales worth of telling in the days of the King's Peace." He continues that his father disparaged the story that he had begun saying that "I could have written a 'thriller' about the plot and its discovery and overthrown—but it would be just that. Not worth doing." Christopher Tolkien points out that it would nonetheless have been a very remarkable thriller, and that one may well view its early abandonment with regret (Tolkien 2002f: 418). Tolkien's fantasy therefore never fully moves in the direction of that genre, but that kind of works, such as Bram Stoker's *Dracula* (1897) have been very successful inside the genre of fantastic literature.

If all three separate main works (*The Hobbit*, *The Lord of the Rings*, and *The Silmarillion*) of Tolkien's fiction shall be taken as contemporary 20th-century fantasy or fantastic literature, then what is the exact fantasy genre or sub-genre that for example *The Lord of the Rings* is written in? I take the opportunity to use Farah Mendlesohn's definitions of fantasy from her *Rhetorics of Fantasy*, which introduces a functional system of classification for the genre. In the book, basically, Mendlesohn introduces four different categories of fantasy: *The Portal-Quest*

The Mythopoeic Code of Tolkien

Fantasy, The Immersive Fantasy, The Intrusion Fantasy, and *The Liminal Fantasy*.

The Portal-Quest Fantasy is "simply a fantastic world entered through a portal.... Crucially, the fantastic is on the other side and does not 'leak.' Although individuals may cross both ways, the magic does not" (Mendlesohn 2008: xx).

The Immersive Fantasy "invites us to share not merely a world, but a set of assumptions. At its best, it presents the fantastic without comment as the norm both for the protagonist and for the reader: we sit on the protagonist's shoulder and while we have access to his eyes and ears, we are not provided with an explanatory narrative." *The Immersive Fantasy* Mendlesohn holds out closest to science fiction: "once the fantastic becomes assumed, it acquires a scientific cohesion all of its own" (Mendlesohn 2008: xx).

In *Intrusion Fantasy*, Mendlesohn sees the fantastic as the bringer of chaos. She explains that "fantastic" could be "the beast in the bottom of the garden, or the Elf seeking assistance. It is horror and amazement. It takes us out of safety without taking us from our place. It is recursive," but not necessarily unpleasant (Mendlesohn 2008: xxi–xxii).

The *Liminal Fantasy* is rare. As M. John Harrison has said, of the existence of the transliminal moment, the points when we are invited to cross the threshold into the fantastic, "but choose not do so." The result is that the fantastic leaks back through the portal. Mendlesohn prefers the concept of liminal to Tzvetan Todorov's hesitation or uncertainty because she thinks that "hesitation" is only one strategy employed by these writers (Mendlesohn 2008: xxiii).

Mendlesohn sees Tolkien's *The Lord of the Rings* as a *Portal-Quest Fantasy* and *The Silmarillion* as *Immersive Fantasy*. She goes on to explain that, despite the reputation as a "full secondary world" *The Lord of the Rings* is in fact a *Quest Fantasy*—most familiar of the kind. The structure of the narrative outlined is: "Frodo moves from a small, safe, and understood world in the wild, unfamiliar world of Middle-earth" (Mendlesohn 2008: 2–3). The same can be said of *The Hobbit*, which is clearly a Quest Fantasy,

1. Construction of Mythology

although as I earlier declared, it has more to do with Adventure, than a Quest. The point of moving through a "portal," for example "the boundaries of The Shire," into the un- and defamiliar "Outside World" is of course the point that I make. *The Silmarillion*, Mendlesohn describes as the Immersive Fantasy: "the book told within the world, about people who know their world" (Mendlesohn 2008: 2–3). Then again, Mendlesohn (2008: 67) goes as far as to argue that in the creating The Shire, Tolkien found immersive depth that cannot be found in the other parts of *The Lord of the Rings*. Mendlesohn (2008: 32) sees that the Hobbit sections are written in the immersive style.

Once again, Mendlesohn's analysis of Tolkien's fiction shows clearly that Tolkien's fiction acts within the scope of many genres and sub-genres. The Portal-Quest Fantasy converges with immersive style, and heroic fantasy elements are woven within a Quest Fantasy. This clash of genres has been noted widely by Tolkien scholars. For example, Lin Carter sees the elements of epic, chanson de geste and romance working in Tolkien's fiction. He sees these elements of chanson de geste and romance borrowed from heroic and epic narrative, for example "the larger-than-life hero, heroine, and villain, as well as the strong element of the supernatural, the occasional act of direct divine intervention into mortal affairs, and the preoccupation with the dual epic themes of quest and warfare as standard plot motifs" (Carter 1969: 121–122). These elements, modes and motifs can of course all be found in Tolkien's fiction.

Tolkien's fantasy fiction is a complex fictional mythology written by the author in many different modes and driven by different motifs. In order to illuminate Tolkien's fantasy's modes and motifs, with the contrast of different contexts, I use, once again, Northrop Frye's theory of the fictional modes as a baseline, as it is also fitting for Tolkien's own Christian Platonic poetics.

Frye in his *Anatomy of Criticism* declares that fictions "may be classified, not morally, but by the hero's power of action, which may be greater than ours, less, or roughly the same" (Frye 1967:

33). Summarily, Frye separates fiction into five categories: (1) Myth, when the protagonist is superior in kind to "us," and to the fictional environment, a divine being, as Frye says. (2) Romance, when the protagonist is superior in degree to "us" and to the fictional environment, moving from "myth" into "legend" of fantasy. (3) High mimetic mode, when the protagonist is superior in degree to "us," and other men, but not to his environment, a leader and hero of most epic and tragedy. (4) Low mimetic mode, when the protagonist is not superior to "us," other men, or his environment—a hero of realistic fiction. And lastly: (5) Ironic mode, when the protagonist is inferior to "us."

Tolkien's mode of writing in his fiction varies. Shippey sees that Frye's framework allows us to place *The Lord of the Rings* and lets us see "why it is an anomaly" (Shippey 2001: 221). Shippey sees *The Lord of the Rings* functioning in all the five levels of Frye's framework.[28] Shippey's thoughts on *The Lord of the Rings* are convincing. Of course, we can itemize some of the wordings, such as that Gandalf, Bombadil and Sauron, characters very close to the level of myth, are not "exactly divine beings," which they, in fact, inside Tolkien's cosmology are. They are all immortals. Shippey addresses the class of Maiar, invented by Tolkien, as "something intermediate," not quite "divine."

Then again, as mythic characters,[29] Gandalf's, Bombadil's and Sauron's level of function differs from each other. The scenes where Tom Bombadil appears in the first book of *The Lord of the Rings* the text itself still functions in very much a fairy-tale mode. Bombadil, despite his "shrouded power" and elemental force as perhaps a spirit of nature, is still quite a humoristic and comical character. On the scenes of his first appearance in the story, Tom Bombadil sings a tune Tolkien describes as "nonsense": "Hey dol! merry dol! ring a dong dillo! Ring a dong! hop along! fal lal the willow! Tom Bom, jolly tom, Tom bombadillo!" (Tolkien 2008: 161).

This is quite far away from the mythic tone, but closer to some Victorian fantasy and Lewis Carroll's style nonsense fantasy fiction for adolescence audiences. Then again, Tom Bombadil, is inside Tolkien's fantasy world "superior in kind both to other men and to the environment," as Frye (1967: 33–34) states the protagonist

1. Construction of Mythology

of mythic mode to be. In *The Lord of the Rings*, Tom Bombadil is referred to quite prestigious or even divine names: he is called "the Master of wood, water, and hill" (Tolkien 2008: 168), and Frodo calls him "Master" almost every time addressing him (see Tolkien 2008: 170, 171, 176). When Frodo asks Bombadil's wife Goldberry who Tom Bombadil is, Goldberry answers in a quite Biblical way. Goldberry just simply answers that "he is" (Tolkien 2008: 168). This expression of Bombadil as "he is" caused some trouble with the Catholic readers and clusters because for some, the phrasing resembles too much the nomination God uses in "The Book of Exodus," in Hebrew "ehje ašer ehje"—"I am that I am," referring to Yahweh (Exodus 3:14).[30] In 1954, in a letter to Catholic book dealer Peter Hastings, Tolkien (1981: 191–192) defended himself philologically, saying that "[w]e need not go into the sublimates of 'I am that am'—which is quite different from *he is*."

Despite the answer, there is definitely something "divine" in Tom Bombadil. Even in Tom Bombadil's own answer later to Frodo's question "Who are you" makes it clear that he is in fact not a mortal, referring that he was in Middle-earth before both the Big People (Men) and little People (Hobbits), or Kings (referring to Númenorean Men), or the Dark Lord (meaning Morgoth, the first Enemy, or Sauron, his apprentice): "Eldest, that's what I am" (Tolkien 2008: 176).

The phrasing that Bombadil uses, that he was here before the Dark Lord came from Outside, hints that Bombadil has existed since the creation of Middle-earth. He is not an analogy of a Christian or Jewish God, but in the cosmology he is a definite "power," maybe a spirit of Pacifism as Tolkien alluded in his letter to Naomi Mitchison in 1954, calling Bombadil's "a natural pacifist view, which always arises in the mind when there is a war" (Tolkien 1981: 178–179). Bombadil, Tolkien says, has renounced control and takes delights in things for themselves, since control and means of power has become utterly meaningless to him.

The character of Tom Bombadil is written on the level of myth: he is a mythic figure of pacifism, an anthropomorphized view of "peace," but not a clear allegory as such. In a way, he represents

The Mythopoeic Code of Tolkien

peace and Christian Platonic concept of harmony. He discussed that *The Lord of the Rings* is basically, as a narrative, a story of good versus evil and both sides focus on the concept of "control." The modes and motifs of the epic are, as Tolkien phrases (1981: 178–179): "beauty against ugliness," "tyranny against kingship," and "conservative or destructive" measure of control.

Another non-human character in *The Lord of the Rings* who can be discussed as an example of an almost neutral position is the leader of the Ents, Treebeard. The ents are anthropomorphized tree-like creatures in Tolkien's fantasy, representing "talking trees" in folk tales around Europe. In Tolkien's fantasy fiction they are giant sized powerful "Shepherds of the Trees," who watch over the trees and flora in certain remote areas of the Middle-earth. In the story, at first Treebeard does not choose a side in the war although he declares that he is not on the side of Orcs. Treebeard comments on that saying: "I am not altogether on anybody's side, because nobody is altogether on my side, if you understand me: nobody cares for the woods as I care for them, not even Elves nowadays" (Tolkien 2009a: 82).

In the end, Treebeard does not remain neutral in the War of the Rings. In *The Two Towers*, the Ents attack Saruman's fortress of Isengard and in a dramatic scene Saruman's power is destroyed by these creatures that symbolize "wild nature." Simply put, in Tolkien's mythopoeic vision, Saruman, symbolizing industrialization and mechanized "modernism" is destroyed by the Ents, symbolizing the counterblow of Nature.

Shippey's discussion on Fryean theory of modes is mostly concerned with characters of Tolkien's fiction, but Frye's theory of modes and symbols can be researched also from the context of Tolkien's fiction's constructive shape and on the contextual field of motifs. In *Anatomy of Criticism*, Frye's purpose is clearly to form a structural theory for the principles of literature. Frye saw mythical archetypes as an important part of this structural theory, they are recurring images and symbols which occur in the texts. Archetype is something "original," or at least a prototype that other objects (knowingly or unknowingly) either copy or emulate.

1. Construction of Mythology

For Northrop Frye, archetype is a "symbol, usually an image, which recurs often enough in literature to be recognizable as an element of one's literary experience as a whole" (Frye 1967: 365). Frye discusses that these patters of imaginary, or fragments of significance, are oracular in origin, deriving from epiphanic, unhistorical times (see Frye 1951). On philosophical and metaphysical level, these "original" archetypes can be also compared to Plato's theory of pure forms and theory of *ideal* that encapsulate the true and essential nature of things, for example as discussed in Plato's *Cratylus* 439–440, *Sophist* 246–250, and *Republic* 472c–480e.

On the following chart, I demonstrate that Frye's theory of modes and of the archetypal imaginary could be applied with modifications to Tolkien's fiction's structural elements as well. There, different mythic "worlds" in literature are divided in the chart, on the vertical scale, to Divine World, Human World, Animal World, Vegetable World, Mineral World, Fire World and Watery World, depending on which elements and elemental characters are central. On the horizontal scale, there are different modes of text: Apocalyptic, Romantic, High Mimetic, Realistic and Demonic. These examples are then compared with elements of Tolkien's fantasy fiction, and examination of these chosen elements is given after the chart.

Explanations should be given to understand this large chart. First, the examples of characters or "creatures" and elements or metaphors of Tolkien's fiction work in many different modes and genres. In the Divine World, the mode moves from Ainur and Eru to the Romantic mode of Gandalf and to the High Mimetic mode of Aragorn, the idealized king, and to the (more) realistic and familiar mode of Frodo as a Realistic—but Divine—element. Frodo represents the "divine world," because in the book, he first becomes the Ring Bearer, a carrier of unearthly power, and in the end of *The Lord of the Rings* leaves the Middle-earth and joins The Undying Lands with other immortal characters. There is of course intermingling between the modes. Frodo, for example, in the narrative, moves from Realistic to High Mimetic, or at some point to the Romantic mode.

Chart 2: Frye's Structures of Archetypal Imagery (adjusted from Denham 1979: 61) and Archetypal Equivalents in Tolkien's Fantasy Fiction

	Apocalyptic	Romantic	High Mimetic	Realistic	Demonic
Divine World	Society of Gods	Parental wise men with magical powers	King idealized as divine	Spiritual vision anchored in empirical psychological experience	Stupid powers of nature, machinery of fate
In Tolkien's fiction (as the "immortal world")	Eru, Ainur	Gandalf	Aragorn, Galadriel	Frodo	Ungoliant / Melkor
Human World	Society of Men	Children and innocence	Idealized human forms	Common, typical human situations, parody of (idealistic) romance	Society of ecos in tension / Tyrant-leader
In Tolkien's fiction (as the "mortal world")	Númenor—the greatest kingdom of Men	Men before the Fall, The Shire (at some point)	"The Reunited kingdom" (or Arnor and Gondor)	The Shire (at some point)	Isengard, Gondor under the rule of Denethor
Animal World	Lamb of God / Dove	Pastoral lamb, birds, horses, hounds	Eagle, lion, horse, swan, falcon, etc.	Ape, tiger	Beast of prey, tiger, wolf, vulture, dragon
In Tolkien's fiction	Great Eagles / Huan	Eagles and ravens in *The Hobbit*	Horses of Gandalf and Glorfindel	"Normal" animals of the Middle-earth	Dragons / Giant Spiders
Vegetable World	Paradisal garden and tree / Arcadian imagery of green world	Garden of Eden (the Bible, Milton) / *Locus amoenus*	Formal gardens (in background)	Farms, painful labor of man / Peasants	Sinister forest or enchanted garden / Tree of forbidden knowledge

In Tolkien's fiction	The Two Trees Valinor	Lórien Cuiviénen, place where the Elves "awoke"	Gardens of Númenor or Gondor	Peasants and farms of the Shire	Old Forest Mirkwood
Mineral World	Jerusalem Highway and road "The Way"	Tower, castle	Capital city with court at center	Labyrinthine modern city Stress of loneliness and lack of communication	Deserts, rocks, waste land
In Tolkien's fiction	The Lost Road Númenor	Towers and castles in *The Lord of the Rings*	Minas Tirith	Cities and villages; for example, Bree, in *The Lord of the Rings*, or Laketown in *The Hobbit*	Mordor
Fire World	Seraphim and Cherubim Saint's Halo	Fire as purifying symbol	King's crown Lady's eyes	Fire as ironic and destructive Prometheus	Malignant demons, will-o'-the-wisps, spirits broke from hell Burning cities
In Tolkien's fiction	Imperishable Flame	Gandalf's "Secret Fire"	Inner fire of the Silmarils (and of the Children of Ilúvatar)	Fire as light or as a mean for heating (for example by the Dwarves in *The Hobbit*)	Balrog Dragon fire The Pyre of Denethor
Watery World	Water of life Baptism	Fountains, pools Fertilizing rains	The disciplined river (Thames)	Sea as destructive element Moby Dick	Water of death Spilled blood Sea monsters
In Tolkien's fiction	Ulmo's water	Fountains of the Elves The Mirror of Galadriel	The Great River of Anduin The Sea	Falls of Rauros Places of shipwreck	Watcher in the Water

The Mythopoeic Code of Tolkien

In the Divine World, Melkor is not such a Fryean example of "Stupid powers of nature," but a Divine-Demonic character: distant, chthonic, and terrifying. Ungoliant, for example, is equally suitable. It is a defamiliar "Dark Spider" (which is the meaning of its name in the Elven language of Sindar), a terrible spirit in the shape of a Giant Spider. It (or she) is described as a "shape as spider of monstrous form, weaving her black webs in a cleft of the mountains. There she sucked up all light that she could find, and spun it forth again in dark nets of strangling gloom, until no light more could come to her abode; and she was famished" (Tolkien 1999: 77).

In the Human World of Frye's theory, which I call the "Mortal World" in Tolkien's fiction, the modes range from the "Society of Men" of Númenor through the distant past and Romantic innocence of Men before the Fall, to the High Mimetic model society of The Reunited Kingdom in the end of *The Lord of the Rings*, when the "Return of the King" promises the start of the Age of Men, under the rule of Aragorn. The more Realistic "mortal world" could be seen—at some point—in the portrayal of The Shire in *The Lord of the Rings*, and the Demonic Mortal World could be seen in the depictions of the mortal parts of Mordor, or the tyrant-ruling of Isengard under Saruman and Gondor under the rule of Denethor in *The Lord of the Rings*.

The elements of the Animal World are diverse. For example, Huan, a great wolfhound of Valar Oromë in *The Silmarillion* has been granted special powers by the Valar, for example to speak three times in its lifetime. Huan could easily be an Apocalyptic element of the Animal World and Dragons as well as Giant Spiders could be Demonic elements of the Animal World. Between these extremities are the Romantic archetypes of animals, such as eagles and crows in *The Hobbit*, or High Mimetic almost magical horses of Gandalf and Glorfindel, to name a few. Then again, the Realistic mode in the Animal World is seen in all the so-called "normal" animals of the Middle-earth.

In the Vegetable World, Tolkien's fictive world is as multifaceted as in the Animal World. Tolkien's usage of flora and fauna ranges from the realistic modes of literature to mythical, fantastic and to the genres of medieval romance and fairy-stories. The Vegetable World of Tolkien's

1. Construction of Mythology

fiction has its "paradisal imagery" of Valinor, the Undying Lands, also known as Aman and its mythical era of "The Two Trees," described in *The Silmarillion* (Tolkien 1999: 31–32). Romantic mode can be seen, for example, in the Vegetable World of Lórien in *The Lord of the Rings*. High Mimetic elements can be seen in the sceneries of Númenor and Gondor, Realistic in the elements of peasantry and farming of The Shire and the most revealing examples of "sinister forest" in the milieus of Old Forest in *The Lord of the Rings* or Mirkwood in *The Hobbit*.

The archetypes of the mineral world in the Tolkien's fiction range from the Apocalyptic almost philosophical and metaphysical element of "The Lost Road" to the Demonic wasteland and defamiliar milieu of Mordor. "The Lost Road" in Tolkien's fiction is a reference to a "Straight Road" that once connected the mortal world of Middle-earth with the land of Valar (Valinor), but which had been removed from mortal reach after the Fall of Númenor, after the Fall all roads were bent and the Undying Lands were (mostly) unreachable (Tolkien 1999: 337–338). Then again, Romantic castles and towers are commonplace in heroic romance and new(er) cities and villages depict a more Realistic mode, whereas the High Mimetic tone of Mineral World is most clearly seen in the milieu of Minas Tirith, which in the later Third Age of Middle-earth has become the capital city of Gondor with a fortress at its center.

The Fire World and the Watery World in Tolkien's fiction could be seen in a dichotomic resemblance. In Tolkien's fantasy fiction, fire and water are both frightening, but also noble and even benevolent. For example, Gandalf is "a servant of the Secret Fire, wielder of the flame of Anor," but his enemy the Balrog is of "dark fire" (Tolkien 2008: 412). Hence fire can be either "good" or "evil." Eru Ilúvatar, the creator, is the maker and ruler of "Imperishable Fire" (Tolkien 1999: 4), which is the clearest example of the Apocalyptic mode of the Fire World in Tolkien's fiction. Vala-Ulmo's water an example of the Apocalyptic mode in the Watery World (Tolkien 1999: 8–9) and the Demonic mode of this world is seen in, for example, the monstrous being called the "Watcher in the Water" by the dwarves of Moria in *The Lord of the Rings* (Tolkien 2008: 403).

The Mythopoeic Code of Tolkien

In the Romantic mode, Gandalf's "Secret Fire" is a fire as a purifying symbol and the magical Mirror of Galadriel in *The Lord of the Rings* could be as such in the Watery World. Then again, the High Mimetic mode could be seen in the Inner Fire of both Silmarils and the Elves. Of the Silmarils, Tolkien writes in *The Silmarillion* that they were like crystal of diamonds, which no violence could break, and they had inner fire inside them (Tolkien 1999: 68). The High Mimetic archetype of disciplined form of Watery World could be seen, for example, in the Great River of Anduin in *The Lord of the Rings*. In Tolkien's fiction, Realistic modes of both Fire and Water are seen on many occasions. For example, the dwarves use fire as a giver of light or means of heating in *The Hobbit*. Then again, water is seen in many parts as a realistic and dangerous element, for example by hydrophobic Sam Gamgee in the early parts of *The Lord of the Rings*.

Tolkien's mythopoeics is coherent fictitious work of literary art created from these archetypes and various elements, essentially constructed, and intermingled with different elements in different modes that are restrained by different motifs. Frye, in *Anatomy of Criticism*, uses Dante's *The Divine Comedy* as an example of constructive motifs: a sense of the verbal pattern in a literary text, which, in my view, form a part of the internal reference fields of texts. Frye discusses that the literal meaning of Dante's *The Divine Comedy* is not historical: not at any rate a simple description in a biographical way of what "really happened" to Dante, writer himself. Frye writes (1967: 77) that "if a poem cannot be literally anything but a poem, then the literal basis of meaning in poetry can only be its letters, its inner structure of interlocking motifs."

That assumption forces us to ponder what is "the literal basis of meaning" in Tolkien's fantasy fiction? What are the inner structures of interlocking motifs in Tolkien's texts? Of these, the central motifs of "Creation and Existence" is discussed in the next chapter. The chapter focuses on both Tolkien's fiction's intratextual creation myth and the inner-built cosmology of Tolkien's works, but also on Tolkien's creative methods and aesthetic theory.

2

Creation and Existence

The Song of Ainur: Christian Platonic Creation Myth in *The Silmarillion*

The collection of posthumously published and fragmented stories of *The Silmarillion* form the basis of Tolkien's fictive mythology, since it tells the timeline of Tolkien's fantasy world from the beginning of the World until the end of the Third Age of Middle-earth: the end of *The Lord of the Rings* narrative.

The Silmarillion itself is divided into five parts, of which the first three form "the proper Silmarillion" and the last two, "Akallabêth" (The Downfall of Númenor) and "Of the Rings of Power and Third Age," being separate and independent works (see Tolkien 1999: vii). The so-called "proper Silmarillion" is divided into three parts: "The Ainulindalë" (The Music of the Ainur), "Valaquenta" (Account of the Valar), and "Quenta Silmarillion" (The History of the Silmarils).

"The Ainulindalë," the first part of *The Silmarillion*, contains the cosmogonical Platonic creation story, as well as the beginning of the cosmological account of Tolkien's fantasy world. It starts before the Creation of the World and introduces the creator "God" Eru Ilúvatar, and his offspring the Ainur. Eru and Ainur inhabit a place which is called "The Timeless Halls," which are described as "fair regions that he [Eru] had made for the Ainur" (Tolkien 1999: 6). Initially, outside of these Halls is only "Void" (Tolkien 1999: 6).

In "The Ainulindalë," it is revealed that Evil, in the form of Melkor, has its beginning before Time or the Great Music. At first Melkor is curious and becomes the first "individualist." Before Time was created, or the Music played, he went in the vast emptiness to search for the "Imperishable Flame" but could not find it. Melkor is described as the greatest of the Ainur: he "had been given the greatest gifts of power and knowledge, and he had a share in all the gifts of his brethren" (Tolkien 1999: 4).

After this hint at Melkor's future role, the Song of Ainur, the Great Music, is played. Eru propounds the Ainur with themes of music; and the Ainur sing before him. Later, the Earth, which in Tolkien's fantasy world is called Arda, is created in a "mighty theme" given by Eru. In heaven-like timelessness the Ainur compose their Music, which is later revealed to be a Vision of the later "real" history of Arda. After the Vision, the real, physical beginning of Arda is manifested by a single word of command by Eru: "Eä!"

During the Music, the role of forthcoming Evil is once again revealed. Melkor creates discord in the great theme that forms the Great Music. His first individualistic discord spreads among the Ainur, and Melkor's "own theme" confuses the Music—although later Eru declares that Melkor shall see "that no theme may be played that hath not its uttermost source in me [Eru]" (Tolkien 1999: 5–6). Thus, even though Melkor tries to disobey Eru's original theme, he is ultimately playing his role in the Music. Eru's words fill Melkor with shame, and Tolkien writes that through this shame came also "secret anger" (Tolkien 1999: 6). Thus, the beginning of Evil is woven.

In the evolution of Evil in the fantastic mythology, servitude, curiosity, and individualism lead Melkor into envy; shame leads him into anger; and, later, power, envy, arrogance, and desire turn him into a violent tyrant. It is explained that Melkor turned his powers and knowledge to evil purposes, violence, and tyranny. Melkor the kingship of Manwë, his brother in spirit, to rule the Arda and a dominion over all the realms of other Ainur (Tolkien 1999: 23). Later, when the Ainur take physical and visible form in Arda, the created World, Melkor too takes a visible form, but because of his malice demeanor it was dark and terrible, something very different to other Ainur.

In *The Silmarillion*, The Music of the Ainur itself is divided into four parts: the unveiling of the theme, and then three parts of Music.

2. Creation and Existence

First, the theme is given to the Ainur, and second, the Music is sung. During the Music, Melkor breaks the harmony and tries to develop his own song and deceives some of the Ainur into joining him. In the Music, this occurs three times, but every time Eru successfully overpowers Melkor's "rebellion" with new themes.

Eru is the only being in Tolkien's fantasy world that can give existence to another being.[31] At first this was the reason for Melkor's envy, since "desire grew hot within him to bring into Being things of his own" (Tolkien 1999: 4). Eru creates the concept of the Music: the mighty theme. The Ainur, too, are conceived of Eru's thought, they are his offspring. Eru's mighty theme is the primary essence of the Creation, but each Ainu gives his own secondary idea and theme to the Music, according to their attributes and powers. Thus, for example, Ulmo's music forms the element of Water, Manwë's music the element of Air, and Aulë the substances of which Arda is made, the Earth. Is it possible that Melkor's discords ultimately serve to create the dichotomy of good and evil? And that this dichotomy makes it possible for the World to have its positive "eucatastrophical"[32] ending, since without evil and bad things, we would not have knowledge of the good things, and good endings?

Eru's primary theme is intermingled with each Ainu's secondary theme, and this creates a coherent, complex musical collaboration: Music according to Eru's original design and plan. Even Melkor's discording themes are blended with the original theme. Of his discordant music, the "most triumphant notes were taken by the other [Ainur] and woven into its own solemn pattern" (Tolkien 1999: 5).

In the Music, after the first theme is spoiled by Melkor's discord, Eru gives the Ainur a second theme, but the second theme also becomes corrupted by Melkor. But when Eru gives the Ainur the third theme, which Melkor tries to corrupt by force, it results in a strife that shakes and convulses the Halls. Eru Ilúvatar ends the Music with one single chord: "deeper than the Abyss, higher than the Firmament, piercing as the light of the eye of Ilúvatar" (Tolkien 1999: 5).

After the Music is sung, Eru takes the Ainur from the Timeless

The Mythopoeic Code of Tolkien

Halls into the Void. There, Eru shows them a Vision. The Vision is a transliteration of their collaborative Music, now in a material, realistic form. The Ainur are shown the entire history of a physical, changeable World. In the Vision, the Ainur see Elves and Men, the forthcoming Children of Ilúvatar, and the complexity of the physical World. In the story, it is clearly stated that the creation of the Children of Ilúvatar has nothing to do with the Ainur, since the Children "were conceived by him [Eru Ilúvatar] alone; and they came with the third theme, and were not in the theme which Ilúvatar propounded at the beginning, and none of the Ainur had part in their making" (Tolkien 1999: 7).

After this, Eru removes the Vision and creates an actual World, Arda (or Eä). Tolkien describes (1999: 8) it as a habitation set in vast spaces of the World. And this created world is to be affected by Time. The vision is ideal, a paragon of things to come. But the actual created world is yet to be thoroughly shaped and will require the Ainur a lot of labors to be fully functional.

Because of this need to sculpture the World, later in the "Ainulindalë" some of the Ainur choose to go "down," so to speak, to this World or Earth. These beings are later called Valar, and their subordinates called Maiar. After moving to the physical world, the Valar, who were mesmerized by the beauty of the Vision, are now astounded because "the beginning of the world" is nothing like the vision:

> For the Great Music had been but the growth and flowering of thought in the Timeless Halls, and the Vision only a foreshowing; but now they had entered in at the beginning of Time, and the Valar perceived that the World had been but foreshadowed and foresung, and they must achieve it [Tolkien 1999: 10].

After this, the Valar and Maiar begin to build the World, and to govern it, in accordance with the Fate detailed in the Vision. This part is referred to as the Realization of the Vision. Melkor also descends to this created world, and while the Valar attempt to build the world and to prepare the world for its forthcoming inhabitants (the

2. Creation and Existence

"Children of Ilúvatar," Elves and Men), Melkor attempts to destroy their work and become the ruler of the World. Therefore, the first actual period in the World comprises countless waves of creation, destruction, and re-creation.

The Valar must labor to unfold the foresung history, but Melkor's attempts make this hard. This begets the first War of Time and World. Manwë, the leader of the Valar, and his people fight against Melkor and his forces. The Valar are victorious, and despite Melkor's malice, the Earth is made ready for the Children of Ilúvatar to awaken.

So how is the ideal vision and its realization constructed? The mythic fantasy world in Tolkien's fiction is formed in many cycles. First, there is only Eru Ilúvatar, the God of Tolkien's fantasy world. Then, Eru made the Ainur of his own thought—he imagined them to be. After that, the Music of the Ainur, designed by Eru, is the beginning of the World, but only as a vision. After the vision, Eru "gave to their vision Being, and set it amid the Void, and the Secret Fire was sent to burn at the heart of the World; and it was called Eä" (Tolkien 1999: 15).

As the internal, chronological beginning of Tolkien's fantasy world, there is "pre-existence." The fictional universe's timespan ranges from pre-existence to physical existence, and on to the end of the physical world. It is a linearly constructed worldview. At the beginning of the storyline there is not a physical, "real" world. Before the creation of the so-called physical "world," there is only "God," Eru, and the Ainur, conceived "of his thought." This era—before the Creation—could therefore be called spiritual pre-existence.

The physical world, and the concept of time along with it, is created by these immortal Beings. The cosmogony begins with tunes of Music and a vision of the (later physical) World, and lastly it is completed by the execution, and realization, of this vision. In the last part of creation, the music is "made visible," as "a light in the darkness." The vision is given existence, and this creation—the World—is set at the center of the Void, of emptiness. And at the heart of this World, there is the Secret Fire.

The Mythopoeic Code of Tolkien

Although highly original, the creation myth in Tolkien's *The Silmarillion* is in part intertextually connected with the creation myth in Plato's *Timaeus*. *Timaeus* was a work fundamental in the formation of medieval thought (Eco 1986: 17); and influenced later literary cosmological visions, and, as a 20th-century neo-medievalist writer, Tolkien should know the work. From Orozo Cilli's study *Tolkien's Library. An Annotated Checklist*, we know that Tolkien owned many works of ancient philosophy, although Cilli's book does not list any Plato's works belonging to Tolkien's private libraries. Then again, Plato's cosmological creation myth is, beside the *Bible*'s *Genesis*, the most important external field of reference for Tolkien's cosmogony in *The Silmarillion*: a prime example of Tolkien's mythopoeics, his creation of myths.

Before further examining Tolkien's cosmogonical myth, we might first look at the Christian Platonic theology behind Tolkien's cosmogony. In his survey of Christian theology, Alister E. McGrath highlights the doctrine of the original "goodness" of creation, which is also the central point Plato made in *Timaeus* (29a). McGrath explains that the world "as we see it is not the world as it was intended to be.... The existence of human sin, evil, and death are themselves tokens of the extent of the departure of the created order from its intended pattern" (McGrath 2011: 221). This concept of "restoration of creation to its original integrity" (McGrath 2011: 221), which Tolkien calls "unmarring," is also present in Tolkien's fiction (see McGrath 2011: 314): The World is marred from the beginning, but it will be ultimately restored to its original faultless vision.

For Tolkien's cosmogonic fiction, the link between music and harmony is crucial: in *The Silmarillion*, the fictitious world is indeed created through music, "Ainulindalë," the Music of the Ainur. The fundamental backdrop of Plato's cosmology and Plato's cosmogony is numeric congruence and universal harmony. Umberto Eco notes that the most ancient and best-established concept of this aesthetics of numerology of proportion is congruence (*congruentia*), the proportion of numbers, a concept that has its lineage in pre–Socratic

2. Creation and Existence

times. Congruence expressed the essentially quantitative conception of beauty, which repeatedly crops up in Greek thought, for example in the thinking of philosophers such as Pythagoras, Plato and Aristotle—and, as Eco sees it, received its classical formulation in the canon of Puluclitus and in Galen's subsequent exposition of Polyclitus' doctrines (Eco 1986: 28). Eco sees that the medieval conception of harmony originally derived from the theory of music (Eco 1986: 28–33). In this sense, Tolkien's mythopoeic cosmogony could, once again, be labeled neo-medievalist, but it also has its roots in ancient cosmological thinking.

Two Levels of Creation

In Tolkien's cosmology, the vision that Eru show the Ainur is extremely interesting. It is central for a Christian Platonic reading of the cosmology. As we see, in Tolkien's fiction, the world is created on two levels: the divine vision shown by Eru Ilúvatar and the realization. The problematic part of this creation on two levels is the beginning of Evil. Melkor (later Morgoth), one of the Ainur, rebels against Eru's will and jurisdiction which results in "corruption" and "marring" of the created world. Therefore, the created world is never formed quite as it was intended to be. This section discusses these aspects on two levels, focusing on the dichotomies of physical and spiritual existence, good and evil, and visibility and invisibility.[33]

Cosmogony is an important feature for the construction of a coherent fictional world. Northrop Frye argues that all mythologies begin with cosmogonies, the creation myths, and that there are two main types of these myths, depending on whether men are looking up or down from their "middle earth." On the one hand, if looking down, we see the cycle of animal and plant life, and creation myths suggested by this would naturally be sexual ones, focusing invariably on some kind of earth-mother. On the other hand, if looking up, we see not different forms of life emerging but the same sun rising in the east. Frye (1976: 112) suggests that such creation myths tend to be associated with a sky-father who goes about his mysterious doings without nursing his children. Plato's creation myth in the *Timaeus*, the story of creation in *The Bible*, and Tolkien's creation myth in *The Silmarillion* are of the latter type: myths looking up to the sky, or heavens.

Frye concludes that in the earth-mother creation myths death does not have to be explained: death is built into the whole process; but an intelligently made world of the second type could not have any death or evil at its genesis, so another myth of a fall is needed to complement it (Frye 1976: 112). This is evident in Tolkien's cosmogony and cosmology, where both the creation of evil and the fall, of Men and Elves alike, are described or hinted at. *The Silmarillion* is basically a story of the Fall of the Elves, and the subtext hints at the Fall of Men. In his letter to Milton Waldman in 1951, Tolkien (1981: 146) describes the original fall in his cosmogony as "a sub-creative Fall."

If we look at Tolkien's creation myth, first there is the cosmogony, the creation of the World, and then the cosmology, how the world is at its totality. There are many similarities in the structure of cosmogony, cosmography, and cosmology if we compare Tolkien's *The Silmarillion* and Plato's *Timaeus*. Here, the focus on Plato's *Timaues*' cosmology is not philosophical but structural. In Plato's structure the unique cosmos has a soul, it is spherical, and it is conditioned by time (Vlastos 1975: 29). One main aspect of Plato's cosmogony is that the world is created by the creator (Demiurge) who is good and cannot do anything evil or malevolent. After the creator has created the world, he quits it, and surrenders control to his children, the created gods.

In the *Timaeus* the creator is declared good, and therefore his creation is also good. The World is created on two levels: as the perfect original model on the one hand, and as the physical, changeable world on the other. The created physical world is thus a likeness of the original true being:

> If the world is indeed fair and the artificer good, it is manifest that he must have looked to that which is eternal; but if what cannot be said without blasphemy is true, then to the created pattern. Everyone will see that he

2. Creation and Existence

must have looked to the eternal; for the world is the fairest of creations and he is the best of causes. And having been created in this way, the world has been framed in the likeness of that which is apprehended by reason and mind and is unchangeable, and must therefore of necessity, if this is admitted, be a copy of something [Plato *Timaeus*: 29a].

The structure of the cosmology of Tolkien's fantasy world is essentially the same as Plato's: first the vision, then the realization. The starting point of the cosmogony of Tolkien's fiction is "The Music of the Ainur," which, although it is played by the Ainur, derives entirely from the creator. Eru is the original source of the music. After the music, as stated earlier, it is revealed in *The Silmarillion* that the image is not the real created world, but its model. When the Ainur are still surprisingly gazing upon the vision, Eru takes it away from their sight, because the "history was incomplete and the circles of time not full-wrought" (Tolkien 1999: 9).

The vision is taken away by Eru Ilúvatar and the real creation takes place. In Tolkien's fiction Eru Ilúvatar creates the World in the Judeo-Christian tradition by the power of words. Eru voices "Eä! Let these things Be!" in *The Silmarillion* (Tolkien 1999: 9), as in the Bible (Genesis 1:3), God says "Let there be light" ("genēthētō phōs" in Greek *Septuagint*, or "fiat lux" in Latin).

Although the Words of Creation are important, the main instrument of cosmogony is the music that creates a vision. Without the vision, there could not be a reality. This vision is the fundamental Idea and model for the cosmogony of the physical world. Verlyn Flieger (2002: 141) has pointed out that for Boethius, Dante, Chaucer, and the Scholastics musical harmony was the first principle of cosmic balance. This is clearly important for Tolkien's cosmology as well.

Flieger concentrates on the function of cosmogonical music in Tolkien's fiction and focuses on the aspect of interruptions in creative music. Tolkien tells how Eru presents a musical theme to his celestial progeny, the Ainur, and invites them to make his theme "a Great Music." The Ainur begin this "Music" which will be at once the pattern for and the agency of creation, but as their chorale of interchanging melodies grows in power and beauty, the Music is interrupted by a counter theme and must begin again. This happens twice, and during the last interruption Eru halts the performance furiously. The choir falls silent, the Music ceases, and a concept of sorrow has been foreshadowed and foresung. Flieger comments that the great design of Eru's initial theme is not carried to its proper conclusion, and thus is not fully achieved (Flieger 2005a: xiii).

Because the first music remains unfinished or the idea is unattained in way, in Tolkien's fantasy world, there will be a "Second Music" at the end of the world, at the end of Arda (the Created World). In this Second Music Melkor's discords will be eliminated and with it the corrupting influence that marred the creation of Arda. This Second Great Music will be played by "the sons of Men" and the Ainur together, in the way that the Music originally was meant to be "played" (see Whittingham 2008: 175).

In Tolkien's cosmogony the Platonic creation myth is an inevitable influence. This influence is similarly a long tradition of cosmologies that starts with Plato and is viable for thousands of years in Western thinking. For example, both the central ancient Neoplatonist Plotinus and central renaissance humanist and Neoplatonist Marsilio Ficino saw that music reigns the cosmos:

> Plotinus had posited a harmony of sentient things and forces in the universe. There is an innate drawing power—he thought—in poems, songs, and prayers, and—as they vibrate—they shape the felt harmony of similar and opposite things. In the wake of Plotinus, Ficino casts music and songs as living forms of spirit.
> ...A planetary music, composed of effluvia from above, reigns in the cosmos [Mazzotta 2001: 13].

This is clearly the case in Tolkien's cosmology too. The Music, played at the beginning and given from "above" (or Outside), reigns in Tolkien's fictional cosmos. And in Tolkien's fantasy world the power of words and music is imperative. As Umberto Eco maintains, behind the aesthetics of beauty and reality, there should be congruence (Eco 1986: 28). From this congruence derives the belief in harmony, and harmony is the creative power in Tolkien's fiction.

2. Creation and Existence

The Flame Imperishable, which is the heart of the created world in Tolkien's fiction, could be understood to resemble the Platonic Soul of the World. Plato writes that "in the center he [creator] put the soul, which he diffused throughout the body, making it also to be the exterior environment of it..." (*Timaeus* 34b).

In Tolkien's fiction the Flame Imperishable is the heart of the World, as Eru Ilúvatar (as an active character) declares in *The Silmarillion*: "And I will send forth into the Void the Flame Imperishable, and it shall be at the heart of the World" (Tolkien 1999: 9). The Flame becomes the heart of the world because of its power of creation. As mentioned, Melkor was searching for the Flame in order to create something new but could not find it "for it is with Ilúvatar," which could lead to the interpretation that the heart of the World is "with Ilúvatar" (Tolkien 1999: 4).

Melkor's search for the Flame is still narratively important. He wandered in "often alone into the Void," and "alone ... begun to conceive thoughts of his own" (Tolkien 1999: 4). This first mention of these "thoughts of his own" could also be seen as a kind of individualism compared to the other Ainur. When Melkor creates the discords, which forces Eru to make the interruptions in the Great Music, this first opposition against Eru's thoughts allows some of the Ainur to follow Melkor on his "musical rebellion."

> Some of these thoughts he [Melkor] now wove into his music, and straightway discord arose about him, and many that sang nigh him grew despondent, and their thought was disturbed and their music faltered; but some began to attune their music to his rather than to the thought which they had at first [Tolkien 1999: 4].

As all of this happens before the beginning of time in Tolkien's fantasy world, in "timelessness," it shows that in Tolkien's cosmology time is also created. It only affects the created changeable world, not the unchangeable world where the creator, Eru, lives in a place which is described as the Timeless Halls. This is "divine" since Tolkien in his letter to Milton Waldman (1981: 146) calls divine those that "were originally 'outside' and existed 'before' the making of the world." In *The Silmarillion* time begins after cosmogony, and at the moment the angelic beings enter the physical World. Tolkien (1995: 15) writes how the Ainur enter the created World at the beginning of Time, so they clearly have pre-existed before the time itself. The vision that was shown to the Ainur was a model, how the world should be. After that they "began their great labours in wastes unmeasured and unexplored, and in ages uncounted and forgotten..." (Tolkien 1999: 10).

What then is the role of future in this concept? If Eru dwells in the divine "timelessness" outside the world, what is the part of free will and fate in Tolkien's fiction? Tolkien himself wrote about Fate and Free Will in his text with the same title (Tolkien 2009c) and Verlyn Flieger discusses the topic on her article "The Music and the Task: Fate and Free Will in Middle-earth" (Flieger 2009). Also, Paul Kocher (1973: 12) has pointed out that many of the wise characters in Middle-earth have general glimpses of the future, but they are never more than vague and nonspecific. The future is the property of Eru, the One who plans it. Kocher ponders whether the future is yet fixed in the sense that every link in the chain of its events is foreordained. His answer is that it cannot be, because in his encounter with Gollum Bilbo's choice to kill or not to kill is genuinely free, and only after it has been made is it woven into the guiding scheme. Kocher (1973: 12) concludes that Tolkien leaves it at that. Human, or Hobbitic or Elvish or Dwarvish or Entish, free will coexists with a providential order and promotes rather than frustrates this order.

Christian Platonically thinking, C.S. Lewis has explained this complexity of the concepts of "free will" and "fate" starting from the theory deriving from Boethius, who then again used the theories of Plato, which greatly influenced Lewis' thoughts, too. Lewis, quoting Boethius, discusses that God, as eternal and not perpetual never foresees: "God sees all things that are, were, or will be ... in a single act of mind, and thus foreknows my actions.... Eternity is the actual and timeless fruition of illimitable life.... And God is eternal, not perpetual. Strictly speaking, He never *fore*sees; He simply sees. Your 'future' is only an area, and only for us a special area, of His infinite Now.... Boethius has here expounded a Platonic conception

2. Creation and Existence

more luminously than Plato ever did himself" (Lewis 1964: 88–90. Emphasis original).

The same could be the case with Tolkien's cosmology's Eru. He is free of time since he lives in "Timeless Halls" outside the Created World. In his letter to Milton Waldman, Tolkien describes how his fantasy world is going to end with a vision of the end of the world, and its breaking and remaking (Tolkien 1981, 149). Like his world's fictitious creator Eru, Tolkien as a "Maker" also knows how his world is going to end. Eru (and Tolkien), as well as the God in Boethius' theory, know the future—they do not foresee, but see.

This residing outside the physical world in timelessness relates closely to creation on two levels. In medieval Christian Platonic thought, there was a view of the ideal world as a "plane of existence" that relates to God himself and unreachable for mortal men. John Scotus Eriugene for example espoused this vision (Eco 1986: 57).

In Tolkien's cosmology the "upper" spiritual level and the "lower" physical level can be discerned, but also a kind of "shadow world" in between. On the upper spiritual level, at the starting point of creation, Eru showed the Ainur (later Valar) how the world would grow and develop, but the Idea, the exact ending, was not shown: "the Valar have not seen as with sight the Later Ages or the ending of the World" (Tolkien 1999: 9).

At the beginning of the physical world, the chosen Ainur (Valar and Maiar) moved within the Created World and began their labors there. In Tolkien's fiction, in *The Silmarillion*, after the rebellion of the Númenorean Men, the Undying Lands or Valinor, where the Valar and Maiar dwell, and which Tolkien also calls Paradise, are removed by Eru to beyond the reach of mortal men, they are removed and only remain in the memory. In a way after this Valinor is an interspace between the Ideal World and Changeable World, undying and unreachable,[34] but still part of the World. In a way, perhaps, resembling the plane of "the upper reaches of the world, the lower reaches of the heavens," where Väinämöinen went in the end of the *Kalevala* (1975: 337).

In Tolkien's fantasy world, physical appearance is relevant to the cosmology of "Two Levels": the levels of the visible and the invisible world. In *The Silmarillion*, the immortal beings Valar and Maiar can take a physical form if they want to, but otherwise they are purely spiritual creatures. As regards the Maiar, Tolkien writes that they were seldom visible to mortals (1999: 21) and that the Valar could "change form" or "walk unclad" (1999: 78) without physical form. Quite interestingly, those of the Ainur who turn evil, such as Melkor (later Morgoth) and Sauron, inevitably lose their power to change form or "unclad" themselves.[35]

For Tolkien, the word to describe good is light and the words to describe evil are dark, black, or shadow. The Valar are beings of light, whereas evil forces like Sauron are described as shadows. Shippey sees this as an important feature and goes on to ponder whether the shadows actually "exist." Shadows are the absence of light and thus do not exist but are still visible and palpable all the same. This dichotomy of light and shadow is vital in Tolkien's vision of evil. Mordor is the "Black-Land" where shadows lie, or where the shadows are. When Aragorn reports the assumed death of Gandalf to Galadriel and the Elves of Lothlórien, he says that he "fell into Shadow." Gandalf himself says that if his side loses, "many lands will pass under the shadow." Shippey points out that many times in *The Lord of the Rings* "the Shadow" becomes a personification of Sauron (Shippey 2003: 146–147).

Furthermore, the Balrog, one of the most horrible creatures in *The Lord of the Rings*, is also "a shadow." In the chapter "The Bridge of Khazad-Dûm," in one of most forceful episodes of *The Lord of the Rings*, the monstrous Balrog is described with the words of dark and shadow:

> Something was coming up behind them. What it was could not be seen: *it was like a great shadow*, in the middle of which was a dark form, a man-shape maybe, yet greater; and power and terror seemed to be in it and to go before it....
> The dark figure streaming with fire raced towards them....
> "You cannot pass," he [Gandalf] said.... "I am a servant of the Secret Fire, wielder of the flame of Anor. You cannot pass. The dark fire will not avail you, flame of Udûn. *Go back to the Shadow!* You cannot pass" [Tolkien 2008: 411. Emphasis mine].

2. Creation and Existence

Gandalf orders the Balrog, a great shadow, to go back to the Shadow, to the emptiness. The origins of this terrible creature is described in *The Silmarillion*, where Tolkien writes about the Maiar spirits that fell and joined Melkor's forces: "Dreadful among these spirits were the Valaraukar, the scourges of fire in Middle-earth were called Balrog, demons of terror" (Tolkien 1999: 23).

In *The Silmarillion*, Tolkien writes that number of Maiar spirits is not known to the Elves (Tolkien 1999: 21), but of the Valaraukar Tolkien speculates in *The History of Middle-earth* that "[t]here should not be supposed more than say 3 or at most 7 ever existed" (Tolkien 2002e: 80), so Gandalf faces a rare enemy.

In *The Lord of the Rings*, the Nazgûl, the Ringwraiths, are also described as shadows. Originally, earlier in Tolkien's world's timespan, the Nazgûl were nine mortal men who were given Rings of Power by Sauron and became his slaves and powerful undead[36] forces. Their role is described in the famous poem that is given as an epigraph for all three parts of *The Lord of the Rings*:

> Three Rings for the Elven-kings under the sky,
> Seven for the Dwarf-lords in their halls of stone,
> Nine for Mortal Men doomed to die,
> One for the Dark Lord on his dark throne
> In the Land of Mordor where the Shadows lie.
> One Ring to rule them all, One ring to find them,
> One Ring to bring them all and in the darkness bind them
> In the land of Mordor where the Shadow lie [Tolkien 2009b: 4].

The Nine, the Nazgûl, are ruled by the maker of the One Ring, they are one with the ring, and they are bound in the darkness and shadows by the One Ring. Tolkien (1999: 346) writes that Men proved easier to "ensnare" with the Rings. The took the rings and obtained power, glory and great wealth. But one by one they became slaves to Sauron and his commands. They became invisible to mortal eyes, and they entered "the real of shadows": "The Nazgûl were they, the Ringwraiths, the Enemy's most terrible servants; darkness went with them, and they cried with the voices of death," (Tolkien 1999: 346)

Thus, the Nine, the Ringwraiths, became invisible to mortal

eyes, and they "entered the realm of shadows." In *The Lord of the Rings*, it seems as if the Nazgûl do not have physical shapes at all, but they can sense the physical world and affect it. This provokes a discussion in *The Lord of the Rings*. Merry asks whether the Nazgûl could even see since they seem to use their sense of smell to track down their enemies. There, it is said that the Nazgûl "do not see the world of light as we do" (Tolkien 2008: 247).

Tolkien is addressing a difference between "the world of light" and "the world of shadow," the plane between the planes, in a way. Randel Helms sees that the sense of smell that the Nazgûl use in *The Lord of the Rings* is a reference to Heraclitus who commented that in Hades, the Greek Underworld and the abode of the dead in Greek Mythology, "the souls—being but smoke, know each other only by scent" (Helms 1974: 91). The Nazgûl are no longer mortal or living since they are undead. They have moved farther away from the mortal senses. In Tolkien's fiction this same dichotomy between visible and invisible, and its effect on senses, is also evident in the dichotomy between mortal and immortal.

The Nazgûl could see only those who also inhabit the shadow world. The One Ring, made by Sauron, makes its mortal user invisible to other mortal eyes. It moves its wielder into the shadow world, where the physical plane becomes blurred, and invisible things visible. When Frodo puts on the One Ring in *The Lord of the Rings*, he becomes invisible to mortal eyes, but visible to the eyes of the Nazgûl, and they become visible to Frodo: "There were five tall figures: two standing on the lip of the dell, three advancing. In their white faces burned keen and merciless eyes; under their mantles were long grey robes; upon their grey hairs were helms of silver; in their haggard hands were swords of steel" (Tolkien 2008: 255).

However, the Nazgûl are not the only beings in Middle-earth who are able to see the invisible. The dichotomy between physical and spiritual does not affect the immortal creatures. When the Ainur enter the physical world they take physical shapes which are based on the Idea of Elves and Men—which the Ainur have seen in the Vision of Eru Ilúvatar—but even these shapes are for them like

2. Creation and Existence

clothes are for humans: "the Valar may walk, if they will, unclad, and then even the Eldar cannot clearly perceive them, though they be present" (Tolkien 1999: 11).

The most interesting character in Tolkien's fiction with respect to the dichotomies of good and evil, mortal, and immortal, and physical and spiritual is the Wizard Gandalf. In fact, in Tolkien's fiction physical and spiritual changes are central to the habitus of Gandalf. In the second book of *The Silmarillion*, Gandalf, called Olórin, is mentioned as a Maia spirit who is fond of Elves, who dwelt in Lórien,[37] but prefers to remain unseen to them, or in disguise in Elvish form (Tolkien 1999: 22).

Later, Olórin, now known as Mithrandir or Gandalf, becomes one of the Wizards, the Istari, who come over the Sea from the Undying Lands to help in a war against Sauron. Of the Istari, he is described closest in counsel with the Elves (Tolkien 1999: 360). Then again, in *The Hobbit* Gandalf is an archetypal "helper" for the protagonist, and at the beginning of *The Lord of the Rings*, he is a familiar character to the Hobbits, although the Hobbits did not know how difficult and dangerous his real tasks were (Tolkien 2008: 48).

In fact, in *The Lord of the Rings*, Gandalf is Dark Lord Sauron's main enemy, The Champion of Light, an "angelic being" sent from the West by the Valar. Tolkien even suggested in the posthumously published *Unfinished Tales of Númenor and Middle-earth* that Gandalf himself could have be Manwë, the King of the Valar, disguised as a "regular" angelic being of the race of Maiar and after that taken a mortal shape (1992: 540).

In the beginning of *The Lord of the Rings* Gandalf suggests that he is more than he appears to be in a scene where Bilbo has a problem with freely giving the One Ring to Frodo as an inheritance. This difficulty to "give away the One Ring" has much to do with the "possessiveness" of magical artifacts that Tolkien himself was addressing in "On Fairy-Stories."[38] When Bilbo gets angry in the scene, Gandalf counters, and warns how it will be his turn to be angry and the Hobbit does not want to meet Gandalf the Grey uncloaked (Tolkien 2008: 59). In the scene, in the eyes of Bilbo, Gandalf seems to grow. This

The Mythopoeic Code of Tolkien

impression that characters "grow in size" is a recurring element. Aragorn, the future king of the Kingdom of Men, is described this way when he meets Frodo and his company for the first time: "He stood up, and seemed suddenly to grow taller. In his eyes gleamed a light, keen and commanding. Throwing back his cloak, he laid his hand on the hilt of a sword that had hung concealed by his side. They did not dare to move" (Tolkien 2008: 225). Also, in a memorable scene in which Frodo offers the One Ring to the immortal and extremely powerful elf Galadriel,[39] she is also described as "tall beyond measurement, and beautiful before enduring, terrible and worshipful" (Tolkien 2008: 454).

Gandalf's character in *The Lord of the Rings* goes through a dramatic change during the narrative. That is because he "dies," and afterwards "returns." In the chapter "The Bridge of Khazad-dûm," Gandalf battles with the Balrog and falls into a pit. In the pit, or abyss, he ends up killing the "monster," but his own physical shape dies. Gandalf explains to his friends that he was sent back to do his work: "Naked I was sent back—for a brief time, until my task is done" (Tolkien 2009a: 117). After rising from the "death," Gandalf emphasizes his disparity from the physical world on some occasions. When Aragorn, Gimli, and Legolas mistake him for Saruman and try to attack him, Gandalf tells them that "None of you have any weapons that could hurt me" (Tolkien 2009a: 108).

The opposing (evil) forces of *The Lord of the Rings* are given a different and more tragic ending. Sauron, after the destruction of the One Ring, rises for one last time as a huge shadow and then disappears with a breeze of wind:

> [B]lack against the pall of cloud, there rose a huge shape of shadow, impenetrable, lightning-crowned, filling all the sky. Enormous it reared above the world, and stretched out towards them a vast threatening hand, terrible but impotent: for even as it leaned over them, a great wind took it, and it was blown away, and passed; and then a hush fell [Tolkien 2009b: 251].

Paul Kocher discusses the "deaths" of immortal beings in Tolkien's fiction and the similarities of the destruction of the Witch King

2. Creation and Existence

of Angmar, the leader of the Nazgûl, at the hands of Éowyn, and the death of Saruman at the hands of Grima. Both death scenes focus on perishableness. Kocher sees that Saruman's death completes his downfall. His spirit rising from his shrunken body is dissipated by a wind from the West and the spirit is dissolved into nothing. Kocher (1973: 79) sees that this "nothing" is a general knell for the passing of the lords of evil in *The Lord of the Rings*, but also that Tolkien is careful never to say anything explicit about this "nothingness" to which they go.

Physical and spiritual, visible, and invisible, are also vital concerning the Rings of Power. For example, in *The Lord of the Rings* the One Ring does not affect Tom Bombadil, who is also an immortal creature. When Frodo puts on the One Ring, and becomes invisible to other Hobbits, Tom Bombadil can still see him (Tolkien 2008: 179). Earlier, when Tom Bombadil puts on the One Ring, he does not become invisible, and all of the Hobbits are astonished (Tolkien 2008: 178). Later, during the Council of Elrond, Gandalf explains that Bombadil "is his own master," and "the Ring has no power over him" (Tolkien 2008: 336), which underscores the fact that the One Ring affects mortals and that Tom Bombadil is not mortal.

As an animistic spirit, Tom Bombadil is unaffected by the One Ring of Sauron, but the effect of visibility and invisibility on mortal eyes is even more interesting when it comes to the Elves in Tolkien's fiction. In *The Lord of the Rings* the One Ring has a "magical" capability to transfer its user to "a shadow world," which is something of a plane of existence between, or perhaps under,[40] the physical "middle-world" and spiritual "upper world." Tolkien describes that high Elves, those of the people of Eldar who have lived in both the Undying Lands of Valinor and in Middle-earth, live on "both sides"— in the physical and in the spiritual world (Tolkien 2002d: 212).

In *The Lord of the Rings* when Frodo is attacked by the Nazgûl and is struck with the Morgul knife, he is injured and evil magic pulls him into the shadow life of the Nazgûl, of the undead. He is "beginning to fade," as Gandalf later explains at Rivendell (Tolkien 2008: 280). In an early version of the story, in *The Return of the Shadow*,

The Mythopoeic Code of Tolkien

Gandalf says that Frodo would have himself become an undead person, a shadow, if he would have put on the One Ring: "they would have made a wraith of you before long—certainly if you had put on the Ring again" (Tolkien 2002d: 206).

In the story, Frodo is quickly rushed to the Elves of Rivendell to be healed. On their way, they encounter Elf-lord Glorfindel, who has ridden from Rivendell in search of them. When Frodo, who is at this point "beginning to fade," sees Glorfindel, he sees him as he "really is": "To Frodo it appeared that a white light was shining through the form and raiment of the rider, as if through a thin veil" (Tolkien 2008: 271). Frodo sees the inner light of the Elf, the spiritual—and the immortal—power of the character. Frodo is about to be pulled into the "shadow land" where invisible things become visible, and visible (physical) things invisible.

Later Glorfindel's real being is again revealed when almost completely "faded" Frodo is attacked by the Nazgûl at the Ford of Bruinen. Frodo, nearly unconscious now, is rescued by a miraculous uprising of the river (caused by Elrond) which bears the Black Riders into "the rushing flood" (Tolkien 2008: 277). Losing his last senses, Frodo sees his friends and companions trying to come to his aid:

> With the last failing senses Frodo heard cries, and it seemed to him that he saw, beyond the Riders that hesitated on the shore, *a shining figure of white light*; and beyond it ran small shadowy forms waving flames, that flared red in the grey mist that was falling over the world [Tolkien 2008: 277. Emphasis mine].

Frodo's mortal companions—the three Hobbits Sam, Pippin and Merry, and Aragorn—are the small shadowy forms, the grey mist is the rest of the physical world, and "a shining figure of white light" is Glorfindel. This is later revealed when Frodo asks Gandalf about the incident, and Gandalf explains that Frodo saw Glorfindel "for a moment as he is upon the other side: one of the mighty of the Firstborn" (Tolkien 2008: 284).

This is an informing passage. Gandalf's words confirm Frodo's vision to be a real one, as his words usually refer to real knowledge of cosmology in *The Lord of the Rings*. Frodo saw Glorfindel for a

2. Creation and Existence

moment as he is "upon the other side." In this Platonic view, Frodo sees, one might say, the ideal shape of Glorfindel: as a shining figure, he saw the ideal form of a High Elf (*Calaquendi*, The Elf of the Light), and not just the real-life physical body. Frodo was moving into a chthonic, demonic underworld, a plane for the shadows and undead. However, at the same time as his vision of the physical world is fading, his vision of things invisible to mortal eyes is evolving.

In *The History of Middle-earth* Tolkien discusses the relation of the Elves and undead more thoroughly when Gandalf explains to Frodo why the Elves do not fear the Nazgûl: "They fear no Ringwraiths, for they live at once in both worlds, and each world has only half power over them, while they have double power over both" (Tolkien 2002d: 212). Basically, the Elves live in "two worlds": the physical and unphysical; the ideal and real.

This view of the dead, or undead, is shared in *The Lord of the Rings* by Legolas, who is an Elf of The Woodland Realm and son of Thranduil, King of Northern Mirkwood. Even though Legolas is a Wood Elf and not one of the High Elves, meaning an Elf whose ancestors once traveled to Undying Lands in the Elder Days, Legolas says that he does "not fear the Dead" (Tolkien 2009b: 55) when traveling with Aragorn to the Paths of the Dead in Dunharrow, which is inhabited by undead creatures, the Oathbreakers, the army of the dead. For the immortal Elves, whose souls never leave the world, there is no need to fear the undead.

One could say that Tolkien's Elves, as immortal creatures, are at the same time physical and spiritual. In *Morgoth's Ring*, Tolkien also discusses how the Eldar, the High Elves, will eventually become completely invisible to mortal eyes. Their spiritual side will "consume" their physical side:

> As the weight of the years, with all their changes of desire and thought, gathers upon the spirit of the Eldar, so do the impulses and moods of their bodies change. This the Eldar mean when they speak of their spirits consuming them; and they say that ere Arda ends all *the Eldalië on earth will have become spirits invisible to mortal eyes, unless they will to be seen by some among Men* into whose minds they may enter directly [Tolkien 2002e: 212. Emphasis mine].

The Mythopoeic Code of Tolkien

In the mythopoeics of Tolkien's fantasy fiction there are dichotomies between the physical and the spiritual and between the visible and the invisible realms. These can be seen also in the great division: the dichotomy between mortal and immortal. Tolkien's fantasy fiction unites these elements and motifs of Christian Platonism in a coherent cosmological vision.

Cosmology and the Chain of Being

The most coherent cosmological account of Tolkien's fiction is given as a posthumously published and fragmented version in *The Silmarillion*. An important text in the work is "Valaquenta," the second part of *The Silmarillion*, which is a short (under ten pages long) account of the "Valar and Maiar according to the lore of the Eldar." A story, on inner perspective of Tolkien's fantasy world, is imparted by the Elves (the Eldar) and concerns the Hierarchy of "Gods": Valar and Mair, the divine and angelic beings of Arda. Basically, "Valaquenta" introduces these divine beings and their attributes, areas of responsibility and roles in the mythology. There, accounts of Melkor and each of the fourteen other Valar are given, and some of the "lower" Maiar beings are introduced for the first time. Here, Sauron and Gandalf (under the name of Olórin), the forthcoming archrivals of *The Lord of the Rings*, are also addressed.

The major text of *The Silmarillion* is titled "Quenta Silmarillion," also referred to as "The History of the Silmarils" or "Silmarillion proper." It is a collection of tales and legends set in the so-called First Age of Middle-earth. The central storyline is the tragic story of the three jewels, the Silmarils, which are the most valued artifacts in the whole mythical history Tolkien's fiction.

In "Quenta Silmarillion," the different phases of history before the ages of Sun are described. The first cycle, when the Valar live in a place called Almaren, is the Age of Lamps, also called "The Spring of Arda." These Lamps, Illuin and Ormal, are the first lights in Arda and illuminate the world before the creation of Sun or Moon. The age

2. Creation and Existence

ends when Melkor destroys the Lamps. This foul act of destruction causes such devastation that the whole structure, shape, and landform of Arda is changed permanently. Symmetry of Arda's waters and lands is marred forever and the original design build by Valar and orchestrated by Eru is lost and will never be restored in the timeline of Tolkien's fantasy world (see Tolkien 1999: 29).

In a way, this devastation creates a new world and starts a new phase in the history of Middle-earth. The destruction on itself is not exactly apocalyptic, referring to the Ends of the World since the World is still functional, but the aftermath of the destruction of the Lamps leads Arda and most certainly the Middle-earth in a quite Post-Apocalyptic era. The Valar in a way forsake the Middle-earth, and it is left to ruled by Melkor and his followers. After the catastrophe, the Valar move their seat of power to Aman, a continent far to the west of Middle-earth, and establish there a kingdom called Valinor, The Undying Lands, which in the fantasy world will stand until the end of Time. Melkor's strongholds and fortresses are on the other side of the world, in the Middle-earth. First, Melkor rules in Utumno and later in Angband, in the far north of Middle-earth. After the destruction of the Lamps, the Middle-earth is a devastating place ruled by Evil Dark Lord Melkor and mostly perilous for its inhabitants.

After the destruction of the Lamps, the second cycle of light in Tolkien's fiction is called the Age of Trees, but it only affects the Undying Lands (Valinor). The Middle-earth remains mostly a dark place. In Valinor, Yavanna, one of the Valar, Giver of Fruits and the Queen of the Earth, creates two trees—Telperion and Laurelin—with the power of her song. But the light of the trees created by Yavanna only affects Valinor, and the only light in Middle-earth are the stars that Varda, the Queen of the Valar, creates. The Middle-earth remain "a twilight realm," like places of Faërie (the world of fairies) has been called in old English and Celtic folktales.

In the Age of Trees, the Elves, the first Children of Ilúvatar, awaken in the farthest east of Middle-earth, in a place called Cuiviénen. The awakening of the Elves at last forces the Valar to go to war against Melkor, whose plan is to corrupt the Elves and become their ruler, or "god." This war ends in the victory of Valar and the capture and imprisonment of Melkor. In the cosmological account it is revealed that some of the Elves journey to Valinor and become its residents, the Calaquendi, The Elves of Light or High Elves. Calaquendi themselves are divided into three family groups: the Vanyar, the Noldor, and those of the people of Teleri who traveled to Valinor (some of them did not). The other Elves, those who stayed in the Middle-earth and did not travel to Valinor, are referred in the cosmology as Moriquendi, the Elves of the Darkness, because they lived in the Middle-earth when it was a dark place without daylight. This division by Tolkien into the Elves of Light and the Elves of the Darkness is of course a clear reference to Norse Mythology, and for example to later *Prose Edda* (ca. 1220) by Snorri Sturluson, where the Elves of Norse Mythology are divided into Light Elves (Ljósálfar) and Dark Elves (Dökkálfar).

In the Age of Trees, as a remarkable miraculous individual task, the Silmarils—the magical gems of extreme beauty—are made by Fëanor, the greatest of Elves. For the making of these jewels or gems, Fëanor used all his unearthly skills as a smith (Tolkien 1999: 68). These gems become a magical artifact that decides the fate of the World. Mandos, the Doomsman of the Valar, foretold that "the fates of Arda, earth, and air, lay locked within them" (Tolkien 1999: 69).

This second age of light ends in a story called "The Darkening of Valinor." In the chapter, Melkor is naively released from his imprisonment. The Valar, being pure in their hearts and unfamiliar with deceptive behavior, believe Melkor's appeals for mercy. Melkor is released, and after that, with the help of a horrific spider-like demonic being called Ungoliant, Melkor attacks Valinor and destroys the Trees and steals the Silmarils from Fëanor's father Finwë, whom he kills during the robbery. As a result of this "darkening," the people of Fëanor, the Noldor Elves, declare a "rebellion" against the Valar and decide to pursue Melkor in Middle-earth. Fëanor decides to win back the Silmarils and to avenge his father. The Noldor Elves choose not to listen to Manwë, the King of the Valar. After the rebellion, the

2. Creation and Existence

Valar tell the Elves that if they choose to leave and fight Melkor on their own, they will not help them. Earlier, Manwë has told them that they had come to Valinor of their own free will and that the Valar had no desire to rule or control them.

The destruction of unanimity in Valinor results in the "flight of the Noldor" from Valinor, without the blessing of the Valar. Before fleeing, Fëanor and his seven sons swore a terrible oath of vengeance, to battle anyone who withheld the Silmarils from them, even the Valar. This all functions as the Fall of the Elves, and everything they must endure after this in Middle-earth is part of their struggle. After this, the unsuccessful and tragic war of the Noldor Elves and Melkor (Morgoth) forms a major part of "Quenta Silmarillion." The war is hopeless and nearly all great kings, leaders and wise of the Elves die in the prolonged struggle.

In the history of Tolkien's world, after the Age of Trees come the Ages of Sun. There, after the destruction of the Trees by Melkor and Ungoliant, the Valar create the Moon and the Sun. This age is also the time of the awakening of Men. Thus, in the cosmology the Elves are the people of the Stars, and Men are the people of the Sun. In the fictional history of Middle-earth, as is also the case in our own history, eras usually start and end with wars. The First Age of Sun, and the narrative of "Quenta Silmarillion," ends with the "War of Wrath." In this war the Valar, the Elves and some faithful Men (Elendili, Elf-Friends) finally manage to break Melkor's (Morgoth's) dominion over Middle-earth, and Melkor is "thrust through the Door of Night beyond the Walls of the World, into the Timeless Void" (Tolkien 1999: 306). But the price of victory is high, since the land of Beleriand, the western part of Middle-earth, is also destroyed in the course of the events (Tolkien 1999: 303). Once again in the history of Arda, the landscape is altered because the Valar must battle against Melkor. The shape of the World changes when the Age of the Lamps end and when the War of Wrath ends, and later, when the island of Númenor is destroyed in the end of "Akallabêth."

The fourth part of *The Silmarillion*, the "Akallabêth," deals with the Second Age of Middle-earth, also known as the Second Age of

Sun. It is an account of the rise and fall of Númenor, the island kingdom of the faithful Men, called the Dúnedain. They are the most trusted part of Elendili, Elf-Friends, who battled side by side with the Valar and the Elves in the War of Wrath against Melkor. The fifth part of *The Silmarillion*, "Of the Rings of Power and the Third Age," closely links the legends of *The Silmarillion* with the storyline of *The Hobbit* and *The Lord of the Rings*. This is a short story that describes the events that take place at the end of the Second Age and the main events of The Third Age. Here, the origin of the Rings of Power is described, and the rise and fall of Sauron's evil empire is illuminated. The survey ends with a short summary of the plot of *The Lord of the Rings*.

Considering Tolkien's fiction as a constructed cosmological account (but also as a set of narratives), during its timespan the focus changes from Ainur to Elves, and later from Elves to Men (and to Hobbits). Tolkien himself comments on a letter to Milton Waldman (Tolkien 1983: 147) that *The Silmarillion* is peculiar if compared to other books, since it is not anthropocentric. It is not all that interested in Men. In *The Silmarillion*, the main focus is not on human characters but on the race of Elves—or, earlier in the text, on the creation myth, and the divine spirits of Ainur. There is clearly a chain of being in Tolkien's fiction: a chain in which mortal Men are "lower" than the races of Elves or Ainur.

This chain of being, or scala naturæ ("ladder of being")—the concept of a hierarchical explanation of the universe, is also evident in the cosmology of Tolkien's fantasy fiction. The concept itself is derived from Plato's and Aristotle's cosmological accounts and developed in Neoplatonism and in the Christian Platonism of the medieval era. Plato introduces its basic principles in *Timaeus* and *Republic*, Aristotle theorizes it in *Historia Animalium*, and Plotinus unravels his Neoplatonist doctrines of the chain of being in his *Enneads*. Medieval Christian Platonic thinkers, such as Albertus Magnus, in his translations and commentaries to Aristotle's *De Animalibus* (*The Man and the Beasts* or *On Animals*) in the 13th century, and Nicolas of Cusa in his *On Learned Ignorance* (*De Docta ignorantia*)

2. Creation and Existence

in 1440, developed these ideas further. Essentially, chain of being details a strict hierarchical structure of all matter and life, starting from the creator (or God) and progressing downward from angels and demons to stars, moon, king, nobles, arcane men, animals, trees, plants, stones, metals and minerals (see Lovejoy 1965: 59).

The chain of being in Tolkien's fiction has some of its origins in the Christian Platonic tradition presented above. In Tolkien's cosmology, immortal and mortal races and creatures are higher or lower in hierarchy than others are. Highest in the hierarchy is Eru Ilúvatar, the creator of Middle-earth. After the creator come the Ainur, The Holy Ones, which are akin to Plato's created gods, quite as Eru Ilúvatar resembles Plato's Demiurge. Flieger (2002: 170) sees that Eru's name—maybe originating from Indo-European *er*, "to set in motion," may also relate to the ancient concept of The One, who sets things in motion, the so-called Prime Mover. But if Eru is the Prime Mover, then how did he set the world in motion if he himself is untouched by movement or change? The same question concerning the Prime Mover troubled thinkers of the ancient and medieval world: how have the movement in the changeable world started and what is the thing that does not move? C.S. Lewis argues that the central answer to this question comes from Aristotle:

> [As a] Prime mover he finds in the wholly transcendent and immaterial God who "occupies no place and is not affected by time." But we must not imagine Him moving things by any positive action, for that would be to attribute some kind of motion to Himself and we should then not have reached an utterly unmoving Mover. How then does He move things? Aristotle answers—"He moves as beloved." He moves other things, that is, an object of desire moves those who desire it. The Primum Mobile is moved by its love for God, and being moved, communicates motion to the rest of the universe [Lewis 1964: 113].

To the question that fixated ancient scholars, and still may baffle modern thinkers, "what is behind this moving cosmos," Lewis answers once again with Aristotle's reasoning:

> And beyond the Primum Mobile what? The answer to this unavoidable question has been given, in its first form, by Aristotle. "Outside the

heaven there is neither place nor void nor time. Hence whatever is there is of such a kind as not to occupy space, nor does affect it...." Adopted by Christianity, the doctrine speaks loud and jubilant. What is in one sense "outside heaven" is now, in other sense, "the very Heaven," caelum ipsum, and full of God, as Bernardus says [Lewis 1964: 96–97].

This question (and answer) of the Primum Mobile, and Heaven beyond that, may have influenced Tolkien's imagination too since he places his cosmology's Eru Ilúvatar in the "Timeless Halls" outside the "Created World."

In *The Silmarillion*, the Ainur are described as the offspring of Eru's thought (Tolkien 1999: 3) and in this way they are "a part" of Eru. In *The Book of Lost Tales Part One* Tolkien writes that Eru has created the Ainur by singing before the Creation: "Before all things he sang into being the Ainur first, and greatest is their power and glory of all his creatures within the world and without" (Tolkien 2002a: 52). In this way, the Ainur are also a part of creation, a foreshadowing of it.

Tolkien writes that some of the Ainur went to the created physical world and will remain there as long as the world will exist, their existence and being is contained and bounded to the world (Tolkien 1999: 9–10). As stated earlier, the Ainur who go to the created world, Arda, are divided hierarchically into two categories: the higher Valar (The Powers of the World), and the lower Maiar, who are of the same sort of existence as them but of lesser degree (Tolkien 1999: 21). In Tolkien's fiction Eru Ilúvatar lives "beyond the confines of the World" in the Timeless Halls, which cannot be reached by mortals, just as Plato writes that "the father and maker of all this universe is past finding out; and even if we found him, to tell of him to all men would be impossible" (*Timaeus* 28c).

The Valar are the "Powers of the Earth," but on some occasions they clearly do not, or perhaps cannot, manage all by themselves. The clearest example of this is seen during the "invasion" of Valinor by the rebellious Númenoreans, who demand immortality from Eru and the Powers. The Númenoreans only manage to get to the shore of Valinor before Eru Ilúvatar uses his Divine powers and changes

2. Creation and Existence

the shape of the world (Tolkien 1999: 333–334). In the passage: "the Valar laid down their government of Arda" and called upon the One, who sank Númenor under the waves (Tolkien 1999: 334). Kocher has pointed out that this serves to show us that while the Valar have what Tolkien calls incomprehensibly great "demiurgic" powers, which they use in governing and guarding the affairs of Middle-earth, they are only agents of Eru and are in need of his direct intervention in major emergencies. Kocher (2000: 24) points out that Tolkien does not go beyond this point in defining the relationship of the Valar to their superior, and that he has told us all we need to understand the literary-philosophical framework of his tale.

The Ainur, as the offspring of Eru's thought, are not bound by physical appearances, they are spiritual creatures. The same can be assumed of Eru, too. Anne Freire Ashbaugh interprets (1988: 13) that Plato's Demiurge knows nothing of physical limitations or (human) physical restrictions. Perhaps, then, Eru and Ainur are pure spirits (*mentes*), as Lewis writes Dionysius thought angels to be (1964: 71). Tolkien himself writes in *The Road Goes Ever On* that the Valar (as part of the Ainur) took physical forms after they ended their demiurgic tasks and settled in Arda, the Created World (Tolkien 1967: 74).

In Tolkien's chain of being, after Eru and the Ainur, the spiritual creatures, come the races that Eru Ilúvatar had created, the Elves and the Men, who in *The Silmarillion* are called the Children of Ilúvatar. The Elves are higher in hierarchy than Men because they are created first and resemble more the Ainur than the Men do: Elves are the Firstborn and Men are the followers (Tolkien 1999: 7).

In the cosmology of Tolkien's fantasy fiction, the races of both Elves and Men are formed of soul and body: Fëa and Hröa, as Elves call them (Tolkien 2002e: 304, 309). Through Finrod, an Elf, Tolkien describes how the Elves see these two—body and soul—functioning in perfect harmony: "[H]armony of hröa and fëa is, we [Elves] believe, essential to the true nature unmarred of all the Incarnate: the Mirröanwi as we call the Children of Eru" (Tolkien 2002e: 315).

Men, who are despaired by the fact that they are mortal, whereas Elves are not, believe that their hröar "were not by right nature short-lived, but had been made so by the malice of Melkor" (Tolkien 2002e: 304). To this, Finrod answers that it is impossible:

> You [Andreth, a human] claim, if you fully understand your own words, to have had imperishable bodies, not bounded by the limits of Arda, and yet derived from its matter and sustained by it. And you claim also (though this you may not have perceived) to have had hröar and fëar that were from beginning out of harmony [Tolkien 2002e: 315].

In fact, in Tolkien's cosmology body and soul are inseparable:

> But the body is not an inn to keep a traveller warm for a night, ere he goes on his way, and then to receive another. It is a house made for one dweller only, indeed not only house but raiment also; and it is not clear to me that we should in this case speak only of the raiment being fitted to the wearer rather than of the wearer being fitted to the raiment —. For were it "natural" for the body to be abandoned and die, but "natural" for the fëa to live on, then there would indeed be a disharmony in Man, and his parts would not be united by love. His body would be a hindrance at best, or a chain. An imposition indeed, not a gift [Tolkien 2002e: 317].

This is a classical view of the subject of soul and body. C.S. Lewis notes that "spirits" are the "subtle gumphus" required by Plato and Alanus to keep body and soul together, or as Donne says, "the subtle knot which makes us man" (Lewis 1964: 167).

Plato says in the *Charmides*, in a negative tone against physicians and medicine, that the body cannot be cured without the soul. In *Timaeus*, Plato asserts the symmetry of soul and body. Any defect of either is an occasion of the greatest discord. Thus, for Plato, body and soul are in a way also inseparable (Jowett 1964: 688).

Lewis points out that in the early Middle Ages the Platonic belief that "we" had lived before we were incarnate on earth still hung in the air. For example, Chalcidius, a 4th-century Platonic philosopher who was most like also Christian, had preserved what Plato says about this in *Phaedrus* (245a) and in *Timaeus* (35a, 41d). From early sources, we know that the doctrine of pre-existence was important for the Christian Platonic philosophy of that era. Concerning the concept, Lewis explains that these very difficult passages may not really imply the pre-existence of the individual soul but could easily

2. Creation and Existence

be thought to do so. Lewis sees that Origen held that all those souls which now animate human bodies were created at the same time as the angels and had long existed before their terrestrial birth. Even Augustine maintains that Adam's soul was already in existence while his body still "slept in its causes" (Lewis 1964: 155–156).[41]

In Tolkien's cosmology, the fates of Men and Elves are different. In *The Silmarillion* Tolkien writes that Elves' souls are immortal, and their bodies are immune to illnesses or pestilences, but their physical form could be destroyed. In that aspect they were more like Men than Ainur. Although this dichotomy of body and soul of Elves will change during their lives, and later in Tolkien's legendarium's timeline, since later the bodies of Elves will be consumed by the fire of their spirit (see Tolkien 1999: 117) and their physical form will change. Maybe they will even become invisible to mortal eyes, as Tolkien hints.

Tolkien writes that the "doom of the Elves is to be immortal, to love the beauty of the world, to bring it to full flower with their gifts of delicacy and perfection, to last while it lasts, never leave it even when 'slain,' but returning ... and yet, when the Followers [Men] come, to teach them, and make way for them..." (Tolkien 1999: xv).

Then again, the souls of the Elves are bound to Arda, the created World, but human souls are not bound to it. The World (Arda) "will not endure for ever. It was made by Eru, but He is not in it. The One only has no limits. Arda, and Eä itself, must therefore be bounded" (Tolkien 2002e: 311–312).

Thus, Men are different from Elves because they are mortal. But what does this mortality mean? Are their souls still "immortal" or ever-lasting? In Tolkien's fiction it is emphasized that the Elves do not know what happens to the souls of Men after they die. Will their souls go to halls of Mandos as will happen to Elven souls, or whether they will leave the borders of Arda? The fate of men is completely unknown to Elves and even to Valar, since it was not foretold in the Music of Ainur that showed the idea of the world (see Tolkien 1999: 117). Tolkien therefore describes in his "mythology of Elves" that the fate of Men is unknown. *The Silmarillion* is of course written from the perspective of Elves. It is the mythical history of the Elves and therefore consists of their legends and stories.

Whereas the Elves and Men are described as "Children of Ilúvatar" in the cosmology, the races of Hobbits and Dwarves are essentially outsiders in comparison. At first, they are not a part of the original cosmological Idea or the final cosmogonical Creation. Then again, the Hobbits were originally also outsiders in Tolkien's own mythopoeic creation. They only arrive to Tolkien's fiction as an accidental creation, for the purpose of giving a comic aspect to Tolkien's story for children: *The Hobbit*. After this, due to writing *The Lord of the Rings* as a sequel to *The Hobbit*, the Hobbits are "accidently" written into Tolkien's cosmology, and the fantasy world of Middle-earth was rooted fundamentally within the world of *The Silmarillion* and older parts of the "history of Elves" (see Carpenter 1977: 183–192). From the perspective of contemporary readers, this is a fortunate happening, since without Hobbits Tolkien's fiction would not have become as popular and significant as it is.

Nevertheless, Hobbits are not the only outsiders in Tolkien's constructive mythopoeics. In *The Silmarillion* Dwarves are "created" by Vala Aulë, though their individual life comes from Eru Ilúvatar. Aulë's actions in making the dwarves are at first quite rebellious, since he tries to do it in secrecy, without Eru's knowledge. Aulë makes the Seven Fathers of the Dwarves under mountains in Middle-earth (Tolkien 1999: 37).

However, Eru Ilúvatar as the all-seeing creator know of Aulë's doings, and his speech to Aulë is also quite revealing on the level of authority and the chain of being. Eru is higher in hierarchy, and Aulë, his follower, is of course lower, and it is not in his power to create a race of mortals. Aulë could not give his creations a mind of their own or power of their own; he could only create un-autonomic things, golems[42] in a sense. Eru Ilúvatar then asks Aulë why he has done this deed which is beyond his power and authority (Tolkien 1999: 37). But as Aulë repents and offers to destroy his work, if Eru wishes so, Eru declares that he has accepted Aulë's offer, and the race of Dwarves

2. Creation and Existence

is accepted as a part of the cosmology. Life and individual minds are given to them as a gift from Eru Ilúvatar (Tolkien 1999: 38).

After this Eru Ilúvatar still clarifies the place of the Dwarves in the chain of being. They cannot awaken before the Children of Ilúvatar; thus, they cannot be the Firstborn since this is the place of the Elves in the cosmography. Eru awakens them when the time is right, and he refers to Dwarves as children of Aulë, although "adopted" by Eru Ilúvatar. They wait until the Firstborn Elves are awaken and after that, when Eru wishes, they take their place in the cosmological order. Thus, while in *The Silmarillion* the Dwarves are adopted as Children of Ilúvatar, they are usually not represented as such in the cosmology. It is said in *The Silmarillion* that in the end the Dwarves will receive their place among the Children in the end, when their part will be to serve Aulë and help him in the remaking of Arda (Tolkien 1999: 39).

Dwarves are adopted as children of Ilúvatar, but what then is the position of Hobbits in the chain of being? Hobbits are different compared to other races first in that they have never "been warlike, and they had never fought among themselves" (Tolkien 2008: 30). They do not seem to be habitants of a mythic or heroic world, but of a more peaceful fairy-tale.

In higher mythical *The Silmarillion*, because of the imagined Elvish background of the narrative, the Hobbits are called by an Elvish word Periannath. There is no explanation of the origins of Periannath, but in the last book "Of the Rings of Power" (Tolkien 1999: 364) their position before the War of the Rings as outsiders of the great history of Middle-earth is revealed. In the Third Age of the Sun the Hobbits dwell in the west part of Eriador, and not Elves, Men, Sauron, or any of the Wise save Ganfalf (Mithrandir in the text) have given thought to this little people.

Yet, *The Silmarillion* explains to us that in the War of the Rings that ends the Third Age of Middle-earth, the Hobbits prove their capability of changing the history of Middle-earth, when "Frodo the Halfling" took on himself the burden of The Great Ring of Power and casts it into the Fire of Mount Doom (Tolkien 1999: 365).

In the end, this is of course not what really happens in Mount

Doom. In *The Lord of the Rings*, Frodo does not cast the One Ring (The Great Ring of Power) into the Fire, but, importantly, he fails to do so. After Frodo's "failure," Gollum unwittingly destroys the One Ring, as he takes the One Ring from Frodo and trips and falls into the fire. This "changing" and remodeling of the story and remaking of intratextual myths is a repetitive concept in Tolkien's fiction, where different fictitious stories and sources fluctuate and overlap each other from time to time.

In *The Lord of the Rings*, the Hobbits are explained to be relatives of Men, and more "human" than for example Dwarves or Elves. Hobbits are "relatives of ours: far nearer to us than Elves, or even Dwarves…. The beginning of Hobbits lies far back in the Elder Days that are now lost and forgotten" (Tolkien 2008: 26).

The position of the Hobbits as outsiders is seen in *The Lord of the Rings*, where nobody seems to be able to place the Hobbits in the chain of being, or the cosmological hierarchy. Consider, for instance, the scene where the Ent Treebeard is trying to place the Hobbits in his old lists, but finds this impossible: "What are you, I wonder? I cannot place you. You do not seem to come in the old lists that I learned when I was young. But that was a long, long time ago, and they may have made new lists" (Tolkien 2009a: 72). In response, Merry, one of the Hobbits, then states that "we always seem to have got left out of the old lists, and the old stories" (Tolkien 2009a: 72).

Later Hobbits Merry and Pippin suggest a new chapter for Treebeard's list of beings: "Half-grown hobbits, the hole-dwellers" (Tolkien 2009a: 72). Still later, Treebeard adds Hobbits to the list in his own fashion, saying: "And hungry as hunters, the Hobbit children, the laughing-people, the little people" (Tolkien 2009a: 217). And thus, in a way, Hobbits get their position in the chain of being, as one of the "free peoples" of Middle-earth.

Tolkien's Christian Platonic Mythopoeics

> *We may put a deadly green upon a man's face and produce a horror; we may make the rare and terrible blue moon to shine; or we may*

2. Creation and Existence

> *cause woods to spring with silver leaves and rams to wear fleeces of gold, and put hot fire into the belly of the cold worm. But in such "fantasy," as it is called, new form is made; Faërie begins,* Man becomes a sub-creator.—Tolkien 1983: 122 [emphasis mine]

In "On Fairy-Stories" Tolkien establishes his theory of the writer as a sub-creator comparable to the creator—the God—in Tolkien's own Roman Catholic beliefs. In this theory the author is a sub-creator creating a secondary world, which in the fantasy literature of Tolkien's time was usually known as Faërie.

The view of the author as a creator of (literary) worlds is of course not a new one, but classical. Theories of a world created by a divine spirit or god, and Platonic mimetic versions of that world created by poets and authors are known throughout western civilization. There are similarities in the etymologies of the words poet and creator. In Greek, the word for poet is *poiein*, which at the same time means to make, to create, and to form (Heninger 1974: 287). In *Timaeus* Plato uses demiurge (dēmiourgos) to refer to the creator of the world. The word demiurge is unfortunately usually translated into English as *God*. Originally the word demiurge had the common meaning of an artisan or craftsman, a maker of things. Plato invented the cosmogonical myth to describe how well organized and formed the created world is and that it is made by a "skillful" artisan.

In the renaissance, the Neoplatonic mimetic view of the poet or author as a creator flourished, and God was indeed in some sense likened to a poet. Italian renaissance humanist Christophoro Landino writes that "God is the supreme poet, and the world is His poem" (Heninger 1974: 292). Authors' comparisons and assumed contacts with transcendent divinity were common in the ancient and pre-modern world, where writers were instruments of God or gods, as inspired oracles (Frye 1967: 55, 60). In Platonic poetical inspirations, the author is possessed by a god, who speaks through him, and the author does not even know what he is doing (Tigerstedt 1969: 63). Divine frenzy takes over the poet (Mazzotta 2001: 47), and he composes his works through divine dispensation.

The Mythopoeic Code of Tolkien

C.S. Lewis discusses different passages from Plato's dialogues on the subject. He finds the most interesting is from Plato's *Apology* (31c–d), where Plato explains why Socrates abstained from political life. Plato's Socrates-character in the dialogue says that the reason is that "[s]omething divine and deamoniac[43] ... happens to me.... It has been so ever since I was a boy. There comes a voice which, whenever I hear it, always forbids something I am about to do, but never commands" (Lewis 1964: 40). Could this be seen as a sign of an outside influence on the thinker or writer?

Owen Barfield (1976: 169–170) also cites Plato's treatment of the subject of divine inspiration. In *Timaeus*, Plato points out that the seer needs prophetae to interpret the meaning. Plato writes that no one attains to true and inspired consciousness while in full possession of his wits, but either the power of his intellect is restricted in sleep or is changed by some disease of divine possession. Plato adds that the task of remembering this divine vision, whether it be a waking or a sleeping one, and of understanding it, is reserved for reason and the full consciousness. Barfield illuminates that the seer himself, while he is still "raving" and "remains in the inspiration," cannot be the judge of his own vision (Barfield 1976: 169–170).

Tolkien takes his place in a long tradition of inspired authors. Tolkien writes that his stories "arose in my mind as 'given' things" (1999: xii). In his biography of Tolkien, Humphrey Carpenter goes farther and writes that when Tolkien wrote *The Silmarillion*, he believed that in one sense he was writing the truth. Carpenter (1977: 91) sees that Tolkien hoped his stories were in some sense an embodiment of a profound truth. In "On Fairy-Stories," and in the story "Leaf by Niggle," Tolkien suggests that a man may be given by God the gift of recording "a sudden glimpse of the underlying reality of truth."

In fact, this idea of common discursive property of stories is shared by postmodernism (see Hutcheon 1988: 124). Indeed, the whole subject of "authorship" and "originality" has been a matter of debate for a long time, especially since the era of post-structuralism. Roland Barthes argues that "the text is a tissue of quotations.... The

2. Creation and Existence

Writer can only imitate a gesture that is always anterior, never original. His only power is to mix writing, to counter the ones with the others...." Claude Lévi-Strauss hews closer to Tolkien when he writes that "I don't have the feeling that I write my books, I have the feeling that my books get written through me—I never had, and still do not have, the perception of feeling my personal identity" (Chandler 2004). A similar kind of method is also vital in Tolkien's mythopoeic writings.

In "On Fairy-Stories," Tolkien uses the terms of the author's independent invention, inheritance, and diffusion. All these terms focus on the textual relations of stories, origins of stories, and the intertextual connections between stories. Tolkien writes that fairy-stories are ancient, related texts appear in very early records, and can be found universally wherever there is language (Tolkien 1983: 121).

In Tolkien's view, researchers that try to trace the background of fairy-stories are confronted with the problems of independent invention (or independent evolution) of similar inheritance from a common ancestry, as well as diffusion at various times from one or more centers. All three issues have evidently played a part in producing the intricate web of extant stories. Of these three, in Tolkien's opinion, invention is the most important and fundamental, and the most mysterious. Tolkien writes that the other two must ultimately lead back to an inventor, or storymaker. He writes that diffusion, borrowing in space, only refers to the problem of origin elsewhere. At the center of the supposed diffusion, there is a place where an inventor once lived. It is similarly the case with inheritance, borrowing in time, in that way we arrive at last only at an ancestral inventor. Tolkien therefore believes—quite understandably—that at the origin of any mythopoeia, literary creation, myth-making or fairy-story-making, there is an inventor or creator. Tolkien writes that "if we believe that sometimes there occurred the independent striking out of similar ideas and themes or devices, we simply multiply the ancestral inventor but do not in that way the more clearly understand his gift" (Tolkien 1983: 121).

The Mythopoeic Code of Tolkien
Concerning Sidney and Coleridge

Tolkien's aesthetics in "On Fairy-Stories" ponder the concepts of imagination, literary belief, and literary pleasure. All these concepts can be seen to reflect classical theories which are linked to Tolkien's own theory, such as Samuel Taylor Coleridge's *Biographia Literaria* or Sir Philip Sidney's *The Defence of Poesy*.

In her article "Is Tolkien a Renaissance Man?" Tanya Caroline Wood compares Tolkien's essay "On Fairy-Stories" to Sidney's *The Defence of Poesie*. Wood argues that Sidney is searching for an original meaning of the word poet (*poiein*), as a creator—especially as a creator of another "nature." Wood writes that both Tolkien and Sidney believe that authors create a secondary world with the creative power of imagination that God has given them (T. Wood 2000: 99). As a work concerned with the creative methods and mimetic nature of literature, Sidney's work was the most influential literary theory of the era, where he both respects the tradition and celebrates the poet's willingness to experiment.

In a philosophical tone, Sidney's *The Defence of Poesy* could be seen as a predecessor of Tolkien's literary view. And on some occasions, Sidney writes, in his own way, on the same subjects as I do in this study: on constructive (mytho)poetics. For example, Sidney sees the historical character of Solon as a Poet who wrote in "verse the notable Fable of Atlantick Iland, which was continued by Plato," and quite disappointedly, that Plato's myth, the Ring of Gyges was just a "meere tale," not a "flower" of poetry (Sidney 1968: 5).

Sidney (1968: 9), following Plato and Aristotle's reasoning, sees that "Poesie" is an "Art of Imitation," mimetic, a "representing, counterfeiting, or figuring forth to speak Metaphorically. A speaking Picture, with this end to teach and delight." But despite this "act of imitation," Sidney in his work compares the poet with the historian and philosopher, and comes to the conclusion that the poet is better of the three, and that "no other humaine skill can match him" (Sidney 1968: 13).

Sidney's *Defence of Poesie* is in one sense "a defence of Plato,"

2. Creation and Existence

whose attack on poets in The *Republic* is of course famous. For Sidney, Plato in his attack never meant poets "in general," but only meant those with erring opinions "of the Deitie." Sidney's defense of Plato is justly done in the light of Plato's dialogue *Ion*, where Plato gives—as Sidney points out—"a high, and rightly divine commendation unto Poetrie." Sidney writes that "Plato banished the abuse, not the thing," and that Plato should be the patron of poets, not the adversary (Sidney 1968: 34). This vision was later shared by many thinkers and writers; for example, in the Romantic period Percy Bysshe Shelley in his theories of poetry connected Platonism and poetry, writing on the "Ideal world of the Poet," and saw the writer's imagination in some ways as an ideal "truth" (Schulze 1966: 12).

For Tolkien's poetics and imaginative writing, both truth and belief are important. In "On Fairy-Stories" Tolkien writes about Imagination and the complex human capability to form images of things not actually present (or even real):

> The human mind is capable of forming mental images of things not actually present. The faculty of conceiving the images is (or was) naturally called Imagination. But in recent times, in technical not normal language, Imagination has often been held to be something higher than the mere image-making, ascribed to the operations of Fancy (a reduced and depreciatory form of the older word Fantasy); an attempt is thus made to restrict, I should say misapply, Imagination to "the power of giving to ideal creations the inner consistency of reality" [Tolkien 1983: 138].

Tolkien tries not to restrict artistic imagination to the level of mere images of the real world. Tolkien as a fantasy writer keeps his door open to non-real or sub-realistic fantasy worlds as well. Tolkien writes about the human imagination, and that the fantastic device of human language can create potent and credible secondary belief, and thus can accomplish a rare achievement of art, narrative art, art of story-making, as Tolkien writes, "in its primary and most potent mode" (1983: 140).[44]

Tolkien's mythopoeics, his view on secondary creation, secondary belief and imagination is, in some ways, closely connected to Samuel Taylor Coleridge's often-cited theory of literary aesthetics.

The Mythopoeic Code of Tolkien

In *Biographia Literaria,* Coleridge writes—in a Christian Platonic tone—about primary and secondary imagination; primary imagination Coleridge holds to be a mimetic repetition in the human mind of the infinite imagination of God, and secondary, its echo, a kind of mortal, artistic, re-creative imagination:

> The imagination then I consider either as primary, or secondary. The primary imagination I hold to be the living power and prime agent of all human perception, and as a repetition in the finite mind of the eternal act of creation in the infinite I AM. The secondary I consider as an echo of the former, co-existing with the conscious will, yet still as identical with the primary in the kind of its agency, and differing only in degree, and in the mode of its operation. It dissolves, diffuses, dissipates, in order to re-create; or where this process is rendered impossible, yet still, at all events, it struggles to idealize and to unify [Coleridge 1965: 167].

Here Coleridge is simply rejecting the view, prominent in his era, of the human mind as an empty page (tabula rasa) upon which external impressions are impressed. Coleridge famously divides this phenomenon of creativeness into imagination and fancy. He sees fancy as a mode of human memory, as the employment of passive and mechanical tasks, the accumulation by association of fact and documentation of what is seen:

> Fancy, on the contrary, has no other counters to play with but fixities and definites. The fancy is indeed no other than a mode of memory emancipated from the order of time and space; and blended with, and modified by the empirical phaenomenon of the will which we express by the word choice. But equally with the ordinary memory it must receive all its material ready made from the law of association [Coleridge 1965: 167].

On the one hand, Rosemary Jackson sees that Coleridge's partition of imagination and fancy emphasizes malleable abilities of the human mind (Jackson 1981: 20). Stephen Prickett, on the other hand, writes that Coleridge, as the greatest Victorian theorist of fantasy, conceptualizes the human mind to show how imagination draws us nearer to the divine (Godly) vision (Prickett 1979: 9). This sort of thinking relates to Tolkien's Christian Platonic vision of literary creation.

As a scholar, Owen Barfield could be an intermediary between

2. Creation and Existence

Coleridge and Tolkien's views of creative literary methods. Barfield widely examines Coleridge's ideas of philosophy in a collection of his 1960s lectures taught at Drew University, titled *What Coleridge Thought* (1971), but Barfield's ideas of poetics had already earlier influenced Tolkien's views. Like Coleridge, Barfield sees poetry and artistic creation as an instrument for pondering the marvels of creation. In *Poetic Diction* Barfield writes that "[g]reat poetry is the progressive incarnation of life in consciousness.... It is only when we have risen from beholding the creator into beholding Creation that our morality catches for a moment the music of the turning spheres" (Barfield 1976: 181). This Pythagorean view of music, or cosmic harmony, as a creative form plays a vital part in Tolkien's fiction as well.[45] The cosmogony of Tolkien's fantasy world is affected by music in Tolkien's mythopoeics. The world is created in an event orchestrated by the creator (Eru Ilúvatar).

Barfield goes as far as to declare that imagination—and not for example science—is the only way that the world can be really "known." Barfield (1976: 28) states that how science deals with the world which it perceives, using its own instrument, but only "by imagination ... can the world be known."

This world-knowing poetics is well absorbed in Tolkien's literary theory. Barfield sees this "meaningful" literature as poetic diction, saying that "when the words are selected and arranged in such a way that their meaning either arouses, or is obviously intended to arouse, aesthetic imagination, the result may be described as poetic diction" (Barfield 1976: 41). This literature is seen as a same sort of creative action as Coleridge's vision of poetry as "the best words in the best order," or as Barfield says, "the best language" (1976: 58). Barfield sees that since Plato's time the study of language has been mainly lingual, developed mainly by grammarians and logicians, having their emphasis still, until only recently, on the external *forms* of words. Barfield is in fact quite surprised that the extraordinarily intimate connection between *language* and *thought* (the Greek word logos, λόγος combining, as Barfield sees, both meanings) has not led philosophers to turn their attention to the subject long ago (Barfield 1976: 60).

The Mythopoeic Code of Tolkien

Tolkien comments on Coleridge's theory of literary belief, the concept of "willing suspension of disbelief," in "On Fairy-Stories," in a chapter dealing with children's reading habits. Tolkien sees that children are capable of literary belief when the story-maker's art is good enough to produce it but dislikes the concept of willing suspension of disbelief as imprecise. On the occasion, Tolkien invokes (once again) his theory of secondary creation:

> What really happens, is that the story-maker proves a successful "sub-creator." He makes a Secondary World which your mind can enter. Inside it, what he relates is "true": it accords with the laws of that world. You therefore believe it, while you are, as it were, inside. The moment disbelief arises, the spell is broken; the magic, or rather art, has failed. You are then out in the Primary World again, looking at the little abortive Secondary World from outside. If you are obliged, by kindliness of circumstance, to stay, then disbelief must be suspended (or stifled), otherwise listening and looking would become intolerable. But this suspension of disbelief is a substitute for the genuine thing, a subterfuge we use when condescending to games or make-believe, or when trying (more or less willingly) to find what virtue we can in the work of an art that has for us failed [Tolkien 1983: 132].

Belief in fantasy—what Tolkien calls "secondary belief" to distinguish it from primary belief in experiential reality—arises from the conjunction of psychological affect and ideational structure, and as Tolkien notes, it is quite different from Coleridge's "willing suspension of disbelief."

Therefore, in some ways, Tolkien's vision differs from Coleridge's theory of "suspension of disbelief." Gary K. Wolfe has pointed this out, noting that Tolkien's "secondary belief" is quite a different thing than Coleridge's "suspension of disbelief," in that belief is "what enables genuine emotions to be aroused from impossible circumstances" (Wolfe 1982: 10–11). More recently, Mark J.P. Wolf has written on the subjects and on the differences between these, and how Tolkien reforms the concepts by refining and combining ideas from Coleridge (see Wolf 2012: 19–20).

Tolkien's concept of a credible Secondary World which the reader can relate as true (and therefore to "suspense his disbelief")

2. Creation and Existence

are closely connected to the concept of high fantasy or epic fantasy, the names fantasy researchers nowadays use to refer to literature where consistent and credible fantasy worlds that differ from our (real) physical world are created (see Carter 1973, Gamble & Yates 2008). Tolkien's works are considered archetypical high fantasy.

Wolfe sees that as Tolkien's stories advance, by the time the reader has begun the second volume of *The Lord of the Rings*, he or she "is well located in the author's symbolic universe and does not expect many new 'impossibilities' to occur" (Wolfe 1982: 5). That is to say, the disbelief of the text diminishes during the reading process.

Coleridge used the concept of literary faith, though he called it poetic faith, in *Biographia Literaria* to describe the creative process by which he and William Wordsworth created their classical poetry collection *Lyrical Ballads* (1798). Coleridge writes that his poems were designed to be more of a supernatural model, whereas Wordsworth was writing in a more realistic model:

> In this idea originated the plan of the Lyrical Ballads; in which it was agreed that my endeavours should be directed to persons and characters supernatural, or at least romantic; yet so as to transfer from our inward nature a human interest and a semblance of truth sufficient to procure for these shadows of imagination that *willing suspension of disbelief* for the moment, *which constitutes poetic faith*. Mr Wordsworth, on the other hand, was to propose to himself as his object to give the charm of novelty to things of every day... [Coleridge 1965: 168–169. Emphasis mine].

In addition to this, the aesthetic views of Tolkien and Coleridge seemingly aim at the same purpose: literary pleasure. Coleridge sees that works of science aim at the truth, but works of art aim at pleasure: "[a] poem is that species of composition which is opposed to works of science by proposing for its immediate object pleasure, not truth" (Coleridge 1965: 172).

Tolkien seems to cherish this view, since in the year 1971, in a letter to Peter Szabó Szentmihály, he writes that his books aim strictly at literary pleasure, and his objective is not to preach or teach (1981: 414). Of course, Tolkien's statement notwithstanding, this seems to be a rather simplistic interpretation of his creative oeuvre.

The Mythopoeic Code of Tolkien

In Tolkien's fiction, there are also other, more substantial, elements at work than just simple "literary pleasure," as this study concerning Tolkien's constructive poetics indicates.

Tolkien's aim is thus imaginative fantasy, or *phantasia*, of which the ancient Greek meaning is almost synonymous. In "On Fairy-Stories," Tolkien writes on the concept of fantasy using the word not as a synonym of its contemporary meaning of imagination, but giving the word fantasy a new meaning—at a theoretical extent which he himself does not fully understand at the time—using "fantasy" as a combination of both the older meaning as an equivalent of imagination, but in the same time describing the word in terms of his own sub-creative art form, "the fantasy":

> The mental power of image-making is one thing, or aspect; and it should appropriately be called Imagination. The perception of the image, the grasp of its implications, and the control, which are necessary to a successful expression, may vary in vividness and strength: but this is a difference of degree in Imagination, not a difference in kind. *The achievement of expression, which gives (or seems to give) "the inner consistency of reality," is indeed another thing, or aspect, needing another name: Art, the operative link between Imagination and the final result; Sub-creation.* For my present purpose I require a word which shall embrace both the Sub-creative Art in itself and a quality of strangeness and wonder in the Expression, derived from the Image: a quality essential to fairy-story. *I propose therefore ... to use Fantasy for this purpose*: in a sense, that is, which combines with its older and higher use as an equivalent of Imagination the derived notions of "unreality" (that is, unlikeness of the Primary World), of freedom from the domination of observed "fact," in short of the fantastic.... I do not assent to the depreciative tone. That the images are of things not in the primary world (if that indeed is possible) is a virtue not a vice. *Fantasy (in this sense), is, I think, not a lower but a higher form of Art*, indeed the most nearly pure form, and so (when achieved) the most potent [Tolkien 1983: 138–139. Emphasis mine].

Tolkien therefore sees the unreality of things in literature as a virtue. He sees fantasy as a higher form of art, not lower, as had been declared by many other critics. For example, in the *Republic*, Plato writes disparagingly of poets as "imitators" of real existence and says that imitators of the unrealistic are even worse than other artists (595a–602d). As a fantasist Tolkien of course does not embrace this

2. Creation and Existence

view, but at the same time, in some ways he shares the aesthetical view of the later Platonists and Neoplatonists.

John Dillon (1990b: 55) points out that for Plato and for later Platonism the status and role of imagination (or phantasia) is quite low. The concept is discussed by Plato in the *Sophist* (264a–b) and by Aristotle in *De Anima* (III). For Platonism, imagination is seen as activity of the "lower" soul, dependent upon sense-perception, from which the soul must purify itself (Dillon 1990b: 55). Later, in the Neoplatonic philosophy, Plotinus assigns to phantasia once again its Platonic role, but also in *Enneads* IV speculates on the immortality of an individual soul, and the survival of the personality. For Plotinus memory is functioning in the faculty of imagination, on which he finds memory to be based (see Dillon 1990b: 55).

At this point, we may turn our focus back to Tolkien's fiction, and to the death scene of King Aragorn in Appendix A of *The Lord of the Rings*. There, at his dying moment, Aragorn says that in the afterlife, beyond the circles of earth, there is "more than memory" (Tolkien 2009b: 390). Plotinus sees that memory is based on imagination, and that it is a fundamental part of the immortality of an individual soul. Tolkien's fictive character wants to believe that his soul is in fact immortal, and that beyond this World there is "more than memory." I would argue that the character of Aragorn therefore imagines the possibility of both afterlife and the memory of the lived life before that. What then is this hope of "more than memory"? A Meaning to it all, one assumes? Perhaps that is the "sudden glimpse of the underlying reality of truth" that Tolkien hoped his fiction to imply. At this point, we may turn our attention more thoroughly to Christian Platonism in general.

The Philosophy of Afterlife

The focus here is on the Platonic and Christian Platonic metaphysical, cosmological, philosophical (and in some way theological) logics of the mythopoeics in Tolkien's fiction. There is of course a long leap in tradition, even in the selected aspects, from Plato to Tolkien's aesthetics. My point is not to say that Tolkien unwillingly, or uncritically, drew from the tradition. On the contrary, Tolkien, in my opinion, was in some ways a traditional successor of the aesthetical tradition of Christian Platonism. Then again, it must be stressed that Tolkien was an author of fiction, and not a theologian or philosopher. The range of possible Christian Platonism or any other philosophical influence is only limited to Tolkien's fiction's cosmology and only forms an internal field of reference there. Kocher discusses the underpinnings of this point cleverly, saying that "Tolkien is not a philosopher or a theologian but a literary artist who thinks" (Kocher 2000: 11).

As the first traditional background and a major external reference for Tolkien's mythopoeics, we have Plato's writings. Plato is of course considered one of the main influences among philosophy, learning and critical thinking in the Western world. Plato's dialogues, thirty-six of them known today, lay the foundations of both Western philosophy and science. Plato's influence is major in the tradition of aesthetics, although a major part of the tradition is informed by Neoplatonism and later fundamentally "Platonic" writings on the subject.

Tolkien was a Catholic and his mythopoeics is clearly influenced by both Catholic theology and Platonic philosophy and could be summarized as Christian Platonic in heritage. The term Christian Platonism can be used as a basic name for the combination (in some respects) of Judeo-Christian theology and philosophy and Platonic and Neoplatonic philosophy. It can be said that especially Neoplatonism was a major influence on Christian theology throughout Late Antiquity, for example during the Christian period of the late Roman era, and the Middle Ages, as will be discussed in this section. Next, I illuminate chosen parts of the tradition from Platonism to Christian Platonism that helped to form a common Inkling philosophy of aesthetics, shared in part by both C.S. Lewis and Tolkien, and by Owen Barfield.

This shared influence between the writers has of course been

2. Creation and Existence

argued earlier, and sometimes critically denied, in Tolkien studies. For example, Ralph C. Wood in his article "Conflict and Convergence on Fundamental Matters in C.S. Lewis and J.R.R. Tolkien" sees the matter quite differently than me. Wood claims that "[C.S.] Lewis was a Platonist at heart. For him, the world is the shadow of another. There is an invisible divine realm hovering over the visible world, making the natural order into a land of shadows and reflections of the really real" (R. Wood 2003: 322).

Wood sees that Lewis' Platonism gives him an understanding of the universe as a seamless whole in which the inner and outer, the upper and lower, the divine and the natural are deeply intertwined (R. Wood 2003: 323). Wood sees Lewis not as a Christian Platonist, but as a Platonist Christian. As to Tolkien, Wood argues that he was "no sort of Platonist at all" (R. Wood 2003: 325). Wood sees Tolkien as merely espousing a kind of Aristotelian metaphysics. That is, for Tolkien the "transcendent reality is to be found in the depths of this world rather than in some putative existence beyond it" (R. Wood 2003: 325). Wood explains that this is the reason why Tolkien sets his reader down in the midst of Middle-earth, and why there is no time voyage or space travel in his fiction, no slippage through the back of the wardrobe into a magical realm. Wood sees that Tolkien seeks to convince readers that "his imaginative world is utterly real, having no other foundation than its own laws and conventions" (R. Wood 2003: 325). These are of course valid points, but Tolkien's Platonism should not be overlooked on these statements alone.

For example, as mentioned earlier, Tolkien's fiction's resemblance to a "portal fantasy" has been discussed by Farah Mendlesohn, who views *The Lord of the Rings* as a familiar quest fantasy: Frodo moves from a small, safe, and well-understood world into the wild, unfamiliar world of ... Middle-earth. Mendlesohn (2008: 2–3) sees that only in *The Silmarillion*, a book told from within the world, about people who know their world, does Tolkien create a "full secondary world fantasy."

And as another correction, Tolkien did start a fictional story about time travel. This story was titled "The Lost Road," a fragment of which is published in *The History of Middle-earth* Volume 5, and which was part of a writing project or proposal meant to include both C.S. Lewis and Tolkien. Tolkien writes in a letter to Michael Tolkien in 1963 that "we decided to divide: he [Lewis] was to do space-travel and I time-travel. My book was never finished, but some of it (the Númenorean-Atlantis theme) got into my trilogy eventually" (Tolkien 1981: 342). As a major thematical inspiration, Platonic myth was important for Tolkien, as can be seen from the earlier excerpts in which Tolkien quotes his "Atlantis theme."

C.S. Lewis, a friend and an important figure in the close circle of fellow writers for Tolkien, points out that Plato's visions of ethics and monotheism that were later used by Christian thinkers were in fact received from Plato's predecessors and only later modified by Plato (Lewis 1964: 2). In this way Plato's dialogues are of course a continuum of a long Greek tradition—not just from Heracletian and Socratic philosophy.

For Christian theology, Plato's emphases of monotheism as well as the account of the "afterlife" at the end of the *Republic* were fruitful material. At the end of the *Republic*, Plato put an account of the afterlife in the mouth of Er the Armenian, who had returned from the dead. The influence is felt in Roman literature, as Lewis points out, where Cicero (106–43 BCE) in his own *Republic* ends his story with the similar vision (Lewis 1964: 23). Plato's mythical vision of the afterlife in the myth of Er greatly influenced both the Roman World and the later Christian West.

Cicero also draws on Platonic ethics. Concerning suicide, Cicero writes that we should not "hasten to join the happy company" of heaven. He sees that all good men must retain the soul in the body's fetters and not depart from human life. Otherwise, Cicero says, you may be held to have deserted the duty allotted by God to man. Lewis states that this prohibition of suicide is Platonic. Lewis assumes that Cicero is following a passage from Plato's *Phaedo* in which Socrates makes a remark of suicide as "unlawful." Stating that "whether we accept or not the doctrine that taught the body is a prison and we must not break from it, at any rate we men are certainly the property

2. Creation and Existence

of gods, and property must not dispose of itself," Lewis then declares that this pronouncement of Christian ethics is indisputable (Lewis 1964: 25).

In his fiction, Tolkien discusses attitudes towards death and killing on many occasions. In Gandalf's voice, Tolkien writes that "[m]any that live deserve death. And some that die deserve life. Can you give it to them? Then do not be too eager to deal out death in judgment. For even the wise cannot see all ends" (Tolkien 2008: 90). This both Platonic and Christian attitude towards killing, and suicide, can be seen in Tolkien's fiction on occasion.

In the tale "Of Túrin Turambar" in *The Silmarillion* as well as in *The Children of Húrin*, the tragic story ends in a double-suicide scene of both the human hero Túrin and his sister Nienor. Tolkien describes the bitter aftermath of Túrin's suicide:

> But Mablung and the Elves came and looked ... upon the body of Túrin, and they grieved; and when Men of Brethil came thither, and they learned the reasons of Túrin's madness and death, they were aghast; and Mablung said bitterly: "I also have been meshed in the doom of the Children of Húrin, and thus with my tidings have slain one that I loved" [Tolkien 1999: 270].

Another revealing scene in Tolkien's fiction about suicide is Denethor's death scene in *The Lord of the Rings*. Denethor, Lord of the City of Minas Tirith and Steward of Gondor, once a perhaps valiant "defender of the West," now devastated and grim, chooses as his last desperate act to burn himself and his son Faramir in self-immolation. Denethor's rather insane monologue, with yelling and repetition, addresses the question of dying and the difference of dying like a "heathen king" or dying and being embalmed like Númenorean and Gondorian civilized people are accustomed to do:

> "Why? Why do the fools fly?" said Denethor. "Better to burn sooner than late, for burn we must. Go back to your bonfire. And I? I will go now to my pyre. To my pyre! No tomb for Denethor and Faramir. No tomb! No long slow sleep of death embalmed. We will burn like heathen kings before ever a ship sailed hither from the West. The West has failed. Go back and burn!" [Tolkien 2009b: 106].

The Mythopoeic Code of Tolkien

In the end of the scene Gandalf, with the help of Pippin, manages to save Faramir from death, but Denethor still commits suicide by self-immolation on a pyre. His ending is tragic, as it is of course for those that commit suicide in Tolkien's fantasy world.

Tolkien writes graphic visions of death and afterlife in his fiction, and so does his fellow-Inkling C.S. Lewis in Lewis' Narnia series. In the seventh book of the Narnia series, *The Last Battle* (1956), the story ends in the final chapter titled "Farewell to the Shadowlands." In a Christian Platonic ending, Lewis describes the "Changeable World" as "Shadowlands" and the Heaven-like afterlife, where the children in the Narnia series can be analyzed to be moving to, as the "Ideal" world. Lewis gives his series a fictitious and more completely "happy-ever-after" ending than perhaps any other fairy-story:

> And as He [the lion Aslan] spoke, He no longer looked to them like a lion; but the things that began to happen after that were so great and beautiful that I cannot write them. And for us this is the end of all the stories, and we can most truly say that they all lived happily ever after. But for them it was only the beginning of the real story. All their life in this world and all their adventures in Narnia had only been the cover and the title page: now at last they were beginning Chapter One of the Great Story which no one on earth has read: which goes on for ever: in which every chapter is better than the one before [Lewis 1974: 165].

Tolkien uses the same kinds of allegorical depths when imaging "afterlife." In the end of *The Lord of the Rings* Tolkien describes main protagonist Frodo Baggins sailing away to the divine West (away from the mortal world) in Christian and Platonic way. Of course, the influence of both the Legend of Elysium and the Legend of Avalon can also be seen in the chapter. There are many other such references to *Locus amoenus* ("a pleasant place") in mythological, epical and Utopia literature such as Gimlé mentioned in *Prose Edda* and *Völuspá*, or Aaru in the Nile Delta myths. In Ancient Greek and Roman legend Elysium refers to an island, the resting place or afterlife for the blessed ones, described by writers such as Hesiod, Virgil, and Plutarch. Avalon, from the Arthurian legendarium, refers to the resting place of King Arthur, where he is taken to recover after the Battle of Camlann.

2. Creation and Existence

In *The Lord of the Rings* Frodo Baggins cannot stay in Middle-earth because he is "too deeply hurt" (Tolkien 2009b: 348). Frodo sails to the far West, to the land of Valinor in the ships of the Elves, who are leaving Middle-earth. Tolkien describes the events as follows:

> [T]he sails were drawn up, and the wind blew, and slowly the ship slipped away down the long grey firth; and the light of the glass of Galadriel that Frodo bore glimmered and was lost. And the ship went out into the High Sea and passed on into the West, until at last on a night of rain Frodo smelled a sweet fragrance on the air and heard the sound of singing that came over the water. And then it seemed to him that as in his dream in the house of Bombadil, the grey rain-curtain turned all to silver glass and was rolled back, and he beheld white shores and beyond them a far green country under a swift sunrise [Tolkien 2009b: 349].

The place where Frodo is going is as divine as Tolkien can let his Hobbit characters into. The glass of light of Galadriel, which Frodo has earlier received as a present in the story, disappears when moving to the "Undying Lands," because it belongs to mortal Middle-earth, and not to the immortal lands. The Elvish culture of Tolkien's fiction mixed with heavenly visions of singing, sweet flavors and dream-like atmosphere captivates Frodo. The "grey rain-curtain turned all to silver glass and was rolled back," writes Tolkien in delicately chosen words. The almost heavenly resting place for Frodo is the "white shores" and "far green country" of Valinor.

Quite interestingly, in the extremely popular movie series representation *of The Lord of the Rings* (2001–2003), directed by Peter Jackson, the chosen narration parts are taken out of the original context and some parts of the text are given even more Christian Platonic meaning. In the third movie, *The Return of the King*, the phrases from the book, originally told by the narrator are moved (and rendered) and put into the mouth of Gandalf to give a theological and philosophical view of the afterlife to a Hobbit, Peregrin "Pippin" Took:

> End? No, the journey doesn't end here. Death is just another path. One that we all must take. The grey rain-curtain of this world rolls back, and all turns to silver glass. And then you see it.... White shores, and beyond, a

far green country, under a swift sunrise [*The Lord of the Rings: The Return of the King* 2003].

Tolkien himself writes on the human and non-human afterlife of his fictional characters on many occasions, for example in *The Silmarillion* when describing The Halls of Mandos, the waiting place of the souls of the Elves. I have mentioned already the death scene of King Aragorn, found in full length in Appendix A, part v, of *The Lord of the Rings* titled "Here Follows a Part of the Tale of Aragorn and Arwen." At the end of this emotional, romantic, and tragic short story, Tolkien describes the death of King Aragorn. On his deathbed, Aragorn encourages his beloved wife Arwen to believe that they will meet again in the afterlife, beyond "the circles of the world": "Behold! we are not bound for ever to the circles of the world, and beyond them is more than memory. Farewell!" (Tolkien 2009: 390).

The allegorical textualities of all three above citations are remarkable. "The grey rain-curtain ... being rolled back" and "beyond them [the circles of the world] is more than memory" could be seen as a promise of life after death, and as a promise of life after this world—and outside of this world.

Even in the death scene of Boromir in *The Lord of the Rings* one can sense this belief in the afterlife, but also feel the bitterness of death. Boromir has earlier betrayed the Fellowship, but then tries to reconcile this by fighting and dying for the Hobbits. In the scene, Aragorn seems to imply that Boromir is in some ways forgiven. Boromir regrets his previous actions, and Aragorn says that, because of the repentance, he has "conquered." On his deathbed, he is forgiven.

Bitterness of death is of course the inescapable "pain of Men." It is also the reason why the highest Kingdom of Men, Númenor, falls:

> Death was ever present, because the Númenoreans still, as they had in their old kingdom, and so lost it, hungered after endless life unchanging. Kings made tombs more splendid than houses of the living, and counted old names in the rolls of their descent dearer than the names of sons. Childless lords sat in aged halls musing on heraldry; in secret chambers withered men compounded strong elixirs, or in high cold towers asked questions of the stars [Tolkien 2009a: 324].

2. Creation and Existence

In the death scene of Aragorn, "The last of the Númenoreans," Elf-lady Queen Arwen feels the bitterness of death that mortals must come to terms with:

> [ARAGORN:] Nay, lady, I am the last of the Númenoreans and the latest King of the Elder Days; and to me has been given not only a span thrice that of Men of Middle-earth, but also the grace to go at my will, and give back the gift. Now, therefore, I will sleep.
> [ARWEN:] ...But I say to you, King of the Númenoreans, not till now have I understood the tale of your people and their fall. As wicked fools I scorned them, but I pity them at last. For if this indeed is, as the Eldar say, the gift of the One to Men, it is bitter to receive [Tolkien 2009b: 389].

After the bitter death, there is still the hope of the afterlife. Tolkien has outlined for contemporary Christian theology a theory of eucatastrophe, the so-called "good catastrophe." McGrath writes that the success of Tolkien's works has influenced Christian Theology and led some to explore his distinctive literary notion of an eucatastrophe as a means of setting the resurrection in context. For Tolkien, a eucatastrophe is "the joy in a sudden glimpse of the underlying reality or truth" found in a good ending not expected, yet utterly consistent with all that went beforehand (McGrath 2011: 314). This can be seen as a basis of Tolkien's fiction, which Tolkien himself in a letter to Father Robert Murray in 1953 commented on (talking particularly of *The Lord of the Rings*) as a "fundamentally religious and Catholic work" (Tolkien 1981: 172).

The Inklings and the Power of Words

This section illuminates the background of the previously mentioned common Inkling philosophy, shared by the Christian Platonic group of writers "the Inklings," of which Tolkien was part in the early 20th century in Oxford. J.R.R. Tolkien was a crucial part of the informal literary club, and the club's literary views, aesthetics and politics is relevant for the creation of Tolkien's fiction.

Esty writes that "the so-called Oxford Christians," or Inklings,

The Mythopoeic Code of Tolkien

played "popular variations on the domestic quest romance and to re-enchant the English landscape" (Esty 2004: 118). There are similarities in the nativist romance of the Inklings and the later works of T.S. Eliot. They all share conservative and religious formation and were well associated to English literary circles (Esty 2004: 118). Also, Verlyn Flieger (2004: 46) discusses that the Inklings shared together "curiosity about the history of languages, a love for fairy-tales, knowledge of North-West European mythology, and—a highly developed taste for science fiction."

The Inklings were (re)founded by Tolkien and his academic friends in Oxford in the 1930s. The central figures of the Inklings were originally Tolkien and C.S. Lewis. A third noted fantasy writer to participate in the Inklings was Charles Williams (1886–1945), who was taken into the "circle" in 1939 (Carpenter 1978: xiii). The fourth important figure was Owen Barfield.

The original Inklings had been founded by an Oxford student, Edward Tangya Lean, in the 1920s. The club existed so that members could read unpublished compositions aloud and ask for comments and criticism (Carpenter 1978: 57). Later the name Inklings was restored by C.S. Lewis for an undetermined and unelected group of friends who gathered about Lewis and met in his room at Magdalen College in Oxford. Tolkien was an active member since the new beginning (Carpenter 1978: 67). Before that, in 1926, Tolkien himself had formed a reading club called Coalbiters or Kolbítar (a jesting Icelandic name meaning "men who lounge so close to the fire in winter that they bite the coal") in which Old Icelandic sagas and myths were read aloud. Lewis was also a member of the group (Carpenter 1978: 27). After that, the newly formed Inklings started to read aloud the unpublished writings of its members and commented and criticized these. For example, Tolkien's *The Lord of the Rings* was one of the books that were first read aloud to the Inklings (Carpenter 1978: xiii).

Carpenter (1978: 156) sees a certain influence of the group on its members. Tolkien, Williams, and Lewis all later became renowned fantasy writers. Barfield for his part became a well-known philosopher and wrote philological and linguistic books. Carpenter

2. Creation and Existence

discusses the common literary aesthetics and politics of the Inklings, the common Inklings philosophy of aesthetics. Tolkien, Lewis and Williams all wrote stories in which myth plays an important part. Yet each of the three uses myth in quite a different way: Williams takes the already existing Arthurian myth and uses it as a setting for metaphysical odes. Lewis uses Christian myth and reclothes it for his didactic purposes. Tolkien invents his own mythology, his fantasy fiction, and draws stories of many different kinds from it (Carpenter 1978: 156).

Lewis and Williams' usage of myth was of course not as simple as Carpenter thoughts would suggest. For example, Lewis used Christian myths on many occasions, such as in Narnia series, but he also wrote many science fiction novels which are not so simply analyzed. Carpenter also simplifies Tolkien's use of myth. Tolkien did invent his own mythology, but he also used existing myths in forming it. For example, Tolkien, albeit in a somewhat superficial way, uses the most familiar Christian myth, the resurrected Christ. Then again, myths of dying and rising god, undying god or death-rebirth-deity can be found in many religions and mythologies, Christ is just one of the examples. Other examples include mythic stories such as Norse god Baldr, Greek Dionysus or Semitic goddess Ishtar. In *The Lord of the Rings* Gandalf the Grey "dies" in the mine of Moria but returns for a short while as Gandalf the White, like a resurrected Christ, to fulfill his task. In the text, Gandalf explains what happened to his companions: "darkness took me, and I strayed out of thought and time, and I wandered far on roads that I will not tell—naked I was sent back—for a brief time, until my task is done" (Tolkien 2009a: 117). But Gandalf's part as an allegorization of Christ should not be so easily pronounced since the differences between the characters are of course more notable than the similarities.

One of the points that explain the aesthetics and literary similarities and common philosophy of Tolkien and Lewis is to be found in their literary background. Both had since childhood been interested in the "Northern writings" of the Old Norse and Icelandic sagas and myths, and also in the fantasy books of William Morris, who himself was influenced by Norse-style poetry and drama (Carpenter 1978: 29). This of course also explains why both were members of Coalbiters.

For Tolkien, C.S. Lewis was not a literary influence as it is ordinarily understood, but sheer encouragement. Carpenter writes that Tolkien thought he owed Lewis an unpayable debt, since Lewis was for a long time Tolkien's only audience (Carpenter 1978: 32). But Charles Williams was never appreciated by Tolkien. Carpenter writes (1978: 121) that Tolkien found Williams' books wholly alien, and sometimes very distasteful, occasionally ridiculous.

Owen Barfield was only a rare visitor to the Inklings, but he still was a respected member. Barfield's books influenced Tolkien a great deal and Barfield was the only one (as Tolkien saw) that could "tackle C.S. Lewis, making him define everything" (Carpenter 1978: 177). Lewis did not accept all of Barfield's points, but it might be said that Tolkien did on many occasions. This can be seen in Tolkien's theory of sub-creation, which tried to achieve fundamental truth. Barfield therefore was an important part of the Inklings, even though he was only a rare guest, and he himself only seldom wrote fiction.

Tolkien was aware of Barfield's influence. Tolkien himself wrote that the only philological remark he thinks of in The Hobbit is on page 221 of the first edition, and it is a point that will be missed by any who have not read Barfield, and probably by those who have (Tolkien 1981: 22). The lines in question, describing Bilbo's reaction to his first defamiliar sight of the dragon Smaug and his treasure, read as follows: "There are no words left to express his staggerment, since Men changed the language that they learned of elves in the days when all the world was wonderful" (see Flieger 2002: xxi). Here, Tolkien is of course describing the "evolution" of language, which for Tolkien is a "marring," or corruption, of language.

Barfield's *Poetic Diction* is the center of his theory of philological Platonism, focusing on the area between word and meaning. In the book, Barfield concludes that myths are closely associated with the very origin of all speech and literature (Carpenter 1978: 41). Flieger writes that Barfield's theory holds that myth, language, and

2. Creation and Existence

humanity's perception of the world are interlocked and inseparable. Language in its beginnings made no distinction between the literal and metaphoric meaning of a word, as it does today (Flieger 2002: 37–38). That is just what Tolkien means by stating that the language has changed, and there are no words to express the precise feeling (Flieger 2002: xxi). Flieger uses the Gospel of Saint John as an example. The opening sentence—very meaningful for the Christian Platonists—says: "In the beginning was the Word," translating the Greek logos as "word." To John and his audience, logos would have conveyed (along with word), "speech," "reason," "organizing principle," and "cosmic harmony." Nowadays people must choose one of the meanings, because word, percept and concept have altered so that the former wholeness has been fragmented (Flieger 2002: 38–39).

Both the secondary world of Tolkien's fiction and the force field that holds it are built out of words (Flieger 2002: 33). Tolkien's response to words, to their shape and sound and meaning, was closer to that of a musician than a grammarian. Tolkien writes in "On Fairy-Stories" that God is the first creator and the writer is the secondary creator, sub-creator. The writer's tools of sub-creation are words (Flieger 2002: 41). This theory of a secondary world created by words is, on these grounds, constantly Christian Platonic.

The power of names and words can be seen in Tolkien's mythopoeic fiction. In Chapter IV of *The Two Towers* Treebeard discusses names and meanings on many occasions. In a dialogue between the Ent Treebeard and Hobbits, Treebeard indirectly declares that names are important, and that they do have power. He is in fact quite surprised when the Hobbits are so eager to openly pronounce their names to him. Treebeard takes this as a compliment, saying: "I am honoured by your confidence." Soon after, concerning his own name, he declares the following:

> For I am not going to tell you my name, not yet at any rate.... "For one thing it would take a long while: my name is growing all the time, and I've lived a very long, long time; so my name is like a story. Real names tell you the story of the things they belong to in my language, in the Old Entish as you might say" [Tolkien 2009a: 73].

The Mythopoeic Code of Tolkien

In Tolkien's fiction names really are important, and they do have some strange power in them.[46] This can be seen on many other occasions, for example in the chapters concerning Dwarf names and Elf names. On the Dwarf names, Tolkien writes that "Gimli's own name, however, and the names of all his kin, are of Northern (Mannish) origin. Their own secret and 'inner' names, their true names, the Dwarves have never revealed to any one of alien races. Not even on their tombs do they inscribe them" (Tolkien 2002f: 296).

The Elves in Tolkien's fiction are not as secretive about their real names, but it is also made clear that the names of the Elves are quite special too. Concerning the Elven names, Tolkien writes that:

> The Eldar in Valinor had as a rule two names, or essi. The first-given was the father-name, received at birth. It usually recalled the father's name, resembling it in sense or form; sometimes it was simply the father's name, to which some distinguishing pre-fix in the case of a son might be added later when the child was fullygrown. The mother-name was given later, often some years later, by the mother; but sometimes it was given soon after birth. For the mothers of the Eldar were gifted with deep insight into their children's characters and abilities, and many had also the gift of prophetic foresight [Tolkien 2002f: 339].

Later, Tolkien describes that in exile (in Middle-earth) some of the Elves also used "self names" (kilmessi) and "after names" or "nicknames" (epessë) (Tolkien 2002f: 339). Therefore, it was possible for an Elf to have three or more names, as can be seen from the Elven lady Galadriel, who is described to be known by names such as Alatáriel, Artanis and Nerwen.

The uniqueness and even magicality of names are seen throughout the classical mythologies, and even in Platonic and later in Christian Platonic theology and philosophy. Dillon comments that the power of names, or the "magician's knowledge of names," was one of the basic presuppositions of magical practice in the antique world. "This applies to knowing the proper name or names of a given god or daemon, or to being in possession of the formulae of power, strings of meaningless words or sounds designed to capture the attention and compel the services of some supernatural or natural force"

2. Creation and Existence

(Dillon 1990a: 203). The theory of magical power of names was later used by later Platonists and seen used in combination with the "doctrine of cosmic sympathy" (Dillon 1990a: 207).

Words are extremely important also in Tolkien's world. For example—keeping in mind the etymologies of both "spell" as a mystical or magical aspect, and "spelling" as a formulating (for example writing or speaking) of words—in *The Lord of the Rings*, in the chapter "A Journey in the Dark," Gandalf is trying to find the right words to open the doors of Moria, the greatest of Dwarven mines. Gandalf's precise words are "I once knew every spell in all the tongues of Elves or Men or Orcs, that was ever used for such a purpose" (Tolkien 2008: 384).

In the next chapter, "The Bridge of Khazad-Dûm," Gandalf again uses lingual spells. This time Gandalf, trying to keep the Orcs away from the Fellowship, is trying to close a certain door with "a shutting-spell." But fearfully, a demonic creature called Balrog comes to the other side of the door and tries to open the door with its mighty "counter-spell." Gandalf describes how Balrog's terrible counter-spell nearly breaks him. The attack is mental but can also affect physical world since the door moves as wished. After this, Gandalf uses even more powerful words—"a word of Command," a mighty spell that finally destroys the door. The spell destroys the door and the whole corridor collapses (Tolkien 2008: 408). Words, lingual spells, are power in Tolkien's fantasy world.

Words in Tolkien's fiction are even cosmological crafting material. In Tolkien's cosmology, the world is created with words and music. The creator, Eru Ilúvatar, the One, gives the Ainur themes and they form the world with their voices. And in the final and the most important phase of creation, Eru uses words to create the visible world. With a single word Eru creates the physical world (Tolkien 1999: 319).

After the Creation, the Ainur (Valar and Maiar) also use words, and songs of power, as Bradford Lee Eden has pointed out: "creational energy is demonstrated by means of the Valar's respective powers in singing" (Eden 2003: 186). Lingual spells and words of power are functional in Tolkien's fantastic fiction. The same can be seen in many North European mythologies, for example in the *Kalevala*, where lingual spells and powerful singing is the force of magic. The key character Väinämöinen is described as an "Eternal Bard" and his power is in his powerful voice, which in the cosmogonical beginning exerts order over chaos (*Kalevala* 1975:8–14). In the same way, powerful characters such as Gandalf in *The Lord of the Rings*, defeats his foes with words of command, or Elven Princess Lúthien sings Dark Lord Morgoth and his minions to sleep in *The Silmarillion*, or Elf King Findor Felagund challenges Sauron, the Necromancer, in a terrible singing contest which ends in Finrod's undoing. The power of words is pivotal in Tolkien's fantasy world.

3

Fall and Struggle

Long Defeat

The recurring elements and motifs that have symbolic significance in Tolkien's texts are comprehensive. Through the modes of myth, fairy-tale, and epic fantasy, Tolkien uses in his fiction the motifs of loss and victory, tragedy and eucatastrophe, the promise of a better future, but then again, the feeling of permanent loss or "marring." Repetitions of these motifs form a literary mood for Tolkien's collection of myths.

Constant marring, weariness and corruption of the created world are recurring motifs in Tolkien's fantasy (see Korpua 2016). In *Morgoth's Ring*, Tolkien writes that "in Eä [meaning the World] according to the Tale nothing endures endlessly without weariness and corruption" (Tolkien 2002e: 376).

The same motif can be seen in *The Lord of the Rings* when the character Galadriel, the ruler of the Elves of Lórien, discusses both her and her husband Celeborn's past life and fate in Middle-earth. Galadriel recalls her life as "the long defeat" by saying that "He [Celeborn] has dwelt in the West since the days of dawn, and I [Galadriel] have dwelt with him years uncounted; for ere the fall of Nargothrond or Gondolin I passed over the mountains, and together through ages of the world we have fought the long defeat" (Tolkien 2008: 443).

This vision of life as a long defeat is shared by Elrond, another powerful Elf character, and the ruler of the Elven people of Rivendell (Imladris) in the times of *The Lord of the Rings*. In the epic, in the chapter "The Council of Elrond" (Tolkien 2008: 309–310), Elrond reminisces the (seemingly) pointless victories and many defeats in the history of Elves and Men with a melancholic tone. Elrond remembers the splendor of old armies and the glory of the old times. His memory reaches to the Elder Days, and in the timeline of *The Lord of the Rings* he is a "relic" of the old world, of the world of *The Silmarillion*.

As an internal theme, one might suggest that this motif of "loss" and "long defeat" is a Christian and Catholic one. One of the basic assumptions in the Christian faith is that true mercy, salvation, and happiness can only be found in the afterlife. Alister McGrath discusses this eschatological vision in his *Christian Theology*. The term *eschatology*, meaning a "discourse about the end," derived from the Greek term ta eschata, "the last things," and in the Christian faith relates to matters such as expectations of resurrection and judgment. For the Christian belief, it is characteristic that time is linear, not cyclical.

McGrath writes that "[h]istory had a beginning: it will one day come to an end." McGrath discusses the distinction in contemporary theology on the concept of eschatology and the concept of apocalypsis, meaning "unveiling," "disclosure" or "revelation." Nowadays eschatology refers to a branch of Christian theology concerned with the "last things," such as the resurrection of the dead, Heaven and Hell. The term "apocalyptic," however, is sometimes used to refer to a particular genre or type of literature that has an interest with the "last things" (McGrath 2011: 444–445).

Tolkien writes about the eschatological ending of his mythology in a quite apocalyptic way, although this mythical ending also has something to do with the Scandinavian myth Ragnarök.[47] Tolkien writes that in the end the evil (and its personification Melkor) will come to a final end and the world of Men shall be "avenged":

> Then shall the last battle be gathered on the fields of Valinor. In that day Tulkas shall strive with Melko[r], and on his right shall stand Fionwë and on his left Túrin Turambar, son of Húrin, Conqueror of Fate, coming from the halls of Mandos; and it shall be the black sword of Túrin that deals unto Melko[r] his death and final end; and so shall the children of Húrin and all Men be avenged [Tolkien 2002e: 76].

3. Fall and Struggle

Though Tolkien's mythopoeic fiction is full of stories of pessimistic life visions, despair, and defeat, still in the end, all shall be avenged, and the world made anew. In Christian worldview, there is always the possibility of "ultimate victory" (see Whittingham 2008: 9).

In a way, death and loss are the main motifs of Tolkien's fiction. Tolkien himself was of course concerned with this kind of "excessive interest" in personal details. In his letter to Deborah Webster in 1958, Tolkien writes that this kind of interest "distracts attention from the author's works." Tolkien sees that only "one's guardian Angel, or indeed God Himself, could unravel the real relationship between personal facts and an author's work. Not the author himself (though he knows more than any investigator), and certainly not so-called 'psychologists'" (Tolkien 1981: 288).

In his letter to Father Robert Murray in 1953, Tolkien writes that "*The Lord of the Rings* is of course a fundamentally religious and Catholic work; unconsciously so at first, but consciously in the revision" (Tolkien 1981: 172). Tolkien writes that "[t]hat is why I have not put in, or have cut out, practically all references to anything like 'religion,' to cults or practices, in the imaginary world. For the religious element is absorbed into the story and the symbolism" (Tolkien 1981: 172).

These absorbed elements in the stories are formed in different overlapping motifs, different referents and frames of referents that form an internal field of reference. Motifs, such as a "quest to save our (way of thinking of the) world," "eucatastrophe" in the end of the quest that gives a glimpse of the "real truth behind the story"—in this case kind of a Christian faith—and motif-elements such as "death and loss," "marring of the world," and in the end an eschatological "ultimate hope" are fundamental in Tolkien's fiction. These motifs could be seen forming a theme for the story, the central topic or subject of constructed mythopoeia.

Frye (1967: 52) discusses this term of mode by using as a background the classical concept of dianoia: "the idea or poetic thought (something quite different, of course, from other kinds of thought) that the reader gets from the writer." Frye discusses that the best translation of dianoia is "theme," and that literature with this ideal or conceptual interest may be called thematic. Frye (1967: 52) further explains that when readers ask: "How is this story going to turn out?," they are asking a question about the plot, but when the readers ask: "What's the point of this story?," the question relates to dianoia, and indicates that themes have their elements of discovery just as plots do.

In Tolkien's fiction, the narrative plots can usually be easily defined. In *The Hobbit*, the plot can be summarized quite simply as follows: a middle-class, early middle aged and quite comic protagonist Bilbo Baggins is lured to an adventure with the wizard Gandalf and a band of dwarves. The adventure's objective is to get back the Dwarf treasure, which an evil dragon, Smaug, has stolen. Bilbo leaves his idyllic and familiar home, does some adventuring in unfamiliar surroundings, including encounters with trolls, goblins, eagles and finally the dragon. In the end, Bilbo returns to his idyllic home, but he is a somewhat changed character. The story is a classical "there and back again"–styled fairy-story.

As a narrative, *The Lord of the Rings* is quite simply a "there and back again" story. Essentially, the objective of the epic's quest is to destroy the evil One Ring that can bring destruction to all "good peoples" of Middle-earth. The plot follows the Hobbit protagonist Frodo Baggins' and his varying companions' quest to destroy the One Ring. In the narrative, it takes the protagonists more than 250 pages to understand that their task is to "destroy" the One Ring in the chapter "The Council of Elrond," which is the fourteenth chapter in the book. To simplify the plot, the protagonists destroy the One Ring, and in the end return to their idyllic home of the Shire, however, the Shire has changed during their absence, and they must "reconstruct" it.

The plots can be easy to describe, but the themes are not so easily interpreted. *The Hobbit* is a fairy-story adventure. Perhaps the original theme of *The Hobbit* is comically adventurous. Then again, originally, in a sub-theme there could be a guideline that it is possible and useful to leave your comfortable lifestyle, in a kind of carpe diem way, and find your own adventure. Later, when *The Hobbit* became

3. Fall and Struggle

intertextualized and mingled with *The Lord of the Rings* and the rest of Tolkien's fiction, the theme changed once again. There can be seen a glimpse of the forthcoming *The Lord of the Rings*. The first edition of *The Hobbit*, published in 1937, was at first not intended to be a part of Tolkien's larger mythological fantasy. Next editions intertextualized *The Hobbit* with *The Lord of the Rings*, changed both the character Gollum and the role of the One Ring itself, and changed the theme of the latter part of *The Hobbit* (after the fifth chapter "Riddles in the Dark") into somewhat darker; as can be seen from Tolkien's changes to the manuscripts in "The Return of the Shadow" (Tolkien 2002d: 75, 79–81, 261). The theme changes because Tolkien began writing *The Hobbit* and *The Lord of the Rings* to be a part of the same mythology.

Then again, in *The Lord of the Rings* the major theme is essentially the same as in *The Silmarillion*. As the motifs mentioned earlier indicate, Middle-earth is a place of constant struggle, of constant change, and "marring." It is a place of "many defeats" and "fruitless victories" as Elrond states in *The Lord of the Rings* (Tolkien 2008: 310–311); an existential battlefield, or a place of "long defeat," as Galadriel says; and a changing plane of evident destruction, where "nothing can endure endlessly without weariness and corruption" (Tolkien 2002e: 376).

In the end, Tolkien's fantasy fiction promises a "final victory" against evil and a eucatastrophic apocalypsis. But in the stories, for the reader, the major theme is sad and melancholic. The third part of *The Silmarillion*, "Quenta Silmarillion," ends in a manifestation of a theme that is not promising of a joyful end to the world. In this manifestation the melancholic vision of Tolkien's fictive universe is quite clearly declared. Passing from high and beautiful to darkness and ruin is the fate of Arda Marred (Tolkien 1999: 306).

From this manifestation of the Fall, next, I focus on the motif of fall in Tolkien's fiction. Here, I research the main functions of good and evil, and heroic, mythic heroes. I start with Tolkien's mythopoeic allegories and how this reflects to the mythic heroes of Tolkien's fiction.

The Mythopoeic Code of Tolkien

The concept of allegory in Tolkien's works has been a critical and difficult point in Tolkien studies. Tolkien himself said on many occasions that he disliked allegory—conscious and intentional allegory—in all its possible forms (Tolkien 1999: xii). These comments notwithstanding, he also produced at least one clearly allegorical text in his career: "Leaf by Niggle" (1945), a short story where an artist named Niggle lives in a world that does not appreciate art, but Niggle himself is an obsessive, meticulous artist who has difficulties finishing his great art work because of constant interruptions. An allegory describing Tolkien's own artistic pursuit, perhaps.

Then again, for all his dislike of "intentional allegory," Tolkien could be seen as sharing a view, once again, with Coleridge who saw on the one hand "symbolism" as emerging spontaneously out of imagination, and "allegory," on the other hand, as artificial and conscious, almost mechanical, construction.

Tolkien's approach to allegory is arguably very strict and limited. For example, he disliked C.S. Lewis' latter Narnia texts, which he thought were too allegorical. As Shippey points out, medieval and renaissance allegorical texts such as Edmund Spenser's *The Faerie Queene* (1590) and Middle English poems *Pearl* (ca.1400) had an influence on Tolkien's works (Shippey 2003: 5). Added to this, many chapters in Tolkien's books could easily be understood allegorically—even primarily—in terms of Christian allegory. The next section delineates why these parts of Tolkien's fiction should nonetheless be read as myths and part of Tolkien's mythopoeic vision—rather than solely allegorically.

Mythopoeic Allegories

How does mythopoeics between internal and external references manifest in Tolkien's texts? A clear example of this is the metaphorical and (even) allegorical language that Tolkien is using when addressing important elements and examples. Tolkien's texts, especially *The Lord of the Rings*, have been judged by some critics

3. Fall and Struggle

as allegorical texts. For example, when it was first published in the 1950s, it was criticized as an allegorical narrative about the Second World War and the "threat" of the Atomic Bomb. Tolkien of course objected to these views unconditionally. Tolkien writes, in his foreword for the second edition of *The Lord of the Rings* that there is no inner meaning or message in the text (Tolkien 1995: xvi). Tolkien goes on convincing his readers that the main parts of the works have been created before the Second World War started in 1939 and was not modified by the war or its sequels (Tolkien 1995: xvi).

Then again, all the main works of the 18th- or 19th-century fantasy have been included in the list of allegorical texts: For example Tolkien's *The Lord of the Rings*, C.S. Lewis's *The Last Battle*, Roald Dahl's *James and the Giant Peach*, Lewis Carroll's *Alice in Wonderland*, George MacDonald's *Princess and the Goblin*, and Antoine de Saint-Exupéry's *The Little Prince*. Fantasy, therefore, on some level, certainly has something to do with allegory. And the dichotomy between the mimetic level of text and the allegorical level of text has been an important critical debate in fantasy research for the last century.

In Tolkien's fiction, textual allegories, and metaphorical language function as a part of the writer's constructive mythopoeics—as Tolkien's own intention as a builder of a fictive fantasy world, a secondary creator. Therefore, the secondary creator becomes the creator of a secondary creation, as the mythopoeia in effect evokes.

Ponder for a while on this quote from *The Lord of the Rings*:

"It is said that the Hornburg has never fallen for assault," said Théoden; "but now my heart is doubtful. The world changes, and all that once was strong now proves unsure. How shall any tower withstand such numbers and such reckless hate? Had I known that the strength of Isengard was grown so great, maybe I should not so rashly have ridden forth to meet it, for all the arts of Gandalf. His counsel seems not now so good as it did under the morning sun."

"Do not judge the counsel of Gandalf, until all is over, lord," said Aragorn.

"The end will not be long," said the king. "But I will not end here, taken like an old badger in a trap. Snowmane and Hasufel and the horses of my

guard are in the inner court. When dawn comes, I will bid men sound Helm's horn, and I will ride forth. Will you ride with me then, son of Arathorn? Maybe we shall cleave a road, or make such an end as will be worth a song—if any be left to sing of us hereafter."
"I will ride with you," said Aragorn [Tolkien 2009a: 161].

There are external and internal references and even metaphorical and allegorical language in the quote above. Théoden, the king of Rohan, is surrounded by the opposing Saruman's forces, who in quite an allegorical way use fire and the "devilry from Orthanc," orcish weapons of "mass-destruction." Théoden swears that he will not have his end here, metaphorically "taken like an old badger in a trap." That proves to be true later when he dies in the Battle of the Pelennor Fields. His ending, as he predicted, will later be worth a song since a song was made on the death of the king and others lying in the Mounds of Mundburg (Tolkien 2008: 135). In the quote above, one could see references to the wars of the 20th century, which Tolkien of course knew closely from his own personal context.

As Jeremy Tambling (2010: 1) sees, allegory has been, until recently, neglected by the modern study of literature, and reading for allegory has been regarded "as getting in the way of an immediate response to a text, missing out on its vital, literal sense." Tolkien also disliked this "mechanical," "artificial," and "predictable" allegory, as did Coleridge earlier (see Tambling 2010: 77–80).

What is then the relationship of allegory and Tolkien's use of mythopoeics? The use of allegory in Tolkien's fiction has become a critical and difficult point in Tolkien studies. Still, some parts in Tolkien's texts could be easily understood allegorically—and even majorly as a Christian, or Christian Platonic, allegory.[48] Allegory is something that is typical for both Plato's texts and traditional Christian theology. However, next I delineate why these parts of Tolkien's fiction could be read as myths and part of Tolkien's vision—rather than (solely) allegorically.

Allegory as a term, as a Latin version of a Greek word, appears in Cicero's (106–43 BCE) *De Oratore* and in the work of his near contemporary Philodemus of Gadara (ca. 110–35 BCE) (Tambling

3. Fall and Struggle

2010: 20). Coulter in his study on Neoplatonism sees the tradition of allegorical reading of texts as indisputably important. Coulter discusses allegory in the sense of allegorism or allegorization (German Allegorese):

> The systematic interpretation of a text (usually of considerable length) on the assumption that the author intended that the reader seek beneath the surface some second or indirect meaning, or meanings, which, in the view of the interpreter, can be related to the apparent or direct meaning in a fairly systematic way [Coulter 1976: 25].

Coulter's strict way of allegory and allegorization could be seen in a reference to Tolkien's view of the subject. Coulter discusses that allegory in this sense differs, at least in an extent, from the "figure allegory," as it was understood by the ancient rhetoricians. Coulter (1976: 25) sees that the genuine difference is the fact that they mostly concerned themselves with "figures" and limited allegorical "passages," not entire works. Ancient rhetoricians therefore were looking for simply allegorical "elements." This style of reading was criticized by Tolkien, for example, when he commented that Rayner Unwin was doing the same when he assimilated *The Lord of the Rings* with *Nibelungenlied* and Wagner. In a letter to Rayner Unwin's father, publisher Stanley Unwin, Tolkien commented that Stanley Unwin should not let Rayner to read text allegorically (Carpenter 1977: 202).

There is also the question of the so-called Christian allegory, which was a problem for Tolkien, as can be seen in his dislike for C.S. Lewis' Narnia series. Perhaps that was a major reason for Tolkien's dislike of the term allegory? In his study, *Piers Plowman and Christian Allegory*, David Aers (1975: 15) discusses the ideological history of Christian allegorization. As a key to the theory of Christian allegory Aers sees the so-called "historical Incarnation of God." Aers quotes M-D. Chenu, who argued that medieval culture had inherited a situation where the *Bible* and Christianity were "blocked up by the categories of Hellenistic culture deployed by Philo and Origen." Chenu attributed this process explicitly to the effects of Platonism and as a modern theologian finds it incongruous with the historicity of Christianity (Aers 1975: 16).

The Mythopoeic Code of Tolkien

Therefore, it is almost impossible, or unimportant, to detect any difference in Christian allegorization and Neoplatonic or Christian Platonic concept of allegory. But then again, many scholars have seen a great difference between old Ancient usage of allegory and later Christian allegory.

M.W. Bloomfield discusses that ancient Greeks and Romans managed history by "reducing it to nature." On the contrary, he discusses that the Christian tradition, following the Hebraic emphasis, sees history revealing religious truth and God's will. Discussing Bloomfield's conceptualization Aers asks, where lays the unique role of history and events in Christian allegory? (Aers 1975: 18–19). As discussed earlier in this book, Tolkien saw his fiction hinting a glimpse of "Truth" and even God's will. Maybe this could be a key point for possible allegorization in Tolkien's texts.

In *The Inklings*, Humphrey Carpenter fictionalizes conversations between participants of the Inklings group in their meeting on Thursday evenings. In one of those conversations, Carpenter illustrates his vision of Tolkien's concept of allegory. In a fictional dialogue Carpenter says, through the mouth of his Tolkien-character that "any attempt to explain the purport of myth or fairytale must use allegorical language." He continues that "the more 'life' a story has, the more readily it will be susceptible of allegorical interpretations." Later Carpenter makes his Tolkien-character also say that "I suppose all my stuff—is mainly concerned with the Fall, with mortality, and with the Machine.... [B]y the Machine I mean the use of all external plans or devices, instead of the development of inner powers and talents.... The Machine is merely our more obvious modern form" (Carpenter 1978: 140). In my opinion, Carpenter's fictionalized vision could be quite accurate, since the main internal motifs in Tolkien's fiction are Fall, mortality—or "Escape from Death"[49]—, and an anti-modernistic tone of cosmography.

As Carpenter argues, Tolkien saw the story of Christ from the *Bible* as a "true myth," as a myth that "really happened" (Carpenter 1978: 148). The eucatastrophical myth of the Christian theology—a true myth in Tolkien's opinion—of Christ's incarnation as a man

3. Fall and Struggle

and his later martyr death for the sake of all mankind was central for Tolkien.[50]

This Christian theory was searching for the literal and allegorical levels of the text. G.W.H. Lampe argues that the approach "rests, not on an interpretation of history but on a particular quasi-Platonist doctrine of the literal sense of Scripture—the outward form or 'letter' of the sacred writings—to the eternal spiritual reality concealed, as it were, beneath the literal sense." For medieval thinkers, the *Bible* was "a mysterious collection of enigmas" and history became "the outward shell or husk containing and hiding from the uninstructed the inner truth of mystery" (Aers 1975: 17).

As an example of the allegorization of the *Bible* in the later Middle Ages, there is the theory of Denis the Carthusian, a 15th-century theologian and mystic who is most famous for his synthesis' on doctrines of spiritual life. Denis' exegesis of the third chapter of "Genesis" shows his interpretation of the allegorical level of the *Bible*. For example, "tree of Life" equals Christ, but also the death-dealing "tree of Knowledge" is Christ in an allegorical level. Following the medieval tradition, Denis sees that "as in Adam all die, so also in Christ all shall be made alive" (see 1 Corinthians 15: 22). Therefore, God's action "in history will transform the first great 'sin,' enacted around the tree of Knowledge, into a felix culpa, and so, in a way, the tree of Knowledge will become the tree of life" (Aers 1975: 29–30). In Tolkien's mythopoeic fiction there is also "a Fall"—mythical, if not strictly allegorical. Tolkien writes that there is the "fall of Angels," which is "quite different in form, of course, to that of Christian myth" (Tolkien 1999: xv–xvi).

Therefore, allegory and myth should be at some point considered in the same context. Clifford (1974: 36), for example, sees that the concept of allegory is closing on to a concept of myth. Allegory, like myth, "presupposes an audience who will respond to it in specific ways: to consider its authors' conception of this response is not necessarily to indulge in the 'intentional fallacy'" (Clifford 1974: 36).

Myth, like allegory, is concerned with a complex system of explanation. They both attempt to offer means by which we can

The Mythopoeic Code of Tolkien

interpret "our relationship to the past, to the forces operating in the psyche, and to the facts and processes of the world around us." The essential difference between them is that "myth is in an important sense pre-literary, while allegory is a literary mode that borrows from myth, subordinating it to its own purposes" (Clifford 1974: 54).

Tolkien's mythopoeics, the creative myth-making, is therefore in many ways connected to the allegorization of language. Symbols, myths, and allegory are difficult concepts to differentiate and should therefore be treated as loosely intermingling tropes as Frye does in his theory.

Tolkien admits that his text uses symbols. For example, in his letter to Milton Waldman, Tolkien declares that Elrond, the mythical Half-Elf lord of Rivendell, symbolizes ancient wisdom and lore, the preservation of all tradition concerning the good, wise, and beautiful (Tolkien 1983: 153).

Tolkien, therefore, understood the symbolic, or even allegorical, level of his text, and the whole body of his fiction could be read as such. In *The Lord of the Rings*, as discussed earlier, Tom Bombadil could be "a spirit of pacifism," or Saruman could be allegorized as a malevolent "spirit of industrialization."

Moreover, Tolkien himself would not approve of such a simple allegorization. In "On Fairy-Stories," he writes about seeing the gods of mythologies as "nature-myths" or "personifications" of some functions. Jeremy Tambling writes that these personifications could be seen as different from allegory, or they may be "the essence of allegory," as it was for artist and poet John Ruskin (1819–1900) (Tambling 2010: 42–43).

For example, the Greek Olympian gods could be seen as personifications of the sun, of dawn, of night, etc. Or the Norse god Thórr could be seen as a personification of thunder, and his hammer, Mjölnir as lightning. Tolkien contradicts this and discusses that even as such presumptions could be made, Thórr has a very marked character, or personality, which "cannot be found in thunder or in lightning" (Tolkien 1983: 123). Therefore, allegorical reading of these mythological texts is possible, put this reading is not the final rendition of the

3. Fall and Struggle

text. Thus, Saruman could be seen as echoing the negative spirit of industrialization and "Machine," but it is not all that Saruman, as a character, is.

In his foreword to the second edition of *The Lord of the Rings*, Tolkien wrote that he preferred history, true or feigned, and that many of the readers might confuse "applicability" with "allegory." He understood that "applicability" resides in the freedom of the reader, and allegory in the purposed domination of the author (Tolkien 1995: xvii).

Additionally, Tom Shippey has made some allegorical assumptions concerning *The Lord of the Rings*. Shippey (2001: 70) points out that the example of the character Saruman certainly stands for some kind of "mechanical ingenuity, smithcraft developed into engineering skills." In *The Lord of the Rings*, Treebeard says regarding Saruman that "He has a mind of metal and wheels"; Saruman's Orcs use a kind of gunpowder at the Battle of Helm's Deep, and later Saruman uses a kind of napalm against the Ents.

Engineering skills, industrialism or mechanical innovations in the hands of "evil forces" is of course not a new point in epic literature; the same tone against modern inventions could be seen in John Milton's *Paradise Lost*, where Satan in the Sixth Book invents "devilish machines" against his enemies for the War in Heaven.

Shippey also discusses views of the "socialistic suggestions" clinging to Saruman, and compares him to Denethor, the Steward of Gondor, whom Shippey sees as an "arch-conservative" character (Shippey 2001: 171–172). Denethor is an "anti-modern character of the past." When, in *The Lord of the Rings*, in the last moments of his life, Gandalf asks Denethor "what then would you have … if your will could have its way?" Denethor answers: "I would have things as they were in all the days of my life—and in the days of my longfathers before me" (Tolkien 2009b: 143). Although Denethor is a character of the past, and against the modern, he is not, for Tolkien, or for most of the readers, a positively received character. In fact, he is a negative character, an antagonist.

Yet again, in many parts, Tolkien's fiction is (pro-)conservative, anti-modernistic, and in some themes Christian. But is it theologically Christian? Tolkien writes that *The Lord of the Rings* is fundamentally religious and Catholic, saying that it was first unconsciously so, and consciously in the revision work (Tolkien 1981: 172). Of course, we must see this statement also in its context, since it was written in a letter to Father Robert Murray, S.J., a close friend of the Tolkien family and a Catholic priest. For a friend and a priest, in my mind, Tolkien wanted to explain his fiction's absence of religious elements to his benefit.

One might ask if *The Lord of the Rings* is a fundamentally religious work, is it so allegorically? Dante has distinguished two forms of allegory: "the allegory of poets," and "the allegory of theologians." He writes that in the allegory of the poets, the truth is "hidden under a beautiful fiction," and that there is no necessary truth in the literal story being told. But for Dante, the *Bible* is characterized by the allegory of theologians, and in there, both the literal level and the allegorical level are true (Tambling 2010: 26). Although Dante is speaking of allegory, and not of myth, Dante's vision still draws closer to Tolkien's vision of the "myth of Christ" as a "True Myth."

Shippey has pondered on this question of Tolkien's works "fundamental" religiousness. Shippey (2001: 179) sees that *The Lord of the Rings* is not Catholic, nor religious, nor even Christian. As Tolkien himself says, there is almost no hint of any religious feeling at all in the characters or in their societies, not even where one would most likely expect it. Shippey points out that this absence of religion in the societies of Middle-earth—for example the society of the Hobbits—is unlike any human societies we know of; and in this sense he calls Middle-earth a "Never-never Land" (Shippey 2001: 179).

That is not the whole truth, of course. One might object that there are the semi-religious funeral traditions, such as, for example, the ones seen in *The Lord of the Rings* by the Men of Rohan, or by the Dwarves in Moria, or in the scene of Túrin Turambar's death in *The Silmarillion*. And there are of course the religious elements in the lifestyles of the people of Gondor, and of Númenoreans; both Black

3. Fall and Struggle

(and evil) Númenoreans worshipping Morgoth, or the so-called Faithfull (and good) Númenoreans, worshipping the Valar.

Furthermore, the character Frodo in *The Lord of the Rings* is in some ways almost a Christ-like figure.[51] Frodo is not an allegory of Christ, but in some ways perhaps an analog. Frodo of course is not messianically killed for the "sins of the humankind," but he tries to deliver the Free People of Middle-earth from Evil by fulfilling a Quest to destroy the One Ring—although, in the end Frodo himself does not succeed in destroying it. In the final dramatic scene in the Crack of Doom, Frodo loses his will to destroy the One Ring and instead claims it for himself. He fails his Quest, but in a miraculous eucatastrophic moment this "failing" is forgiven. In one of the most physically mimetic scenes of *The Lord of the Rings* Gollum—Frodo's "nemesis" and previous holder of the One Ring before the Hobbits Frodo and Bilbo—attacks Frodo and regains the long-lost Ring. After regaining the One Ring, Gollum, overwhelmed with joy and excitement, loses his balance while dancing and falls with the One Ring into the Pit, thus destroying both himself and the One Ring.

After the destruction of the One Ring, Frodo is somewhat psychologically changed. He becomes a distant character who rarely acts in any of the forthcoming chapters. He is calm, wise, and even philosophical, "grown," as Saruman later describes: "You have grown, Halfling—You are wise, and cruel. You have robbed my revenge of sweetness, and now must go hence in bitterness, in debt to your mercy" (Tolkien 2009b: 335).

Frodo never completely recovers from the physical and emotional stress of the quest, from his many injuries sustained during the quest and, finally and most severely, from the destruction of the One Ring itself. In the end of *The Lord of the Rings*, as mentioned earlier, Frodo sails to the West, to the Undying Lands, where he can find peace and rest. For Sam Gamgee, Frodo's loyal companion, the most troubling thing after the War of the Ring is the fact that the people of Shire—the fellow Hobbits—do not appreciate Frodo's quest and his sacrifices. This is reminiscent of the *Bible*, where Jesus testifies that "a prophet hath no honour in his own country" (John 4: 44).

The Mythopoeic Code of Tolkien

Myths of Middle-earth (and Arda as whole) could be discussed allegorically, but these could also be seen in metaphorical language as examples of Platonic myth, which is later discussed. For example, the Atlantis myth of Númenor is simply in its mode a story of "fall from the grace." The myth of invisibility concerning Plato's Ring of Gyges and Tolkien's The Great Ring is basically a myth of "moral agendas," of "right and wrong," and of "good and evil." The Myth of Creation in both Plato and Tolkien deals with the difference between the "ideal" world and the "real" world. Or: How can the original ideas of the World be achieved, or is it even possible?

Ralph C. Wood (2003: 318) discusses the Catholic elements of Tolkien's fiction, discussing that, as a Roman Catholic, Tolkien's conviction was that God's implanted natural law underlies everything created. Wood sees that Tolkien was not troubled by the fact that readers failed to perceive the implicitly Christian character of *The Lord of the Rings*, because he wanted his work to stand on its own merits: "to glorify God as a compelling and convincing story, not it to be propped up with even so noble a purpose as evangelism" (R. Wood 2003: 318). Wood sees communal life and ecclesial company at the very center of *The Lord of the Rings*, saying that there is nothing individualistic to be found anywhere in Tolkien. The Fellowship of the Ring always functions as a unity. Even when the Fellowship is split—after "the betrayal of the Judas-like Boromir"—there is no solitude. Frodo and Sam serve as companions, and Aragorn and the other separated members of the Fellowship also act communally (R. Wood 2003: 320).

As for the myth of Christ, Wood claims that Tolkien is not writing an allegory. Gandalf, as well as Frodo, could be compared to Christ: Gandalf dies in the battle with the Balrog and descents into an abyss, just as he is resuscitated from death to newness of life. Yet Wood sees that Gandalf "is not resurrected to die no more." Wood claims that while Gandalf possesses Christ-like qualities, so do Aragorn and, by the end, Sam Gamgee. Wood sees that there is no clear equivalence between Gandalf and Christ, whereas Aslan in C.S. Lewis' Narnia series is clearly an allegory of Christ (R. Wood 2003: 328–329).

3. Fall and Struggle

Conversely, there are of course many, in some way, biblical chapters in *The Lord of the Rings* after Gandalf is "returned from the Death." The most striking is the one when Gandalf appears to the party of Aragorn, Gimli, and Legolas. Tolkien writes that the three cannot recognize Gandalf mistaking him for the other wizard, Saruman. "What veil was over my sight," cries Aragorn wondering why he could not identify Gandalf at first (Tolkien 2009a: 108).

This scene has a close resemblance to the Biblical account of Christ's appearance on the Road to Emmaus, where, after his crucifixion, Christ appears to the disciples, who do not recognize him. At first, when they met Christ on the road, their "eyes were holden." And afterwards, when Christ disappears from their sight during an evening meal, they finally recognize him and "their eyes were opened" (Luke 24: 13–32, Mark 16: 12–13).

One certainly religious element in Tolkien's fantasy fiction, forming a continuous internal field, seems to be the fundamental belief that the Elves and some of Men (the faithful ones) have on Eru Ilúvatar, the creator. In *The History of Middle-earth* series, in *Morgoth's Ring*, Tolkien makes his characters Andreth and Finrod discuss Eru, the One, in quite a theological level. In Tolkien's mythology, Andreth is a wisewoman of Men from the House of Bëor,[52] who lives in the First Age of the Sun, in an era when Middle-earth is largely dominated by the evil Vala Morgoth. Finrod Felagund is the King of Nargothrond, an Elven lord and brother of Galadriel.

In the intratextual reference text, which was published posthumously, Andreth and Finrod discuss, one might say, religious beliefs of both Men and Elves. Andreth says that those of the "Old Hope" say that one day "the One will himself enter into Arda, and heal Men and all the Marring from the beginning to the end" (Tolkien 2002e: 321).This certainly eschatological view is then contradicted by Finrod, who does not think that Eru could "fit" inside Middle-earth. He says: "How could Eru enter into the thing that He has made, and then which He is beyond measure greater? Can the singer enter into his tale or the designer into his picture?" (Tolkien 2002e: 322).

The Mythopoeic Code of Tolkien

Afterwards, Finrod discusses his vision, shared perhaps by most of the Elves that Eru is "in" Middle-earth already:

> "He is already in it, as well as outside," said Finrod. "But indeed the 'in-dwelling' and the 'out-living' are not in the same mode."
> ...But they speak of Eru Himself entering into Arda, and that is a thing wholly different. How could He the greater do this? Would it not shatter Arda, or indeed all Eä? [Tolkien 2002e: 322].

After this, Finrod sees that the ways of Eru are, of course, mysterious and cannot be predicted: "If Eru wishes to do this, I do not doubt that He would find a way, though I cannot foresee it. For, as it seems to me, even if He in Himself were to enter in, He must still remain also as He is: the Author without" (Tolkien 2002e: 322).

What is the interesting "Author without" that Finrod is referring to? Is this once again a reference to Tolkien's theory of secondary creation? Theologically God could be seen as a creator of the story of life, the Author of everything. An author of fiction could be seen as a secondary creator creating a secondary world, a fictional world. Could the fictional creator—in this case Eru—of the (secondary) fictitious world be seen also as a kind of "tertiary creator"?

Eru is absent from the text of *The Lord of the Rings* and *The Hobbit*, appearing only in secondhand references, but in the text of *The Silmarillion*, he is present. In the first section "Ainulindalë," Eru is one of the functional characters of the text. In this sense, the character Eru, in my opinion, cannot represent the authority of the writer. In the latter part of Tolkien's fiction, however, Eru could be seen as a kind of "author of the story": the future is described to be only known by Eru, and fate and history are, in a way, in his dominion. Fleming Rutledge, in his theological survey of Tolkien's texts *The Battle for Middle-Earth. Tolkien's Divine Design in The Lord of the Rings* sees that Tolkien's references to "God" in *The Lord of the Rings* are explicit. Rutledge (2004: 21) points out that Tolkien is referring to "the Writer of the Story," "the Great Author," and "the supreme Artist," and sees that Tolkien came to think of "his story as a reflection of, or adumbration of, the biblical drama of redemption."

3. Fall and Struggle

As for the external references, Whittingham (2008: 39) discusses that Tolkien, as a devout Catholic, knew the two Genesis creation stories and other references to the formation of the world in the Jewish Scriptures, known to Christians as the Old Testament, and in the Christian New Testament. Whittingham (2008: 39) points out that Deborah Webster and Ivor A. Rogers refer to the *Bible* of Judaism and Christianity as a "principal mythic" source for Tolkien's mythology. These various texts contributed to what Tolkien calls the "Cauldron of Story," from which he drew in developing his mythology. Shippey notes in *The Road to Middle-earth* that "the design of The Silmarillion" parallels "the history of Genesis" (Shippey 2003: 235). Similarly, Brian Rosebury has referred to the first part of *The Silmarillion*, "Ainulindalë," as "the Elves' version of Genesis" (Whittingham 2008: 44).

But these are not certain elements of Christian allegory, but more or less elements of cosmogonical and cosmological myths. But as such, these are in fact Christian Platonic in many ways. Therefore, with all this in consideration, it is possible to say that in Tolkien's fiction, the religious and semi-religious elements are used on the level of myth and mythopoeia, and not on the level of precise allegory.

Mythic and Biblical Heroes

One could say that Tolkien's *The Hobbit* and *The Lord of the Rings* are 20th-century's ultimate quest fantasies. The plots in both texts are basically the same: the Hobbit protagonist/protagonists start in idyllic, familiar Hobbiton (or Shire), and travel into archaic wild lands to confront many dangers. In the end of the stories, the heroes—Bilbo Baggins in *The Hobbit*, and Frodo Baggins and his companions in *The Lord of the Rings*—have completed their quest and return back to the familiar Shire. In both cases, the heroes have grown and changed in the journey, but at the same time, something has happened back in the Shire. In *The Hobbit*, fellow Hobbits think that Bilbo is dead and try to sell his properties. In *The Lord of the*

Rings, Saruman and other "bad people" have taken control of the Shire, and the Hobbits must reclaim their own country.

In *The Hobbit*, Bilbo Baggins' journey as a proper hero starts only after he finds the One Ring, and after he finds his own courage. Before that, Bilbo encounters some dangerous situations involving trolls and goblins, but in the encounters, he is more of an unsuccessful bystander. In the latter part of the book, Bilbo becomes the hero, and he is also declared a hero by his fellow companions, the dwarves, and the wizard Gandalf. *The Hobbit* is thus a classical "hero's journey," resembling ancient heroic myths and legends, and medieval fairy story motifs, and showing growth of the character.

In *The Lord of the Rings*, the hero's journey is essentially the same as in *The Hobbit*: the two main protagonists, Frodo Baggins, and Sam Gamgee, grow to be real heroes and save the world. Their quest is so difficult that it is easy to say that they could not have completed it solely by themselves. *The Lord of the Rings* is a classic example of the value of friendship and of "team spirit" in a quest fantasy. As in *The Hobbit*, as well in *The Lord of the Rings*, the hero's journey does not really begin until the latter part of the book.

It is also interesting to examine the hero's journey in Tolkien's *The Silmarillion*, which is a different kind of narrative, written in the purest epic high fantasy tone that cannot be easily matched to any other work of the genre. There is not much growth of character in the hero's journey in *The Silmarillion*, since the "journey" appears to be predestined to fail, or to succeed.

The heroic legend "Of Beren and Lúthien," in the heart of *The Silmarillion*, is written in Tolkien's fiction's most romantic tone. In its context, it is a story of a human hero's (Beren) great adventures to gain a possibility to marry an Elvish "princess" (Lúthien). It deals with a classical human myth of escape from death, but also with an Elvish myth of escape from immortality, or "deathlessness," as Flieger sees it (2005a: 46). The purpose of Beren and Lúthien's journey is to make it possible to stay together in life and there-after, and in this, their journey is successful. In the end of the story, after Beren's death and Lúthien's return to the Blessed Lands of Valinor, they are joined

3. Fall and Struggle

in the afterlife, their fates and paths are joined (see Tolkien 1999: 221).

A clear hero's journey is seen also in *The Silmarillion*'s chapter "Of the Voyage of Eärendil and the War of Wrath." In the story, Eärendil is an offspring of both Elves and Men, who inherits from his father one of the three Silmarills: the mystical and powerful elven-gems, which—by some point—rule the fate of the Elves of Middle-earth in *The Silmarillion*.

Eärendil's fate is to make a journey to the Undying, Blessed Lands of Valinor and plead for the Valar to come to Middle-earth and overthrow Morgoth, The Dark Lord. Eärendil sails to Valinor in his great ship Vingilot, and is confronted with many adventures in his journey, both on land and at sea. Eärendil's plea for the Valar is successful because he represents both Men and Elves. The Valar decide to destroy Morgoth's oppression and ruling in Middle-earth by war, which is named the War of Wrath, and which ends the main story of *The Silmarillion*, the "Quenta Silmarillion."

In the end Morgoth is overthrown and thrust into the Timeless Void. Eärendil is promoted to the skies, where he forever journeys with his ship, Vingilot, and together they form a new star: Gil-Estel, the Star of High Hope. The Silmaril is bound in Eärendil's brow and he now sails the sky as a glitter of hope for all the people of the Middle-earth (Tolkien 1999: 300–301).

In addition to being a mariner and a voyager who brings salvation to the free people of Middle-earth, Eärendil also does a superb heroic act in the War of Wrath. He leads the birds, along with Thorondor, the King of the Eagles, in the battle with Morgoth's dragons in the sky. Eärendil becomes a dragon slayer by slaying the mightiest dragon of all time in the Middle-earth, Ancalagon the Black. When Eärendil casts the Dragon from the sky its body falls to the towers of Thangorodrim, mighty vulcanic mountains raised by Morgoth, and all that Morgoth has build is broken in to ruins (Tolkien 1999: 302–303).

Eärendil is a great voyager and his journey as a hero is straightforward. Like in classical myths, he becomes a star in the sky,[53] and he brings hope to the hearts of Elves and Men. He becomes a dragon slayer and a great hero in the greatest of all wars in Middle-earth, the War of Wrath. In the end, he is the greatest champion of both Elves and Men. The character Eärendil assimilates with many mythical heroes from other fields of reference; for example, such characters as Saint George the Dragon Slayer, Jason, Baldr or even Apollo.

Heroes in Tolkien's fiction could be references to older mythologies and having common features and attributes with these. Tolkien addresses these intertextualities in his created myths, how for example tragic tale of Túrin Turambar is derived from elements in Sigurd the Volsung, Oedipus, and the Finnish Kullervo (Tolkien 1999: xix). Here, we see that Tolkien is addressing the question of both intertextuality and intratextuality. Tolkien argues that his "independent" stories are linked to the general history inside Tolkien's fantasy world: the internal references, but also that these stories are deriving from intertextual (outer) elements.

Tolkien's narrative and linguistic tone changes from text to text, but still his aesthetic background stays the same. That is because intertextual references in Tolkien's texts are drawn from the same sources even though he is writing a fairy-story in *The Hobbit* or higher mythology in *The Silmarillion*.

William Blisset calls *The Lord of the Rings* the last masterpiece of medieval literature (Timmons 2000: 1). Tolkien took his main influences from medieval literature and wrote in kind of a medieval tone. Still Tolkien's traditional background is not as easily pronounced. In *The Silmarillion*, there are intertextual similarities and reflections to many mythologies and myths. In *The Silmarillion*, there are reflections of the Judeo-Christian *Bible*, Icelandic sagas, Finnish the *Kalevala*, Ancient Greek myths, and other sources. Next, it will be discussed how Tolkien's fiction reads the *Bible* from its chosen parts.

Straight elements from the *Bible* are not that easy to find in Tolkien's fiction, because Tolkien tried to make his Middle-earth into a fantasy world without direct religious connotations. Tolkien wrote that he disliked the Arthurian world, because it explicitly contains the Christian religion, and that, to Tolkien, seemed a fatal mistake.

3. Fall and Struggle

He wrote that myth and fairy-story must reflect and contain in solution elements of moral and religious truth, but not explicit religions in the form of the primary real world (Tolkien 1999: xi). Therefore, some elements of the *Bible* can be found in Tolkien's fiction, but not that many directly religious elements.

There are many strong heroic, symbolic characters in Tolkien's fantasy, since Tolkien's fiction reads the *Bible* at level of symbols. Tolkien's fantasy fiction uses some powerful characters from it, such as Dragon, Satan, and Christ. Tolkien's dragons are mainly derived from *Beowulf* and Icelandic, Norse, and Germanic myths, but they also have the same symbolic value as snakes and dragons in the *Bible*. In the *Bible*, the snake is the most evil of all animals (Genesis 3: 1). In "The Book of Revelation," the (seemingly) same ancient snake is now known as the dragon, the devil and Satan (Rev. 12: 7–9). In the Christian mythology, Satan used to be the chief angel of God, but then revolted against God and was cast out of Heaven. In *The Silmarillion*, Melkor used to be the highest angelic being, Ainur (or Valar in Middle-earth), after the creator, Eru, God of Tolkien's world. Tolkien wrote that "Melkor is the supreme spirit of Pride and Revolt, not just the chief Vala of the Earth, who has turned to evil" (Tolkien 2002a: 375). Melkor and Satan both symbolize pride and evil.

As discussed earlier, Tolkien uses the old myth of a dying god in *The Lord of the Rings*. In the New Testament of the Christian *Bible*, resurrected Christ is the personification of God (and "The Son of God"), who dies, and by dying, brings salvation to all mankind who believe in Him. This myth of dying god/gods can be also found in the stories of Hercules, Orpheus, and Balder, as well as in the *Bible* (Frye 1967: 36). In Tolkien's fiction, the Christ myth and even "dying god" myth is represented by both the characters Frodo and Gandalf in *The Lord of the Rings*.

Analogical and mythological similarities between Frodo and Christ were discussed in the earlier chapter, but in *The Lord of the Rings*, the character Gandalf resembles Christ in some ways even more than Frodo does. In *The Lord of the Rings*, the wizard Gandalf is the Dark Lord Sauron's main enemy, The Champion of Light, a divine

The Mythopoeic Code of Tolkien

angelic being, sent from the West by the Valar, the God-like powers of Middle-earth. As mentioned earlier, Tolkien suggested in the posthumous *Unfinished Tales of Númenor and Middle-earth* (1980) that Gandalf could have even been Manwë, the King of Valar himself, disguised as a "regular" angelic being of the race of Maiar, and taken a mortal shape (Tolkien 1992: 540). If that really were the case, then even Gandalf's arrival in Middle-earth would further still resemble Christ's incarnation as a normal human in the *Bible*.

In *The Lord of the Rings*, Gandalf dies in the mines of Moria, and returns from the dead afterwards. When he returns, he is stronger, better, and glorified, even Christ-like. In the *Bible*, after Christ is resurrected from the death and returns, he is more like The God that he originally is. Likewise, in *The Lord of the Rings*, Gandalf is more angelic after his resurrection. He uses his original angelic power more openly.

In Tolkien's fiction, the influence of the Valar in Middle-earth is also much like God's influence on humans in the *Bible*. In the Christian *Bible*, in the Old Testament, God affects the lives of normal humans much more directly, as in *The Silmarillion*, the Valar still have direct contact with Elves and Men. In the New Testament of the *Bible*, God does not affect humans as directly anymore. God's direct influence is the sending of Christ, His only Son. Similarly, after the first ages of *The Silmarillion*, Valar have changed their strategy. Their influence changes to more indirect, and they only fight the Dark Lord Sauron by sending to Middle-earth five of their own kind in human shape and form, Istari or the Wizards, among whom Saruman and Gandalf are the greatest. Tolkien writes that the Istari were restricted from using force against the enemy, their purpose was to unite all the free people to fight against Sauron, and not to become their leaders (Tolkien 1992: 535). Saruman fails his tasks and betrays his cause by becoming evil, but Gandalf stays remains intact and later in the end of *The Lord of the Rings* triumphantly returns to The Undying Lands. Saruman ends up building his own kingdom and take power over mortals. But Gandalf's influence in *The Lord of the Rings* is not as much in force and power, but in wisdom and speech; much like the

3. Fall and Struggle

power of Christ in the *Bible*. Although Christ wields hidden divine power, his force is in wisdom.

Christ is not the only character from the *Bible* and Christian mythology that has traces or analogs in Tolkien's fiction. In his letter to Ruth Austin in the year 1971, Tolkien admitted that he used Virgin Mary as a background for Galadriel, the most powerful Elf in *The Lord of the Rings* and in the Third Age of Middle-earth. Tolkien (1981: 407) writes that it is based to Christian and Cathlogic teaching and imagination about Virgin Mary, but there is an important difference: Galadriel in the mythology is now penitent, she used to be one of leaders of Elvish rebellion against Valar, which led by her uncle Fëanor.[54]

Of course, the similarities of Mary and Galadriel are only superficial, and in the level of image, not in the level of narrative. Galadriel is not a virgin who gives birth to the Son of God. In *The Silmarillion* she is a powerful Elf leader from the House of Finwë. In *The Lord of the Rings* she is the ruler of the hidden Wood-Elf realm of Lórien, an important aid for the Fellowship of the Ring during their quest, and also grandmother of Arwen, the future Queen of Gondor (and Free Men). Like Mary, Galadriel is extremely respected. Galadriel has concrete power, which Mary is also found to have in Catholic myths. In *The Lord of the Rings* Galadriel's function is to be an encourager and almost a motherly figure for the messianic Frodo, on his last great quest to Mordor to destroy the One Ring.[55]

There is still one more biblical character that Tolkien himself used to describe as a character from his fiction, and that is Noah (or Noach). Tolkien's Noachian figure is found in his Atlantis myth of the island of Númenór. Númenór was the greatest civilizations of Men and was placed halfway between Middle-earth and Valinor, the land of immortals and home to the Valar. In the end of the story of Númenór, the island sinks into the sea, and only the so-called Faithful survive. These Faithful Númenóreans, known as Dúnedain, did not turn evil and worship Sauron and Darkness, as the Kings of Númenór did, but remained faithful to Valar and Eru. And because they were faithful, they were spared, and when the devouring wave

The Mythopoeic Code of Tolkien

of water rolled over Númenór, the Faithful were aboard their nine ships, and great western wind swept their ships away from the island and saved their lives (Tolkien 1999: 335). In this instance, Tolkien's fiction's "Noah" is Elendil, the leader of the Faithful. Later in the text he establishes a new kingdom and civilization and becomes the King of Gondor and leader of the Dúnedain in Middle-earth, just like the biblical Noah is the founder of the new human civilization after the Flood.

Tolkien was aware of the similarities between the mythological images of Noah and Elendil, because, in his letter to Milton Waldman, he called the situation Noachian:

> So ended Númenor-Atlantis and all its glory. But in a kind of Noachian situation the small party of the faithful in Númenor, who had refused to take part in the rebellion (though many of them had been sacrificed in the Temple by the Sauronians) escaped in Nine Ships (Vol. I. 379, II. 202) under the leadership of Elendil (= Ælfwine, Elf-friend) and his sons Isildur and Anárion... [Tolkien 1981: 206].

There are also clear external mythic references from the *Kalevala* in Tolkien's fantasy fiction. On a large scale of Tolkien's mythopoeics, these are most important references. As early as in the year 1911, Tolkien discovered the *Kalevala*, the poems which are the central collection of Finnish mythology, and he was thrilled about it. In the *Kalevala*, Tolkien saw a complete and important mythology that he thought England lacked (Carpenter 1977: 49 & 59). It was because of the *Kalevala* that Tolkien first tried writing a legend in verse and prose. In 1914, Tolkien wrote his own "The Story of Kullervo" based on *Kalevala*'s character Kullervo (Carpenter 1977: 73), which later became the foundation of the Tolkien's story of Túrin Turambar.

"Of Túrin Turambar" is written in a tone of tragedy. The story's central character, Túrin, is an anti-hero who wants to be a hero, whose life is tragic from the start to finish. Turin's tale deals with the Finnish national epic *Kalevala's* story of Kullervo, with the same myths of a slave-prince and an oedipalian myth of incest, but also deals with the heroic myths of dragon slayers, deriving mostly from Scandinavian and Germanic myths (see Flieger 2005a: 32, 41, Ship-

3. Fall and Struggle

pey 2003: 261, 265–266). The story itself is dark, gloomy, and joyless. Turin's terrific but tragic journey affects the reader's emotions. In the predestined story, since after Túrin's mother has sent his young son over the mountains, his fate is woven (Tolkien 1999: 236). Later, Túrin is cursed and doomed from the beginning by an evil fate, constructed by the Dark Lord Morgoth. Túrin's journey, therefore, is to fulfill his tragic tale.

In the story, Túrin loses his family, and he is raised as a slave, and constantly tormented by his oppressors. Like Kullervo from the *Kalevala*, Túrin seeks revenge and finds it. He manages to kill the great dragon Glaurung in a great heroic deed. But before that, in the middle of his tragic adventures, Túrin also weds a lady, who is—unknowingly to both—his sister. When the truth is revealed, the sister kills herself. Afterwards, because of his act, Túrin commits suicide.

By Tolkien, the myth of Túrin Turambar is often called "The Children of Húrin" because it tells the story of the hero Húrin's two children, Túrin and his sister Nienor (known also as Níniel). Tolkien's biographer Humphrey Carpenter writes that Túrin's fight with the great dragon inevitably suggests comparison with Sigurd and Beowulf, while Túrin's unknowing incest with his sister and his suicide were derived quite consciously from the *Kalevala* (Carpenter 1977: 96). Incest has been a popular mythological theme since the beginning of literature and human culture, in a kind of an "alarming myth," as a myth of moral tuition. Túrin's tragic life may also have some echoes from the myth of Oedipus from Sophocles' famous tragedy *Oedipus the King* (ca. 429 BCE).

Túrin's suicide and Kullervo's suicide are in the end very similar in style and narrative. Both heroes kill themselves with a sword, by first asking the sword to take their lives.[56] Both kill themselves because of their act of incest, and because their sisters have also committed suicide. Both heroes' sisters also commit suicide by drowning themselves. Túrin Turambar is a classic tragic hero. His story is influenced by the stories of Oedipus, Kullervo, Beowulf, Sigurd and Saint George. Tolkien himself wrote that the story is derived from

The Mythopoeic Code of Tolkien

elements of Sigurd, Oedipus and Kullervo (Tolkien 1999: xix). Túrin's suicide is more intimately connected, in my view, to the story of Kullervo than any of Tolkien's stories to any other mythological elements. In the scene where Túrin commits suicide, he asks his mythical sword Gurthang to kill him:

> Then he drew forth his sword, and said: "Hail Gurthang, iron of death, you alone now remain! But what lord of loyalty do you know, save the hand that wields you? From no blood will you shrink. Will you take Túrin Turambar? Will you slay me swiftly?"
> And from the blade rang a cold voice in answer: "Yes, I will drink your blood, that I may forget the blood of Beleg my master, and the blood of Brandir slain unjustly. I will slay you swiftly."
> Then Túrin Turambar set the hilts upon the ground, and cast himself upon the point of Gurthang, and the black blade took his life [Tolkien 2007: 256].

In the *Kalevala*, in a similar way, Kullervo asks his sword, whether it will kill him:

> Kullervo Kalervon poika, tempasi terävän miekan;
> katselevi, kääntelevi, kyselevi, tietelevi.
> Kysyi mieltä miekaltansa, tokko tuon tekisi mieli
> syöä syyllistä lihoa, viallista verta juoa.
> Miekka mietti miehen mielen, arvasi uron pakinan.
> Vastasi sanalla tuolla: »Miks en söisi mielelläni,
> söisi syyllistä lihoa, viallista verta joisi?
> Syön lihoa syyttömänki, juon verta viattomanki.«
> Kullervo, Kalervon poika, sinisukka äijön lapsi,
> pään on peltohon sysäsi, perän painoi kankahasen,
> kären käänti rintahansa, itse iskihe kärelle.
> Siihen surmansa sukesi, kuolemansa kohtaeli [*Kalevala* 1992: 321].

In the English version, Francis Peabody Magoun Jr.'s translation, the scene is as follows:

> Kullervo, son of Kalervo, drew his sharp sword;
> he looks at it, turns it over, questions it, inquires of it.
> He asked the sword its wish, whether it wanted
> to eat guilty flesh, drink sinful blood. The sword knew the man's mind,
>   understood what the warrior said:
> it answered with these words: "Why should I not eat as I want,

3. Fall and Struggle

> eat guilty flesh, drink sinful blood? I eat the flesh of an innocent person,
> drink the blood of a sinless one, too."
> Kullervo, son of Kalervo, blue-stocking son of an old man,
> pushed the hilt into the field, pressed the butt into the heath,
> turned the point against his breast, struck himself onto the point.
> On that he contrived his death, met his end [*Kalevala* 1975: 255].

However, even after his tragic death and many anti-heroic acts, Túrin's reputation inside the fictive world of Middle-earth is not "anti-heroic" since Elrond in *The Lord of the Rings* calls him one of the great human warriors. Intratextually, Túrin is a "hero," despite his many villainous acts. This has perhaps something to do with Tolkien's own sympathies for the misunderstood and mistreated tragic characters such as Kullervo, Túrin, or even Beowulf (see Flieger 2003b). And as stated earlier, Tolkien still planned an important role for Túrin also after his death in the after life. In *The History of Middle-earth*, Tolkien writes that in the End of the World, in the Last Battle, Túrin will be the avenger of all Men, and by that their greatest hero (Tolkien 2002c: 76).

Kalevala based Túrin Turambar is a great example of a mythic hero in Tolkien's fantasy, but Tolkien's fiction reads the *Kalevala* in other aspects as well. The greatest Elven smith of all time, Fëanor, resembles the great smith Ilmarinen of the *Kalevala*, and Fëanor's greatest achievement and labor, the Silmarils, resemble the Sampo of the *Kalevala*, which was the greatest single work done by Ilmarinen.

Both the Silmarils, which were three great jewels, and the Sampo are objects desired and wanted by anyone who sees them. They both also have some great and unknown powers. *The Silmarillion* deals greatly with the war of the Silmarils, as the *Kalevala* deals with the theft of the Sampo. Furthermore, the theft of one of the Silmarils in the story of Beren and Lúthien is an important part of *The Silmarillion*. And in the end of both stories, they are forever lost from their makers and are disintegrated all over the world.

Before that, when the Sampo is stolen from the Northern Land back to Kalevala, the land of the *Kalevala*'s heroes, the theft follows the same path as the theft of one of the Silmarils in *The Silmarillion*. In the *Kalevala*, the heroes manage to steal the Sampo because Väinämöinen puts to sleep the people of Pohjola ("North Farm") by playing his kantele, a lute-like instrument: "The whole household of North Farm and all the people of the community he put into a long sleep, put to sleep for quite a long time" (*Kalevala* 1975: 281).

This is echoed in *The Silmarillion*, where Beren and Lúthien steal one of the Silmarils back from Melkor. Beren is the greatest human hero in *The Silmarillion*, and Lúthien is a "semi-angelic" being, because her father is the Elven king Thingol, and her mother, Melian, is one the Maiar, the spirits who govern Middle-earth. Beren and Lúthien manage to steal one of the Silmarils from Melkor's crown, because Lúthien sings and thus puts Melkor and all his court to sleep. She sings a song of surpassing loveliness and blinding power that even Melkor, the mighty daemonic Dark Lord, falls to sleep (see Tolkien 1999: 212–213).

Beren and Lúthien run away after they have managed to take one of the Silmarils. This Silmaril is later inherited by their son, Dior, and after him by his daughter, Elwing. In the end of "Quenta Silmarillion," the third book of *The Silmarillion*, Elwing bears the Silmaril when she and her husband Eärendil travel to the Undying Lands of Valinor and ask the Valar to aid in the desperate struggle against Melkor. After this, the Valar finally decide to destroy Melkor, and aid Men and Elves in their war.

Because of that, Eärendil and Elwing became the saviors of Middle-earth, but they could never again return to Middle-earth from the Undying Lands. As discussed earlier, Eärendil later rises to the sky with his ship Vingilot and becomes a star of new hope, bearing the Silmaril with him, and illuminating all of Middle-earth. The sons of Fëanor, who had fought long and hard to get the Silmarils from anyone keeping them, could now see where the Silmaril is, unreachable in the sky. Maedhros and Maglor, the last surviving sons of Fëanor who swore the oath to forever hunt the Silmarils stolen from their father, see the star and understand that it is a Silmaril that shines in the sky (Tolkien 1999: 300–301).

3. Fall and Struggle

In the *Kalevala*, the Sampo breaks in a fight, and its pieces spread in all directions. Väinämöinen takes some of the parts, his enemy Louhi gets the handle, and other pieces fall into the water and create a wealth in the lakes and rivers (*Kalevala* 1975: 367–369). This distribution of valuables is also seen in *The Silmarillion*. In the end of "Quenta Silmarillion" the Silmarils are also spread all over the world. The Dark Lord Melkor is vanquished by the Valar, and the last two Silmarils are taken from his crown. After that, Maedhros and Maglor attack the forces of the Valar, Maiar and Elves and steal the Silmarils.

This is actually the fourth stealing of the Silmarils in *The Silmarillion*: Originally Melkor stole the Silmarils from Fëanor's father Finwë in Valinor, and after that Beren and Lúthien stole one of the Silmarils back from Melkor, and thirdly the Forces of Valinor took the Silmarils back from Melkor. However, in this last "reclaiming" of the Silmarils, because of their evil deeds, the sons of Fëanor have lost their right to the jewels, and the Silmarils have their own different destiny. Because there are two of them, both Maedhros and Maglor take himself a single Silmaril. But the jewels burned their hands with terrible pain and torment. Maedhros could not deal with the pain, so he tragically casts himself into a fiery chasm. Maglor too could not take the pain caused by the gem and so he thrusts it into the sea and wandered thereafter upon the seashores singing in pain and regret (Tolkien 1999: 304–305). So, one of the Silmarils ends up in the bosom of the Earth, one in the Sea, and one as earlier mentioned into the Sky with Eärendil. Just like the Sampo in the *Kalevala*,[57] the Silmarils in the end are scattered all over the world, into three different elements.

Another intertextual similarity between the *Kalevala* and Tolkien's text has been seen by Shippey in the departing of Väinämöinen in the end of the *Kalevala* and the departing of the Elves in Tolkien's *legendarium* (Shippey 2007: 34). In the *Kalevala*'s hubristic end, Väinämöinen is disappointed with the appearance of the Christ-figure, the new king of Kalevala, and sails away from the mortal realms.

In a kind of Arthurian, or even Christ-like, way, Väinämöinen promises to return if his crafts and might will be needed again. Like Tolkien's High Elves, who sail to the West but do not completely leave the worlds boundaries, Väinämöinen does not either leave the plane of this world completely. Väinämöinen goes into "yläisihin maaemihin, alaisihin taivosihin" (*Kalevala* 1992: 427), "toward the upper reaches of the world, to the lower reaches of the heavens" (*Kalevala* 1975: 337).

In the case of intertextualities between Tolkien's fantasy fiction and the *Kalevala*, it should be added that Tolkien's name for the creator, Eru Ilúvatar, resembles the air spirit Ilmatar (or Luonnotar), mother of Väinämöinen, the Eternal Bard, the chief protagonist of the *Kalevala*. In the *Kalevala*, Ilmatar is impregnated by a storm, and when Ilmatar drifts into the sea, a scaup (or a duck in some translations) settles on Ilmatar's knee, mistaking it for an island, an lays seven eggs which she then begins to brood. The brooding makes Ilmatar move her leg and the eggs break, becoming the created universe. Hence, there is certainly something in common with Ilmatar, who is responsible for the creation of the world of the *Kalevala*, and Ilúvatar, the creator in Tolkien's fantasy fiction.

Next, after these examples, I discuss three main examples of how Christian Platonic mythopoeics function in Tolkien's fantasy fiction. Examples of these motifs are numerous. First, as an example of the Fall, the motif of a "drowned land," or Atlantis, is discussed more closely in the next section. Then, the motif dealing with morality or amorality and the concept of the One Ring is discussed. That is an interesting example of Tolkien's mythopoeics, since it is, on the one hand, deriving partly from Plato's dialogues. And on the other hand, it is a crucial storyline for *The Lord of the Rings*, Tolkien's major work on the fantasy genre. The final section focuses on familiarization of myth in Tolkien's fantasy fiction. This illuminates how mythopoeics and contemporary language works as tools to familiarize elements of the fantastic for the reading audience. For the reader, this is the most important part of Tolkien's mythopoeics, since without these familiarizing elements in the fantasy the text would become defamiliar and alien to us, even unreadable, some might say.

3. Fall and Struggle

The Fall: Númenor as an Atlantis Myth

In Tolkien's fantasy fiction, in the Second Age of the Sun, Númenor was a utopian island raised from the sea as a gift for the "Loyal Men," who fought on the side of the Valar in the War of Wrath that ended Morgoth's reign of evil and the First Age of Middle-earth. It was given to the loyal three houses of Men because of their valor and faithful alliance. The Númenorean were blessed by Valar since for mortals they had a great span of life (Tolkien 1999: xx). Later, thousands of years afterwards, the people of Númenor were corrupted by Sauron, and started a war against the Valar, and that led to the downfall of the island and to the destruction of Númenorean culture. Only a small party of survivors, those loyal to the Valar survived, and later formed the Kingdom of Gondor, and later Arnor, in Middle-earth.[58]

Númenor is mentioned many times in Tolkien's fiction. Its fall is the central story of *The Silmarillion's* fourth part "Akallabêth." Its milieu is described in a posthumous romantic story "Aldarion and Erendis" that was published in the *Unfinished Tales of Númenor and Middle-earth*, a posthumous collection of essays edited by Christopher Tolkien and published in the year 1980. Númenor is also featured in the appendices to *The Lord of the Rings* and in many parts of *The History of Middle-earth* series.

Essentially, the story of Númenor is a Platonic Atlantis myth. Next, for the understanding of the concept, I discuss Plato's myth of the Atlantis in the dialogues *Timaeus* and *Critias* and Tolkien's story of the downfall of Númenor in *The Silmarillion*. Both Plato's myth and Tolkien's story deal with an island in the west, which is occupied by an advanced human civilization that has divine genealogy. In both stories, the inhabitants of the island turn greedy and proud, and try to rule all the other nations. Both stories end with a divine intervention of gods (or God) that destroys the island—Eru Ilúvatar in Tolkien's mythology, and presumably Zeus in Plato's story. "Akallabêth," as an Atlantis myth, has indisputably been influenced by Plato's story of Atlantis. Plato's Atlantis is one of the most known literary utopias and island utopias.

The Mythopoeic Code of Tolkien

The tradition of literary utopias is long and versatile, and the history of utopias is much older than the word utopia itself. The Greek word *utopia* (ūtopos) means a place which does not exist. Nowadays utopia is commonly understood to be a place that is at once imaginary and ideal (see Carey 2000). The word utopia itself was created by English Renaissance humanist Thomas More (1478–1535), whose novel *Utopia* (1516) is one of the basic works of utopian literature. Although More's work was genre-defining, the field of utopian literature is of course much wider including, for example, Plato's myth of Atlantis, and, as *The Cambridge Companion to Utopian Literature* edited by Gregory Clayes argues, "Platonism, classical mythology, golden ages of both eastern and western, ideals of lost worlds, fantastic voyages, inhabited moons and planets, imaginary social and political experiments, nations, empires and ideal commonwealths" (Clayes 2010a: xi). In other words: almost every kind of literature focusing on imaginary, ideal, and fantastic landscapes. Significant works in the tradition of the literary utopia are also Plato's dialogues *The Republic, Critias* and *Timaeus*; Tomaso Campanella's (1568–1639) *The City of the Sun* (*La citta del Sole* 1611); Francis Bacon's (1561–1626) *The New Atlantis* (1627); and David Hume's (1711–1776) *The Idea of a Perfect Commonwealth* (1752).

Krishan Kumar (1987: 2) discusses that "Utopian ideas and fantasies, like all ideas and fantasies, grow out of the society to which they are a response," and that Utopian "Arcadian idyll is apparent in the anti-urban (and later anti-industrial) fantasies of scores of later writers up to our own time, most notoriously perhaps in England" (Kumar 1987: 3). Tolkien's (at the start) utopian fantasy of arcadian Númenor, and Tolkien's anti-industrial sceneries, therefore, were quite typical for English writers of earlier literary periods. Tolkien is once again taking his place in a long tradition of myth-makers and mythographers of the English language.

Then again, Tolkien's Númenor is intertextually connected to the Platonic myth of Atlantis. In the long tradition of utopias, Plato comes rather late, since utopian themes reach back to the earliest

3. Fall and Struggle

Greek writings, such as Hesiod's *Works and Days* (see Kumar 1987: 3), but the influence of Plato's writings for the tradition is huge.

In the end of Tolkien's story of Númenor and Plato's myth of Atlantis, the described ideal utopian society of the fantastic island turns bad, evil, and malevolent. The ideal society turns upside down, and negative developments—both political and philosophical— change the progress.

In this way, Tolkien's Númenor also reads and re-imagines the external reference field of Plato's Atlantis myth. Plato's dialogues *Timaeus* and *Critias* include all Plato's textual material dealing with Atlantis. In *Timaeus*, Plato explains the creation of the universe and the order of nature, and, therefore, *Timaeus* is often considered to be the center of his cosmogonies, cosmologies and natural sciences.[59] At the beginning of the dialogue, Plato puts the story of Atlantis to emphasize the meaning of the city of Athens in his cosmology, and to warn that every great civilization in the changeable world could fall quickly from grace.

Plato writes that "in this island of Atlantis there was a great and wonderful empire which had rule over the whole island and several others, and over parts of the continent.... This vast power, gathered into one, endeavoured to subdue at a blow our country and yours and the whole of the region within the straits" (*Timaeus* 25a–b). Later Plato describes how Atlantis was destroyed: "there occurred violent earthquakes and floods; and in a single day and night of misfortune all your warlike men in a body sank into the earth, and the island of Atlantis in like manner disappeared in the depths of the sea" (*Timaeus* 25d).

The reasons for the destruction of Atlantis remain unclear in *Timaeus*, but are revealed in *Critias*, which is a fragment designed to be the second part of a trilogy, of which Timaeus was the first part (Jowett 1964: 781). In *Critias*, Plato describes the geography of Atlantis, and of the beauty and greatness of the island's inhabitants. To prove the divine background of the kings of Atlantis, Plato describes how the first king of Atlantis, Atlas, descended directly from Poseidon, the god of sea in the Greek mythology. But at the time as Atlantis was destroyed, this divine heredity had declined:

The Mythopoeic Code of Tolkien

> For many generations, as long as the divine nature lasted in them, they were obedient to the laws, and well-affectioned towards the god, whose seed they were; for they possessed true and in every way great spirits, uniting gentleness with wisdom in the various chances of life, and in their intercourse with one another ... but when the divine portion began to fade away, and became diluted too often and too much with the mortal admixture, and the human nature got the upper hand, they then, being unable to bear their fortune, behaved unseemly, and to him who had an eye to see grew visible debased, for they were losing the fairest of their precious gifts; but those who had no eye to see the true happiness, they appeared glorious and blessed at the very time when they were becoming tainted with unrighteous ambition and power [Plato: *Critias* 120e–121b].

Critias ends in the middle of the sentence, but right before the ending, it is told that Zeus, the king of gods in the Greek mythology, paid special attention to Atlantis and its inhabitants because of their "woeful plight" and decided to inflict punishment on them. Therefore, the destruction of Atlantis, described in Timaeus, could be interpreted as having been conducted by Zeus.

Both Plato's Atlantis and Tolkien's Númenor are great island kingdoms in the far west. In Tolkien's fiction, Númenor is described as a gift from the Valar to the only faithful Human tribe (called Edain). It was a land that was neither part of the Middle-earth nor Valinor, the Undying Lands. It was sundered from both of those by a wide sea, but it was closer to Valinor than the Middle-earth (Tolkien 1999: 310).[60]

Like the king of Atlantis, the first king of Númenor, Elros, although partly a mortal descendant from the Third House of the Edain, also had a divine background. His foremothers were from the immortal races of Eldar Elves and Maiar: his grandmother from the father's side was Elven Princess Idril of Gondolin and his great grandmother from mother's side was Lúthien, daughter of a Maiar spirit Melian, the mighties Elven Lady of all time. Eärendil, the savior of all Men and Elves in the end of "Quenta Silmarillion" was his father, and Elwë Thingol, the King of Doriath, possibly the greatest Elven Kingdom in the history of Middle-earth, was his great grandfather.

The Númenóreans lived on an island near Valinor, the undying lands of the Valar, and after thousands of years of glory, they became envious of the immortals living there, because they were mortals and

3. Fall and Struggle

even their kings' divine heredity was fading: "They said to themselves: 'Why do the Lords of the West sit there in peace unending, while we must die and go we know not whither, leaving our home and all that we have made?'" (Tolkien 1999: 315) The Númenóreans were banned by the Valar to sail to the undying lands, and that also disturbed them, because immortal Elves (Eldar) sailed from time to time to Númenor from the undying lands. Tolkien describes that the Númenóreans became restless because they began to hunger for the Undying lands and cities that saw from afar when sailing near to Valinor, and they become jealous for the everlasting life of the Elves that was unreachable for them as mortals (Tolkien 1999: 315). The Númenoreans started to talk against dying, the doom of Men, and the Ban set by Valar, which forbade the Númenoreans to sail into the West.

Both Tolkien's Númenor and Plato's Atlantis are destroyed by divine intervention. In "Akallabêth," the people of Númenor wage war against the Valar because Sauron persuades them to do so. Sauron uses the unrest attitude that the Númenoreans feel for the Elves and Valar, their immortality, and the Undying Lands in general.

Eru Ilúvatar destroys the beautiful island of Númenor because of the Númenóreans' attack against the Undying Lands. In a dramatic scene Manwë, the King of the Valar, asks Eru for a guidance in the dire situation and Eru Ilúvatar shows his omnipotent powers. Eru refashions the World, creates a great chasm that separates the Middle-earth from the Undying Lands, and sinks the island kingdom of Númenor (Tolkien 1999: 334). Like the destruction of Atlantis, it is a complete destruction of the beautiful milieu of Númenor.

C.S. Lewis writes that, according to Macrobius, nearly the whole human race has frequently been destroyed by great global catastrophes; nearly, because there has always been a remnant. Macrobius sees that Egypt has never been destroyed; that is why Egyptian records remount to an antiquity elsewhere unknown. According to Lewis (1964: 61–62), this idea goes back to Plato's *Timaeus* which in its turn may have been influenced by the story in Herodotus: the story of Hecataeus the historian, visiting the Egyptian city of Thebes. In Tolkien's fiction, this kind of constant destruction of old kingdoms and realms is apparent. There are many destroyed kingdoms of both Elves and Men in the fictitious history of Middle-earth, but of all the kingdoms of Men, Númenor is the most famous of them all.

Tolkien's "Akallabêth" is also a story of fall from greatness, of which remnants remain. The stories of the glory of Númenor, but also the remnants and descendants of the Númenoreans: the kingdom of Gondor, for example, in the Third Age of Middle-earth, and King Aragorn in the end of *The Lord of the Rings*. "Akallabêth" as a story of fall is clearly a Christian Platonic view of a changeable world, but it could be the main theme of *The Silmarillion* and Tolkien's mythopoeic fantasy fiction as a whole.

The spirit of Númenor is still felt in *The Lord of the Rings*. In the end of the Second Age of Middle-earth, Sauron is defeated because the Men of Westernesse, from the far West of the World, came to aid the free peoples of Middle-earth. Later, Gondor is described as a land where "the old wisdom and beauty brought out of the West remained long in the realm of the sons of Elendil the Fair, and they linger there still..." (Tolkien 2009a: 324).

Even Sam Gamgee can feel this "air of Númenor" when he and Frodo Baggins meet Faramir from Gondor. When Sam Gamgee comments that Faramir reminds him of Gandalf and wizards, Faramir responds that "Maybe you discern from far away the air of Númenor" (Tolkien 2009a: 329).

Then again, Númenor is an important traditional background for Faramir. He describes this as a recurring dream later in the text to Eowyn in the Houses of Healing in Minas Tirith: "the land of Westernesse that foundered, and of the great dark wave climbing over the green lands and above the hills, and coming on, darkness unescapable. I often dream of it" (Tolkien 2009b: 267).

The Struggle: The One Ring and the Ring Motif

> When Bilbo opened his eyes, he wondered if he had; for it was just as dark as with them shut. No one was anywhere near him. Just imagine his fright!

3. Fall and Struggle

> He could hear nothing, see nothing, and he could feel nothing except the stone of the floor.
> Very slowly he got up and groped about on all fours, till he touched the wall of the tunnel; but neither up nor down it could he find anything: nothing at all, no sight of the goblins, no sign of dwarves. His head was swimming, and he was far from certain even of the direction they had been going in when he had his fall. He guessed as well as he could, and crawled along for a good way, till suddenly his hand met what felt like a tiny ring of cold metal lying on the floor of the tunnel. It was a turning point in his career, but he did not know it. He put the ring in his pocket almost without thinking; certainly it did not seem of any particular use at the moment [Tolkien 1975: 67].

In this scene from *The Hobbit*, Bilbo Baggins finds the One Ring, which is the artifact of vital importance later in *The Lord of the Rings*. Here, the narrator argues that finding the One Ring was, for Bilbo Baggins, "a turning point in his career," but he might as well be writing of Tolkien himself. Since for Tolkien's career as a writer of fiction (and fantasy), the ring-theme starting in The Hobbit, and developing later in *The Lord of the Rings*, was of great importance.

In *The Lord of the Rings*, the One Ring is fatal for mortals. A mortal who keeps one of the Great Rings does not die, but ultimately fades and becomes permanently invisible. And, as Gandalf says, the wielder sooner or later is devoured by the dark power of Sauron (Tolkien 2008: 75). This is what happened to the Nazgûl. They faded and became invisible, undead beings under the power of Sauron.

The One Ring is the central plot motif of the story in *The Lord of the Rings*. It is the Master-ring, the One Ring to rule them all, as the famous poem says. In the story Sauron has lost the Ring many ages ago, because of that has lost an important portion of his powers, and now desires it with all his will. The central theme is that Sauron, the Enemy, tries to get the One Ring back, and the forces opposing Sauron try to prevent it. Later, the opposing (Good) forces decide to destroy the One Ring, and that forms the central quest in the narrative. Sauron's only pursuit is to get the One Ring, since if he gets it back, he could rule all the Middle-earth (Tolkien 2008: 80).

That is the basic plot of the story, but there are also many moral

The Mythopoeic Code of Tolkien

and philosophical questions concerning the ring-motif. Therefore, under the discussion next will be Tolkien's fiction's ring-theme and Plato's myth of The Ring of Gyges from the second book of *the Republic*. In Plato's story, the shepherd Gyges finds a golden ring which makes its user invisible (*Republic* 359d–360d). This shows that Tolkien's ring-theme is not solely derived from Germanic and Scandinavian myths and fairy-stories as some researchers have pointed out but may have some mythological backgrounds in Plato and in the Platonic tradition.

Tolkien's theme of invisibility has similarities to Plato not only in regards of the two levels of ontology (levels of the ideal and changeable world), but also on the level of myth and morality. Tolkien himself wrote many times about the moral aspect of owning a ring of invisibility—for example, think about H.G. Well's *The Invisible Man* (1897). Plato writes about the morality of owning a ring of invisibility:

> Suppose now that there were two such magic rings, and the just put on one of them and the unjust the other; no man can be imagined to be of such an iron nature that he would stand fast in justice. No man would keep his hands off what was not his own when he could safely take what he liked out of the market, or go into houses and lie with any one at his pleasure, or kill or release from prison whom he would, and in all respect be like a god among men. Then the actions of the just would be as the actions of the unjust; they would both tend to the same goal... [Plato: *Republic* 360b–c].

As I mentioned earlier, the invisibility altogether has something to do with two levels of ontology. The Elves in Tolkien's fiction are immortal, and the immortal beings stay visible in "The Shadow world of invisibility" as well, because they live at the same time in "both worlds" and in between.

Furthermore, the discovery of the Ring of Gyges in Plato's *Republic* and the discovery of The Great Ring in Tolkien's *The Hobbit*, and later described in *The Lord the Rings*, resemble each other. In Plato's *Republic*, Gyges is a shepherd and the ancestor of Croesus of Lydia, who finds the ring of invisibility in a cave:

3. Fall and Struggle

[T]here was a great storm, and an earthquake made an opening in the earth at the place where he [Gyges] was feeding his flock. Amazed at the sight, he descended into the opening, where, among other marvels which form part of the story, he beheld a hollow brazen horse, having doors, at which he stooping and looking in saw a dead body of stature, as appeared to him, more than human; he took from the corpse a gold ring that was on the hand, but nothing else, and so reascended [Plato: Republic 359d].

After that, Gyges finds out that the ring can be used to make him invisible:

Now the shepherds met together, according to custom ... into their assembly he [Gyges] came having the ring on his finger, and as he was sitting among them he turn the collet of the ring to the inside of his hand, when instantly he became invisible to the rest of the company and they began to speak of him as if he were no longer present [Plato: Republic 359d].

In *The Hobbit*, the main protagonist Bilbo Baggins gets lost in the mountains after an attack by the evil orcs, and finds The Great Ring in a cave in the mountains, where the ring's previous holder, Gollum, has lost it. As *The Lord of the Rings* (Tolkien 2008: 36) describes, Bilbo at first sees The Great Ring mainly as a ring of gold that made its wearer invisible, not realizing its dark powers.

On the contrary, after finding the One Ring, Bilbo uses it chiefly for helping his friends (Tolkien 2008: 39), as does Bilbo's heir Frodo, who is the protagonist in *The Lord of the Rings* and the next holder of The Great Ring. There is a difference between Plato's story and Tolkien's fiction, mainly because the Hobbits are not so easily corrupted by the ring. Of course, it must be stressed that in the long run also the Hobbits become corrupted. A few times in *The Lord of the Rings* Frodo is unable to withstand the power of the Ring. Most importantly, Frodo fails to destroy the Ring in "The Return of the King." Frodo's words in the scene itself are philosophically (and theologically) very interesting, because Frodo *chooses* not to do his task pointed to him: "I do not choose now to do what I came to do. I will not do this deed" (Tolkien 2009b: 247).

The other magical rings in Tolkien's fantasy fiction also mingle with invisibility and morality. For example, the Nine Rings that were also made by Sauron, and were given to nine powerful human men. In one of the revealing passages in *The Silmarillion*, Tolkien writes that the Nazgûl "could walk, it they would, unseen by all eyes in this world beneath the sun, and they could see things in worlds invisible to mortal men"; and "they became forever invisible save to him that wore the Ruling Ring, and they entered into the realm of shadows" (Tolkien 1999: 346).

This quotation is revealing for two different reasons. First, it reveals that visibility and invisibility are mortal things: the Nazgûl became invisible to "mortal eyes." The Nazgûl "entered into the realm of shadows," which in my point of view is a realm between the real physical world of Tolkien's mythology, and the upper spiritual level. As declared earlier, those of the immortal elven race, which have lived in the undying forbidden lands of the west, live at the same time on both levels.

Secondly, as the chosen passage declares, that mortal men all get corrupted, sooner or later, by the rings, "according to their native strength and the good or evil of their wills in the beginning." This is also the point Plato made in *Republic*:

> And this [the story of Gyges] we may truly affirm to be a great proof that a man is just, not willingly or because he thinks that justice is any good to him individually, but of necessity; for wherever anyone thinks that he can safely be unjust, there he is unjust. For all men believe in their hearts that injustice is far more profitable to the individual than justice, and he who argues as I have been supposing will say that they are right. If you could imagine anyone obtaining this power of becoming invisible, and never doing any wrong or touching what was another's, he would be thought by the lookers-on to be an unhappy man and a fool, although they would praise him to one another's faces, and keep up appearances with one another from a fear that they too might suffer injustice [Plato: *Republic* 360c–d].

For the Elves, the invisibility is a quite different thing. Tolkien writes that, as immortal beings, the Elves will later become altogether invisible if they want to (Tolkien 2002e: 212). The Rings of Power have the power to change their mortal users invisible, and later on, they will become "shadows."

3. Fall and Struggle

In Plato's *Republic*, in his famous simile or allegory of the cave, Plato describes a scenario in which that, which people take to be real, could in fact be an illusion. In the allegory, the people (prisoners) in the cave see only shadows of men and objects, not knowing that they are only shadows. In the dialogue, Plato asks that "do you think they have seen anything of themselves, and of one another, except the shadows?" (*Republic* 515b). The figures of sight (shadows), and the figures of sound (echoes), in the allegory, are only the lowest form of perception—the perception of shadows, as Plato discusses (*Republic* 511e). Plato's Simile of the Cave has been taken in the Christian Platonic theology as a part of the Christian doctrine of the "invisibility" of God.

For Tolkien's fiction, the invisibility is, for mortals, moving from the physical world into the world of shadows. And the world of shadows is, as we have seen, a world of undead and un-life. The obvious intertextual field of reference for Tolkien's ring myth is the Platonic myth of the Ring of Gyges from the *Republic*, but there are many other intertextual references to the ring-motifs. A magical ring, as a referent, has external references to many other myths of magical rings in literary history. The mythic and magical rings have often been important artifacts in mythic and fantastic literature.

The myth of Gyges was not solely Plato's since it was a typical ancient myth. The legend of Gyges as the founder of the Mermnad dynasty of Lydian kings could be found in the stories of Herodotus, Nicolaus of Damascus, Plutarch, as well as in Plato's *Republic* and Cicero's *De Officiis*. In Cicero's version, there is also a magical ring of invisibility (Oksala 1983: 255–256).

The myth was popular in later the Romantic period as well, because it can be found in Hans Sach's poem "Die Nacket Königin aus Lydia," Lafontaine's fable *Le roi Candaule et me maître en droit*, Théophile Gautier's short story "Le roi Candaule" (1844); Friedrich Hebbel's tragedy *Gyges und sein Ring* (1853–1854), and later, André Gide's drama *Le roi Candaule* (1901) (Oksala 1983: 255–256).

In the Greek versions, there is an inscription in the Ring of Gyges that reads εύτυχίανκρύπτω, or, roughly translated, "I shall

The Mythopoeic Code of Tolkien

hide my happiness." In the Herodotus' version, this can be seen in Gyges' words. In the story, Gyges is the bodyguard of king Candaules, who believes his wife to be the most beautiful woman on Earth. The king insists on showing Gyges his wife naked to show her beauty. The queen, who sees Gyges staring at him, gives Gyges the choice of either murdering her husband and making himself the king, or being put to death himself. In the end, Gyges murders Candaules, and becomes the king. At the beginning, Gyges had said the words to Candaules that echoes the later inscriptions in the Ring of Gyges: "Let each look on his own" (Herodotus 1952: 3).

In *The Lord of the Rings*, there is also an inscription on the One Ring, the Ruling Ring. The text, written in an ancient mode of Elvish scripture but in the language of Mordor, is two lines taken from a known Elven poem, which in Common Tongue (here: English) goes: One Ring to bring them all and in the darkness bind them. The One Ring in Tolkien's fiction can "hide" its wielder from mortal eyes, but it also rules and binds.

Another ring myth from *The History* by Herodotus could also form an external reference to Tolkien's fiction—although this intertextuality could be interpreted as a traditional reference. The story in question is the story of Polycrates and Amasis, and the ring of Polycrates.

According to Herodotus, Polycrates was a king of Samos, and a man of good fortune, and his successes were constant, and his prosperity endless. Amasis sends a letter and a counsel to Polycrates saying that Polycrates should be alerted. Amasis' warning says that no one will succeed in all his undertakings, and Polycrates should avoid forthcoming failure by throwing away his most valuable treasure, or possession:

> It is a pleasure to hear of friend and ally prospering, but thy exceeding prosperity does not cause me joy, for as much as I know that the gods are envious. My wish for myself and for those whom I love is to be now successful, and now to meet with a check; thus passing through life amid alternate good and ill, rather with perpetual good fortune. For never yet did I hear tell of any one succeeding in all his undertakings, who did not meet with calamity at last, and come to utter ruin. Now, therefore, give

3. Fall and Struggle

ear to my words, and meet thy good luck in this way: bethink thee which of all thy treasures thou valuest most and canst least bear to part with; take it, whatsoever it be, and throw it away, so that it may be sure never to come any more into the sight of man. Then, if thy good fortune be not thenceforth chequered with ill, save thyself from harm by again doing as I have counseled [Herodotus 1952: 98].

Having read the letter, Polycrates thought that the advice was good, and he chose his signet-ring as his most valuable possession. The ring was said to be an emerald set in gold, and a workmanship of Theodore, son of Têlecles. Polycrates went to the open sea, a long way from any island, and threw the ring into the deep of the ocean. Herodotus (1952: 98) explains that five or six days afterwards a fisherman caught a fish that he held so large and beautiful that it deserved to be a present to the king. So, the fisherman took the fish and gave it to king Polycrates. In the end of the story, the servants cut open the fish, and they found the signet of their master in its belly.

What is the moral of the story? Is it that, what you throw away, you will find awaiting you in the end? That we cannot hide from our old ghosts? Or is it that you cannot (or should not) throw away your good fortune?

Either way, Frye argues that the same theme dominates the story told by Wagner and retold by Tolkien: a story of "a stolen ring that has to be given back, a return that achieves its recreation by a creatively negative act, a cancelling out of a wrong action" (Frye 1976: 185).

Tolkien of course objected to the claims that he "retells a story of Wagner." Shippey has pointed out that connections with Wagner are the most obvious example of dubious references. Tolkien hated that people connected *The Lord of the Rings* with *Der Ring des Nibelungen* (Shippey 2003: 343). Tolkien's famous line from the letter to Allen & Unwin Publishers in 1961 says that "[b]oth rings were round, and there the resemblance ceases" (Tolkien 1981: 306). Shippey discusses that despite this, there are many similarities in the stories as well: for example, the motifs of a riddle contest, the cleansing fire, and the broken weapon preserved for the heir (Shippey 2003: 343–344). But of course, sheer "retelling" of Wagner's story is not the case.

The Mythopoeic Code of Tolkien

Furthermore, throwing the ring into the sea, as Polycrates in the story of Herodotus does, is discussed in *The Lord of the Rings*. In the Council of Elrond, Glorfindel suggests that the One Ring should be tossed to the sea, and there it would be safe for ever (Tolkien 2008: 337).

But as the myth of Polycrates tells us, this is not the right way to act. Wise enough, Gandalf answers to Glorfindel that things thrown away could be found, since there are many creatures living there and seas and lands may change (Tolkien 2008: 337).

The story of Polycrates is well-known and has many independent and related stories in the history of literature, both older and more recent. In the tradition of historical novels, in *Three Musketeers* by Alexander Dumas, the characters refer to the story when planning on throwing a ring into the river Seine. There, the ring acts as a holy and precious relic:

> I don't at all understand you, but I believe all you say to be true. Let us return to my ring, or rather to yours. You shall take half the sum that will be advanced upon it, or I will throw it into the Seine; and I doubt, as was the case of Polycrates, whether any fish be sufficiently complaisant to bring it back [Dumas 1930: 310].

In literary history, magical rings are commonplace: from the folk tales of Aladdin, to mythological accounts of *Edda*, *Volsunga Saga*, or *Nibelungenlied*. For example, in *Nibelungenlied*, the supernatural powers of queen Brunhild (or Brynhildr) come from a magical ring. The Queen loses her powers when Siegfried removes her ring, secretly and carefully: "Einen Ring von Goldezoger von ihrer Hand. So heimlich und behutsam, daβ sie nichts davon empfand" (*Das Nibelungenlied* 1959: 199). Even Gustave Flaubert, who Richard Maxwell sees less inclined to allow supernatural visitations, such as the Ring of Gyges, "emphasizes the fetishistic charisma of his magical artifact" (Maxwell 2009: 205). Intratextually, the One Ring is both an important magical artifact, and an element that functions as a central story motif. *The Lord of the Rings* was written originally as a sequel to *The Hobbit*. It changed from a fairy-tale styled children's book into

3. Fall and Struggle

an epic fantasy because of the One Ring, and because of the connection that the One Ring creates to the earlier parts of the mythology (that was partly later published as *The Silmarillion*). The One Ring functions as a mediator between Tolkien's fiction's mythopoeic epic high fantasy world and of more familiar *The Hobbit*–style characters of *The Lord of the Rings*, especially the Hobbits themselves. The One Ring transfers the story and the characters to a grimmer, more dangerous world of the earlier heroic mythology.

The One Ring is the central plot element in *The Lord of the Rings*. In the intratextual references Tolkien describes how it was made by the evil lord Sauron in the Second Age of Middle-earth. It was designed to deceive the Elves, and to give Sauron dominion over the so-called "Free Peoples of Middle-earth."

In the story, The One Ring is ultimately evil, and it will corrupt its bearer, regardless of the bearer's intentions. Sauron made it for a purpose of ruling. At the end of *The Lord of the Rings*, when the Ring is destroyed, Sauron's dominion ends. Therefore, the power of the One Ring is both Sauron's utmost desire, but at the end also his destruction.

The One Ring is a great example of the motifs of Fall and Struggle in Tolkien's fiction. Its ownership will eventually end in a catastrophic fall. And being a bearer of the One Ring, as Frodo is in *The Lord of the Rings*, is an ultimate struggle. As Frodo describes when he is trying to climb to the Mount of Doom, to destroy the One Ring:

> "I can't manage it, Sam," he said. "It is such a weight to carry, such as weight."
> Sam knew before he spoke, that it was vain, and that such words might do more harm than good, but in his pity he could not keep silent. "Then let me carry it a bit for you, Master," he said. "You know I would, and gladly, as long as I have any strength."
> A wild light came into Frodo's eyes. "Stand away! don't touch me!" he cried. "It is mine, I say. Be off!" His hand strayed to his sword-hilt. But then quickly his voice changed. "No, no, Sam," he said sadly. "But you must understand. It my burden, and no one else can bear it. It is too late now, Sam dear. You can't help me in that way again. I am almost in its power now. I could not give it up, and if you tried to take it I should go mad" [Tolkien 2009b: 237].

Conclusion

This book discusses Christian platonic mythopoeics in J.R.R. Tolkien's fiction; the logic and elements on which Tolkien's texts and his fantasy world is constructed. The research aims to create a constructive, idea historical, and intertextual reading of Tolkien's fiction and to show that it is possible to perceive a clear constructive gestalt in Tolkien's fiction.

My thesis is that Tolkien's mythopoeic fiction is constructed to be coherent on the levels of languages, myths, and inter- and intratextual backgrounds. This coherence can be found throughout the various texts and fragments of Tolkien's fiction. Even when writing in many different tones and modes, Tolkien is the sub-creator of his own fantastic world: he is rewriting or remodeling chosen intertextual references, he is creating new intratextual myths, and he is functioning as a coherent world builder. As part of this sub-creating, Tolkien is "pretending" to be a translator of mythical pseudo-historian documents. This is done to interlink Tolkien's mythology together, but also to give his sub-creating credibility, narrative depth, and a feeling of familiarity. This familiarizing feeling is evident, for example, when reading Tolkien's poem *Bilbo's Last Song* (1990), the reader connects its pseudo-writer "Bilbo" to the character of Bilbo Baggins from *The Hobbit* or *The Lord of the Rings*.

The main chapters of the study follow the inner timeline of Tolkien's fantasy world, but also my individual research logic. Therefore, the text began with the creation of the fictive fantasy world Arda, of which Middle-earth is a part. After that, I moved into the long fall and struggle, and discussed Tolkien's vision for the end of his fictive,

Conclusion

created world, thus creating a reading of Christian Platonic mythopoeics in Tolkien's fiction.

In Tolkien's poetics, there is a vision, the realization of the vision, and the promise of an apocalyptic thereafter that reflects both on the stories of Tolkien's fiction and on the creative work behind these stories. Tolkien's fantasy aims to work in many levels and succeeds in this. Tolkien's mythopoeics create a coherent, understandable, and credible fantasy world with its vivid history and mythical backgrounds, and an apocalyptic future. Through the concepts of the Creation and the Existence we, as readers, are given explanations of the cosmogony and cosmology of Tolkien's fictive world. Then, through the examples of the Fall (or falls), we are given explanations as to why the ideal world became corrupted and marred, and why the lives of the characters in Tolkien's fiction are ruled by continuing Struggle. But then again, according to these mythopoeics, we are also given a glimpse or a hint of eucatastrophic ending and a promise of a better future for the whole fictive creation. Therefore, Tolkien's mythopoeics and his entire fantastic work is ruled by aesthetic and a philosophical (or theological) Christian Platonic vision of creation and recreation.

It has been interesting to read Tolkien's texts as part of Christian Platonic tradition. In closing, I should say that Tolkien's work can be defined in many ways, since the material of his creative work is huge, and the whole amount of his fictive work is not easily methodologically obtained. Therefore, my focus has been on the Christian Platonic essence of Tolkien's fantasy fiction concerning Arda (and Middle-earth as part of it), not in the single details of his creative work. The methods used to achieve this reading originated in constructive mythopoeics and the idea historical literary studies. This is of course not the only way that Tolkien's fiction can be read, and we all know it. But it is for me the best way to see it. It is a methodologically interesting new position. Then again, as Frans Ilkka Mäyrä (1999: 295) comments, the etymology of "method" is illuminating: "the Greek methodos (pursuit) consists of *meta* (with, after) and *hodos* (way, journey)," and in the end "knowledge cannot be found

Conclusion

in explications: it is embodied in the road itself." This Christian Platonic road into Tolkien's fiction has been very interesting to travel, but as Tolkien himself writes, the road itself goes on forever—it is, in its way, eternal:

> The Road goes ever on and on
> Down from the door where it began.
> Now far ahead the Road has gone,
> And I must follow, if I can,
> Pursuit it with eager feet,
> Until it joins some larger way
> Where many paths and errands meet.
> And whither then? I cannot say [Tolkien 2008: 61–62].

Notes

1. As in the Greek word *mythographos*, one who records, narrates, or comments on myths.
2. Although the term intertextuality would normally be used to refer to links to other texts, a related kind of link might be called intratextuality—involving internal relations within the text or texts. See for example Chandler 2004.
3. It should be stressed that although Tolkien is "creating myths" and using extant myths, these (re-)created myths are literary creations and do not derive from any pre-existing cultural tradition.
4. In the year 1595 it was also published with the title *An Apology for Poetry* by Olney. Ponsonby's publication under the title *The Defence of Poesie* is considered the "more authoritative of the two" (Sidney 1968: v).
5. Gergely Nagy has earlier discussed this subject of intertextual relations and "genuine allusions" compared to "pseudo-allusions" in his article "The Great Chain of Reading: (Inter-)textual Relations and the Technique of Mythopoesis in the Túrin Story" (2003). See also Chance 2004: 10.
6. In this case: "the imitation of those linguistic and bibliographic codes that make up an historical literary idiom" (Wisner 2010: 62).
7. Keeping in mind the vast understanding of the word epic. Scholes & Kellogg in their study *The Nature of Narrative* write: "Behind the epic lie a variety of narrative forms, such as sacred myth, quasi-historical legend, and fictional folktale, which have coalesced into a traditional narrative which is an amalgam of myth, history, and fiction" (Scholes & Kellogg 1966: 12).
8. See for example Russell 2000: 82–90. Frye writes on "displacing" and "recovery" of myths in, for example, *The Secular Scripture* (Frye 1976: 159–190), *Anatomy of Criticism* (Frye 1967: 131–223) and in *Myth and Metaphor* (Frye 1990: 3–17).
9. Originally, the so-called "literary constructivism" started in Russia with the *Literaturnyi tsentr konstruktivistov* (Literary Center of Constructivist) in 1923. It perceived "culture as an all-embracing and comprehensive phenomenon, penetrating all spheres of human existence and activity." Hence, it fostered "the idea of creating not only literature but also its broad theoretical foundations" (Możejko1993: 18).
10. I have earlier addressed these elements in an article Korpua, "Tutut vieraat hobitit." See Korpua 2012.
11. On Tolkien's postmodern tones, see also Brljak 2010.
12. I thank Dr Dimitra Fimi for her perceptive views on my previous studies which are also suitable here.
13. Ainur (plural, singular is Ainu) refers to the immortal Spirits, or angelic beings of Tolkien's mythology. The Ainur living in "the created world" (physical world) are usually referred to as either Valar (plural, singular is Vala)—higher angelic beings, or Maiar (plural, singular is Maia)—lower angelic beings.

Notes

14. Elves are immortal, the "first born" race (compared to "second born" Men) in Tolkien's fiction. The distinctions between Elves and Men have been discussed by, for example, Jonathan Evans (2003: 194–224). On the complicated concept of race in Tolkien's fiction, see also Fimi 2009. On Elves and Men, see the chapter "Cosmology and the Chain of Being."

15. These concepts of the Last Battle (*Dagor Dagorath*, "The Battle of all Battles"), and The Second Music that will be played after the battle are of course quite abstruse, since these accounts were left out of *The Silmarillion*. As Christopher Tolkien describes in *The Shaping of Middle-earth* (Tolkien 2002b: 3–11 & 274–280) and in *Morgoth's Ring* (Tolkien 2002e: 199 & 367–433), J.R.R. Tolkien wrote many versions of his myths and abandoned many versions of both the basic text of *The Silmarillion* and accounts of his cosmogony and cosmology. Those stories published in *The Silmarillion*, although very impressive, are just one example of Tolkien's accounts of his mythopoeic cosmological myths. But, for the purpose of this study, it is important to keep in mind that Tolkien thought his fantasy world should have a beginning and an end.

16. Rebecca Ankeny (2005), for example, emphasizes the poetic, lyrical elements in Tolkien's fiction.

17. Frye's theory of literary modes and Tolkien's fiction have been earlier compared in some theoretical discussions, most distinguishingly in Shippey's *The Road to Middle-earth*. The first researcher to address this interesting schema was perhaps Christine Brooke-Rose in her study *A Rhetoric of the Unreal: Studies in Narrative and Structure, Especially of the Fantastic*.

18. For example Paul Kocher states that "the work often puzzles, sometimes repels outright. Those who manage to get past it are likely to go on to the later epic [*The Lord of the Rings*] with preconceptions which they find they must rapidly discard." (Kocher 1973: 19.) On the other hand, Harold Bloom in his introduction to *Modern Critical View: J.R.R. Tolkien* comments—in terms that I cannot fully approve—that he suspects "that *The Lord of the Rings* is fated to become only an intricate Period Piece, while *The Hobbit* may well survive as Children's Literature" (Bloom 2000: 2).

19. The position of Tolkien as the "Godfather of Fantasy" is still very firm in the 21st century among writers and scholars of fantasy. For example, British fantasy writer China Miéville, who is usually considered the chief author among the New Weird genre, writes about Tolkien from this perspective in his article "There and Back Again: Five Reasons Tolkien Rocks" (Miéville 2009). Then again, Miéville had earlier described Tolkien in a famous quote as "the wen on the arse of fantasy literature" (See for example Doctorow 2003).

20. Tolkien here uses the word legendarium that originally meant a book or series of books comprising a collection of legends, for example medieval heroic legends. Later, the word legendarium has become commonly used by Tolkien scholars rather than "Tolkien's mythology." In the scholarship, the term can have different meaning. In some rarer cases it means all the material that deal with his created fantasy world Arda, on which the so-called Middle-earth is part of, including so-called Tolkien's "Elvish legends" (e.g., *The Silmarillion*), and his main works *The Lord of the Rings* and *The Hobbit*. But in most cases, the legendarium means Tolkien's legends that happened before the events described in fictional history of Hobbits, *The Hobbit* and *The Lord of the Rings*, a legendary pre-history of those books. Also, it should be noted that Tolkien's other fantastic fiction that does not deal with this created fantasy world, such as children's books *Smith of Wootton Major* (1967), *Farmer Giles of Ham* (1949), or *The Father Christmas Letters* (1976, posthumously), are never considered part of in his fictious legendarium.

21. Maria Jesus Martinez Alfaro's article "Intertextuality: Origins and Development of

Notes

the Concept" points out that the term was first used in Julia Kristeva's "Word, Dialogue and Novel" (1966) and in "The Bounded Text" (1966–67), essays she wrote shortly after her arrival in Paris from here native Bulgaria (Alfaro 1996: 268).

22. *The Mabinogion*, translated by Gwyn Jones and Thomas Jones (1949), *The Mabinogion* translated by Jeffrey Gantz (1976) and *The Mabinogi and Other Medieval Welsh Tales* translated by Patrick Ford (1977). See also Flieger 2005a: 57.

23. Verlyn Flieger discusses these names and attributes of Ælfwine "an Englishman of the 'Anglo-Saxon period' of English history," and earlier versions of the character as Eriol the Voyager or *Angol* of pre–Anglo-Saxon time (Flieger 2004: 47, 50).

24. In *A Journey to the Western Islands of Scotland* Samuel Johnson writes "I believe they [poems of Ossian] never existed in any other form than what which we have seen. The editor, or author, never could show the original; nor can it be shewn by any other; to revenge reasonable incredulity, by refusing evidence, is a degree of insolence, with which the world is not yet acquainted; and stubborn audacity is the last refuge of guilt" (Johnson 2005).

25. To Shippey's views of Lönnrot's the *Kalevala*, shared by many works in Anglo-American Tolkien studies, it should be stressed that scholars of Finnish culture and literature, as well as Lönnrot did in his time, admit the constructivism of the published the *Kalevala*. As the Finnish Literary Society in its introduction writes: "[in making the expanded version] Lönnrot moved further and further away from his source texts in compiling the New Kalevala. With regard to his method, Lönnrot explained: "I felt myself to have the same right which, according to their conviction, most singers bestow on themselves, namely, to be able to order the runes as they are best suited to be joined together," or, in the words of a rune: "I conjured myself into a conjurer, a singer came of me. That is, I considered myself as good a singer as they" (Finnish Literary Society).

26. This tendency in fairy-stories has been studied vigorously. For example, in the major studies of the genre, such as Vladimir Propp's *The Morphology of the Folk Tale* (1928, in Russian), Joseph Campbell's *The Hero with a Thousand Faces*, or Tzvetan Todorov's narrative theory in *Introduction à la littérature fantastique* (*The Fantastic: A Structural Approach to a Literary Genre*).

27. As has been argued, for example, by Chester N. Scoville in his article "Pastoralia and Perfectability in William Morris and J.R.R. Tolkien" (2005: 93–103), or, in John R. Holmes' article "Tolkien, *Dustsceawung*, and the Gnomic Tense: Is Timelessness Medieval or Victorian?" (2005: 44).

28. The Hobbits, Shippey discusses, are very clearly low mimetic, most of the time. Of the Hobbits, Sam Gamgee, on the other hand, even more than Gollum, tends to sink towards the ironic. Shippey even compares his relationship with Frodo Baggins with the most famous ironic or romantic pairing in the history of Western literature, that of Don Quixote and Sancho Panza from Cervantes' *Don Quixote* (1605–15). Then again, nearly all the human characters of *The Lord of the Rings* occupy a higher level. For example, Éomer or Boromir are characteristic figures of high mimesis: leaders, kings, and heroes, but still mortal, without supernatural powers. However Aragorn, Shippey writes, though staying on the level of other humans much of the time, is still different: "he can summon the dead, he can compel the *palantír* to his will, he lives in full vigour for 210 years, and he is able to control his death." Shippey sees that Aragorn, and his non-human companions like Legolas, Gimli, and Arwen, and all the non-human species of Middle-earth, are figures of *romance*. For Shippey, finally the characters like Gandalf, Bombadil and Sauron, are very close to the level of myth. Shippey writes "that they are not exactly 'divine beings,' but they are not human either, something intermediate (in fact Gandalf and Sauron are both Maiar, a class of being invented by Tolkien)." Shippey even invents a "sixth

Notes

level" outside Frye's categorization, which one could call "true myth," or gospel, or revelation, or (in Tolkien's word) *evangelium*. Then again, Shippey says that Tolkien refuses to reach out for that category, only hinting to that direction—in the direction "of mythic meaning" (Shippey 2001: 222–224).

29. Character being quite a peculiar name to call Sauron (in *the Lord of the Rings*), who only appears narrated by other characters of the story in few shadowy and dreamy scenes, such as the *analeptic* scene where Pippin looks at the Palantír. On the other hand, Sauron (known as Gorthaur the Cruel) is an active character in the later parts of *The Silmarillion*.

30. Frye sees that for scholars this is more accurately rendered "I will be what I will be," meaning that "we might come closer to what is meant by the word "God" if we understood it as a verb, and not a verb of simple asserted existence but a verb implying a process accomplishing itself" (Frye 2006: 35).

31. Despite of course natural reproduction, which is the method of population growth for many of species in Tolkien's world. Family trees of Elves, Men, Hobbits, and Dwarves play a part as a background information in for example *The Silmarillion*, *The Lord of the Rings*, and *The Unfinished Tales of Númenor and Middle-earth*. We also know that there is population growth via reproduction in the species of Orcs, since Bolg, the chief of Goblins (also: Orcs) in *the Hobbit* is described to be the son of the Orc leader Azog (Tolkien 1995: 1052), whose death scene in the hands a Dwarf Dáin Ironfoot is told in Appendix A of *The Lord of the Rings* (Tolkien 1995: 1049). Also, regarding reproduction, the problem with natural reproduction of Ents after they have lost their "wives," the Endwives is addressed in *The Lord of the Rings* (Tolkien 1995: 464–466).

32. Eucatastrophical (or *eucatastrophe*) meaning a positive catastrophe or a good catastrophe. Tolkien used the term in his essay "On Fairy-Stories" (Tolkien 1983: 153–155) to demonstrate a sudden dramatic turn of events in fairy-stories, which resulted in a happy ending for the story. Both the appearing of the Eagles in the end of *The Hobbit's* decisive "Battle of Five Armies" and the destruction of the One Ring and (once again) the appearing of the Eagles in the final battle between forces of Mordor and forces of Gondor in The Field of Cormallen in *The Lord of the Rings* act as eucatastrophical scenes.

33. My interpretation and analysis in this chapter is a continuum on my article "Good and Evil in J.R.R. Tolkien's *Legendarium*: Concerning Dichotomy Between Visible and Invisible." See Korpua 2014.

34. Unreachable for many, but not for all. The High Elves sail to Valinor in the Third Age of Middle-earth, and the bearers of the Great Ring (Bilbo, Frodo, and even Sam Gamgee) travel there according to *The Lord of the Rings*. Also, Gandalf returns there when his "task is done" in *The Lord of the Rings*.

35. For Morgoth's loss of this power, see Tolkien 1999: 78. Sauron lost the power much later. For example, in the beginning of the Second Age, after the defeat of his master, Morgoth, Sauron once again wears his fair appearance (see Tolkien 1999: 341). But after the Fall of Númenor—when his physical form was destroyed by the destruction of the island—Sauron lost his power of shape changing. After that he wrought himself in a new shape that is terrible and defamiliar (see Tolkien 1999: 351). An appearance to fit a Dark Lord of the Middle-earth.

36. Undead meaning a creature (for example in mythic or fantastic literature) which is at the same time dead, but still behaves as if it were alive. Usually functioning as a monstrous creature, an aspect of horror.

37. This is a reference to the original Lórien in Valinor, not to the forest of Lórien or Lothlórien which is one of the milieus in *The Lord of the Rings*. The original Undying Lórien is the name for the gardens of Vala Irmo (known also as Lórien), the master of

Notes

vision and dreams. Lórien is described as "the fairest of all places in the world, filled with many spirits" (Tolkien 1999: 19).

38. Richard Mathews views that this "possessiveness of the ring/rings" is parallel to the "tale of Two Trees" from *The Silmarillion*. Mathews writes that "The Story of the Rings, like the tale of the Two Trees, is in one sense a fable of how advanced technology and craft produce artifacts of great power and temptation but induce theft and war." (Mathews 2002: 63.) Then again, this theme is of course parallel to the effect of the Silmarils in *The Silmarillion*, too.

39. Galadriel's power is almost invincible in Middle-earth. Appendix B of *The Lord of the Rings* says that "Three times Lórien had been assailed from Dol Guldur, but besides the valour of the elven people of that land, the power that dwelt there was too great for any to overcome, unless Sauron had come there himself" (Tolkien 1995: 1069). I assume that "the power" that the text is referring to is Galadriel herself, and the Elven Ring of Power she wields.

40. This could be the case if one compares this with the planes of existence (or "worlds") in Ancient Greek, Scandinavian or Finnish cosmologies, for example. In the Norse cosmology, the Underworld Hel and Nilfheim are the abodes of the dead and in the *Kalevala* the old Finnish underworld is described as Tuonela, the realm of the dead. In Greek mythology the underworld is usually Hades. The world that humans and mortals inhabit is usually, both in Finnish and Scandinavian mythology, called "middle-earth," Midgard in *Eddas*. Originally, though, Midgard did not mean "middle-earth." Webster's dictionary relates that *Midgard* (from the Icelandic *midhgardhr*) literally means "mid-yard," i.e., the middle ground between heaven and hell, where human beings dwell (Carter 1969: 32).

41. Flieger, for example, has pondered on this possibility of reincarnation in Tolkien's fiction. Tolkien himself commented on the possibility of reincarnation as a mode of existence in his letter to Peter Hastings (see Flieger 2004: 59).

42. In Jewish folklore a *golem* is an animated anthropomorphic being, created from matter, such as iron, earth, wood, etc.

43. It has to be stressed that Plato's word *daemoniac* (δαιμόνιον) has very little to do with the later Christian concept of "daemons" or "demons." As Lewis points out, "divine" and "daemoniac" may be synonyms, but Plato later draws a clear distinction between them and declares "daemons" as creatures of a middle nature between gods and men (Lewis 1964: 40).

44. These questions of real and non-real have of course been widely discussed by researchers. One contemporary scholar of these theories was American philosopher Nelson Goodman (1906–1998), whose influential works *Languages of Art: An Approach to a Theory of Symbols* and *Ways of Worldmaking* are seen as a fundamental turning point in the analytic approach to artistic issues in Anglo-American philosophy. For Goodman, "art is not sharply divided, in goals and means, from science and ordinary experience." On the contrary, Goodman sees elements of art as "symbols that classify parts of reality for us, as do such things as scientific theories and what makes up common, ordinary knowledge" (*Stanford Encyclopedia of Philosophy*). Also, Alan Paskow comments in *The Paradoxes of Art: A Phenomelogical Investigation* that we do not need to view artworks as a separate kind of entity from other things in our world. Paskow sees that artworks and fictional characters could be viewed as internal components of the world. Paskow's main interest is on the ways that readers (for example) interact with works of art. Paskow's work is mainly interested in the reality of fictional beings, and on the touching points of "real" and "fiction," the same emotional responses that Kendal Walton is addressing in his *Mimesis as Make-Believe: On the Foundations of the Representational Arts*. Walton

Notes

addresses, for example, the distinction between fiction and nonfiction, and explores the reader's emotional reactions to literary representations (Walton 1990).

45. This was discussed on previous chapter, and Tolkien's theory of music as a creative force and the medieval concept of the "music of spheres" have been discussed in detail by Bradford Lee Eden (2003: 183–193).

46. This is of course an old revelation, which can be found in many religious and mythological texts, such as *The Bible*, the *Quran*, and the *Kalevala*. In fantasy literature such themes can be found for example in Ursula K. Le Guin's *Earthsea* series.

47. Whittingham discusses Tolkien's "end of world," The Second Music, The Last Battle and Arda Healed or New Arda. In the Last Battle, Whittingham sees parallels to the Scandinavian myth Ragnarök and the biblical "Book of Revelation." See Whittingham 2008: 9, 131.

48. Tolkien's texts and connections between them and Christianity have been researched in many studies. See for example *The Ring and the Cross: Christianity and The Lord of the Rings*, edited by Paul E. Kerry (2011).

49. "The Escape from Death," which Tolkien declares in "On Fairy-Stories" to be the "oldest and deepest desire," the "Great Escape" (Tolkien 1983: 153). On the other hand, in the intratextualities of Tolkien's fiction, Tolkien's Elves, since they are *immortal* and do not die, fantasize about the "Escape from Deathlessness." See Shippey 2003: 237 and Flieger 2005a.

50. Also, Aers discusses that medieval theory saw God's historical incarnation as the key to all Christian allegory (Aers 1975: 19).

51. In the intertextual level, Shippey finds lots of similarities and differences between Frodo and Christ. Shippey (2003: 204) writes that, although Frodo is send to his mission, he is not the Son of God, he buys for his people only a limited, worldly and temporary happiness, and in the end, he does not get sacrificed and become "Christ Crucified." Although the rest of Frodo's life in *The Lord of the Rings*, is a kind of sacrifice, because after he has "succeeded" in his task, he has to leave Middle-earth and move to Valinor, the land of immortals, and he does not get the benefits of saving the world in his mortal life. Also, an interesting theological reading on Frodo and Christ is made by Olli-Pekka Vainio in his article "Philomythius Misomythiukselle." Vainio sees Frodo as a character who has to go through a *kenosis* ("the self-emptying" of one's own will in order to become receptive to God's will) and remaking of his personality in his way to Mordor (Vainio 2003: 127).

52. The House of Bëor was the most famous of families of so-called "Faithful Men," for example, the human heroes Húrin, Túrin and Tuor were part of that House. Later descending from Tuor's son Eärendil were the Kings of Men in the Second and Third Age of Middle-earth, such as Elros and later Aragorn, the forthcoming King in *The Lord of the Rings*. In the family tree of the House of Bëor, Andreth was the aunt of Bregolas, the great-grandfather of Túrin Turambar.

53. Common, for example, in the Greek mythology. For example, in the myths of Cassiopeia and Andromeda, or Aquila and Aquarius in the myth of Ganymedes. The most similar myth is perhaps that of Argo which was the ship of the heroic Argonauts that was, after the voyage of the search for the Golden Fleece, placed amongst the stars.

54. Fëanor was the oldest son of Finwë, King of the Noldor Elves. Galadriel was the youngest child of Finarfin, Fëanor's youngest brother. Fëanor and Finarfin had different mothers, Míriel and Indis, but Finwë was the father of both.

55. These analogues have been discussed for example by Michal W. Maher in his article "'A land without stain': Medieval Images of Mary and Their Use in the Characterization of Galadriel" (Maher 2003: 225–236).

Notes

56. Of course, this kind of dialogue with a sword is a recurring scene in epic or fantastic literature. For example, in Shakespeare's *Macbeth* (1606), the play's antihero Macbeth hallucinates seeing a dagger and asks questions from it, although the dagger does not answer. In the 20th and 21st century, fantasy writers such as Terry Pratchett in his *Discworld* series or Mercedes Lackey in *The Heralds of Valdemar* series, and Brent Weeks in *The Night Angel* series use talking swords as "characters"; perhaps as a homage to either Tolkien's fiction, or for the old Anglo-Saxon mythology.

57. Intertextual similarities between the loss of Sampo, and the loss of Silmarils, have been discussed by Shippey 2007: 35. I also addressed these questions in my master's thesis earlier in 2005, and also on my article "The Germ of J.R.R. Tolkien's Fantasy: Elements of *Kalevala* in Tolkien's Fiction." See Korpua 2005: 27–29, and Korpua 2018.

58. In Tolkien's fiction, there are also the so-called "Black Númenoreans," who were not loyalists, but survived in the remote parts of Middle-earth where Númenoreans had colonies at the time of the destruction of the island. One of these, in *The Lord of the Rings*, is "Mouth of Sauron," the Lieutenant of the Tower of Barad-dûr. He is described as a Black Númenorean, a race that established their kingdoms in the Middle-earth, enamored evil knowledge and worshipped Sauron as their god.

59. It is also important to remember that the dialogue is put into the mouth of a Pythagorean philosopher, and not Socrates. Therefore, we should not hastily regard *Timaeus* as the most important of Plato's dialogues. See also Jowett 1964: 631–633.

60. Kingdoms from the history of Elves that might be compared to Númenor are the hidden and closed kingdoms of Gondolin and Doriath. A major part of the tale of Gondolin and the destruction of Gondolin is told in *The Silmarillion* and there are references to the kingdom in both *The Hobbit* and *The Lord of the Rings*. As told in *The Silmarillion*, The Fenced Land of Doriath, ruled by Sindar Elves in the Elder Days of Middle-earth and the First Age of the Sun was destroyed after the War of Wrath when all the land of Beleriand was sunk into the sea.

Works Consulted

Abrams, M.H. 1973. *Natural Supernaturalism: Tradition and Revolution in Romantic Literature.* New York: W.W. Norton & Company.
Abrams, M.H. 1976. *The Mirror and the Lamp: Romantic Theory and the Critical Tradition.* London: Oxford University Press.
Aers, David. 1975. *Piers Plowman and Christian Allegory.* London: Edward Arnold.
Allen, Graham. 2000. *Intertextuality: The New Critical Idiom.* London: Routledge.
Anderson, Douglas A. 2003. "'An Industrious Little Devil': E.V. Gordon as Friend and Collaborator with Tolkien." *Tolkien the Medievalist.* Ed. Jane Chance. New York: Routledge, pp. 15–25.
Ankeny, Rebecca. 2005. "Poem as Sign in the Lord of the Rings." *Journal of the Fantastic in the Arts* Vol. 16, Issue 2, Summer. Pocatello: Idaho State University, pp. 86–95.
Aristotle. 1968. *Poetics: A Translation and Commentary for Students of Literature.* Trans. Leon Golden. Eaglewood Cliffs: Prentice-Hall.
Ashbaugh, Anne Freire. 1988. *Plato's Theory of Explanation: A Study of the Cosmological Account in the Timaeus.* Albany: State University of New York Press.
Atherton, Mark. 2012. *There and Back Again: J.R.R. Tolkien and the Origins of the Hobbit.* London: I.B. Tauris.
Attebery, Brian. 2014. *Stories About Stories: Fantasy and the Remaking of Myth.* Oxford: Oxford University Press.
Baltasar, Michaela. 2004. "The Rediscovery of Myth." *Tolkien and the Invention of Myth.* Ed. Jane Chance. Lexington: The University Press of Kentucky, pp. 19–34.
Barfield, Owen. 1976. *Poetic Diction: A Study in Meaning.* 3rd ed. Middletown: Wesleyan University Press.
Benardete, Seth. 1997. *The Bow and the Lyre: A Platonic Reading of the Odyssey.* Lanham: Rowman and Littlefield.
Blake, William. 2010. "Laocoön." http://en.wikisource.org/wiki/Laocoon_%8Blake%29. Accessed 4 September 2020.
Bloom, Harold. 1973. *The Anxiety of Influence: A Theory of Poetry.* Oxford: Oxford University Press.
Bloom, Harold. 1975. *A Map of Misreading.* Oxford: Oxford University Press.
Bloom, Harold. 1988. *Poetics of Influence.* Ed. John Hollander. New Haven: Henry R. Schwab.
Bloom, Harold. 2000. "Introduction." *Modern Critical Views: J.R.R. Tolkien.* Ed. Harold Bloom. Philadelphia: Chelsea House Publishers, pp. 1–2.
Brisson, Luc. 2004. *How Philosophers Saved the Myths: Allegorical Interpretationsand Classical Mythology.* Chicago: Chicago University Press.
Brljak, Vladimir. 2010. "The Books of Lost Tales: Tolkien as Metafictionist." *Tolkien Studies*, Volume 7, pp. 1–34.

Works Consulted

Brooke-Rose, Christine. 1981. *A Rhetoric of the Unreal: Studies in Narrative and Structure, Especially of the Fantastic.* Cambridge: Cambridge University Press.
Campbell, Joseph. 1973. *The Hero with a Thousand Faces.* 2nd edition. Princeton: Princeton University Press.
Carey, John. 2000. "Introduction." *The Faber Book of Utopias.* Ed. John Carey. London: Faber & Faber.
Carpenter, Humphrey. 1977. *J.R.R. Tolkien: A Biography.* Boston: Houghton Mifflin Company.
Carpenter, Humphrey. 1978. *The Inklings: C.S. Lewis, J.R.R. Tolkien, Charles Williams, and Their Friends.* London: George Allen & Unwin.
Carpenter, Humphrey. 1981. "Notes." Tolkien, J.R.R.: *The Letters of J.R.R. Tolkien.* Ed. Humphrey Carpenter. London: George Allen & Unwin.
Carter, Lin. 1969. *Tolkien: A Look Behind the Lord of the Rings.* New York: Ballantine Books.
Carter, Lin. 1973. *Imaginary Worlds—The Art of Fantasy.* New York: Ballantine Books.
Cassirer, Ernst. 1972. *The Individual and the Cosmos in Renaissance Philosophy.* Trans. Mario Domandi. Philadelphia: University of Pennsylvania Press.
Chance, Jane. 2003. "Introduction." *Tolkien the Medievalist.* Ed. Jane Chance. New York: Routledge.
Chance, Jane. 2004. *Tolkien and the Invention of Myth.* Ed. Jane Chance. Lexington: The University Press of Kentucky.
Chance, Jane, and Siewers, Alfred K. 2005. "Introduction: Tolkien's Modern Medievalism." *Tolkien's Modern Middle Ages.* Ed. Jane Chance and Alfred K. Siewers. New York: Palgrave Macmillan, pp. 1–13.
Chandler, Daniel. 2004. *Semiotics: The Basics.* London: Taylor & Francis Group.
Clayes, Gregory. 2010a. "Preface." *The Cambridge Companion to Utopian Literature.* Ed. Clayes, Gregory. Cambridge: Cambridge University Press, pp. xi–xiii.
Clayes, Gregory. 2010b. "The Origins of Dystopia: Wells, Huxley and Orwell." *The Cambridge Companion to Utopian Literature.* Ed. Gregory Clayes. Cambridge: Cambridge University Press, pp. 107–134.
Clifford, Gay. 1974. *The Transformations of Allegory.* London: Routledge & Kegan Paul.
Clute, John. 1979. "Tolkien, J(ohn) R(onald) R(euel)." *Encyclopedia of Science Fiction.* Ed. Peter Nicholls. London: Granada, pp. 608–609.
Cole, G.D.H. 1948. "Introduction." *William Morris: Selected Writings: Centenary Edition: Stories in Prose: Stories in Verse: Shorter Poems: Lectures and Essays.* Ed. G.D.H. Cole. New York: Random House.
Coleridge, Samuel Taylor. 1965. *Biographia Literaria; Or, Biographical Sketches of My Literary Life and Opinions.* Ed. George Watson. London: J.M. Dent & Sons.
Cotrupi, Caterina Nella. 2000. *Northrop Frye and the Poetics of Process.* Toronto: University of Toronto Press.
Coulter, James A. 1976. *The Literary Microcosmos: Theories of Interpretation of the Later Neoplatonism.* New York: Leiden E.J. Brill.
Denham, Robert D. 1979. *Northrop Frye and Critical Method.* https://macblog.mcmaster.ca/fryeblog/critical-method/preface.html. Accessed 4 September 2020.
Dillon, John. 1990a. "The Magical Power of Names in Origen and Later Platonism." *The Golden Chain: Studies in the Development of Platonism and Christianity.* Aldershot: Variorum.
Dillon, John. 1990b. "Plotinus and the Transcendental Imagination." *The Golden Chain: Studies in the Development of Platonism and Christianity.* Aldershot: Variorum.
Doctorow, Cory. 2003. "Miéville on Tolkien." http://boingboing.net/2003/11/02/mieville-on-tolkien.html. Accessed 4 September 2020.

Works Consulted

Doležel, Lubomír. 1998. *Heterocosmica: Fiction and Possible Worlds*. Baltimore: Johns Hopkins University Press.
Drout, Michael D.C. (ed.) 2006. *J.R.R. Tolkien Encyclopedia: Scholarship and Critical Assessment*. New York: Routledge.
Drout, Michael D.C., Wynne, Hilary, and Higgins, Melissa. 2000. "Scholarly Studies of J.R.R. Tolkien and His Works (in English)." *Envoi* vol. 9, no. 2, Fall. Wilmington: Envoi Publications, pp. 135–165.
DuBois, Nancy. 2001. *Vico and Plato*. New York: Peter Lang.
Dumas, Alexander. 1930. *Three Musketeers Volume II*. New York: J.H. Sears & Company.
Eco, Umberto. 1985. *Reflections on the Name of the Rose*. Trans. William Weaver. London: Secker & Warburg.
Eco, Umberto. 1986. *Art and Beauty in the Middle Ages*. Trans. Hugh Bredin. New Haven: Yale University Press.
Eco, Umberto. 1995. *The Role of the Reader: Explorations in the Semiotics of Texts*. Bloomington: Indiana University Press.
Eden, Bradford Lee. 2003. "The 'Music of the Spheres' Relationships Between Tolkien's *The Silmarillion* and Medieval Cosmological and Religious Theory." *Tolkien the Medievalist*. Ed. Jane Chance. New York: Routledge, pp. 183–193.
Esty, Jed. 2004. *A Shrinking Island: Modernism and National Culture in England*. Princeton: Princeton University Press.
Evans, Jonathan. 2003. "The Anthropology of Arda: Creation, Theology, and the Race of Men." *Tolkien the Medievalist*. Ed. Jane Chance. New York: Routledge, pp. 194–224.
Fimi, Dimitra. 2009. *Tolkien, Race and Cultural History: From Faeries to Hobbits*. London: Palgrave Macmillan.
Fimi, Dimitra. 2015. "Opponent's Assessment for a Doctoral Dissertation." University of Oulu. Unpublished assessment form.
Finnish Literary Society. "The Publification of the Kalevala." http://www.finlit.fi/kalevala/index.php?m=154&s=159&l=2. Accessed 4 September 2020.
Fisher, Jason. 2008a. "The Imaginative and the Imaginary: Northrop Frye and Tolkien." http://lingwe.blogspot.fi/2008/12/imaginative-and-imaginary-northrop-frye.html. Accessed 4 September 2020.
Fisher, Jason. 2008b. "Three Rings For—Whom Exactly? and Why? Justifying the Disposition of the Three Elven Rings." *Tolkien Studies*, Volume 5, pp. 99–108.
Flieger, Verlyn. 1997. *A Question of Time: J.R.R. Tolkien´s Road to Faërie*. Kent: Kent State University Press.
Flieger, Verlyn. 2002. *Splintered Light: Logos and Language in Tolkien's World*. Rev. ed. Kent: Kent State University Press.
Flieger, Verlyn. 2003a. "'There Would Always Be a Fairy-tale': J.R.R. Tolkien and Folklore Controversy." *Tolkien the Medievalist*. Ed. Jane Chance. New York: Routledge, 26–35.
Flieger, Verlyn. 2003b. "Tolkien's Wild Men: From Medieval to Modern." *Tolkien the Medievalist*. Ed. Jane Chance. New York: Routledge, pp. 95–105.
Flieger, Verlyn. 2004. "Do the Atlantis Story and Abandon Eriol-Saga." *Tolkien Studies*, Volume 1, pp. 43–68.
Flieger, Verlyn. 2005a. *Interrupted Music: The Making of Tolkien's Mythology*. Kent: Kent State University Press.
Flieger, Verlyn. 2005b. "A Postmodernist Medievalist?" *Tolkien's Modern Middle Ages*. Ed. Jane Chance and Alfred K. Siewers. New York: Palgrave Macmillan, pp. 17–28.
Flieger, Verlyn. 2009. "The Music and the Task: Fate and Free Will in Middle-earth." *Tolkien Studies*, Volume 6, pp. 151–181.

Works Consulted

Flieger, Verlyn, and Hostetter, Carl F. 2000. "Introduction." *Tolkien's Legendarium: Essays on the History of Middle-earth*. Ed. Verlyn Flieger and Carl F. Hostetter. Westport: Greenwood, pp. xi–xiv.

Fokkema, Douwe W. 1985. "The Concept of Code in the LiteratureStudy." *Poetics Today*, Vol 6. No 4., 1985. Durham: Duke University Press. http://www.jstor.org/stable/1771958. Accessed 4 September 2020.

Frenzel, Elisabeth. 1988. *Stoffe Der Weltliteratur: Ein Lexikon Dichtungsgeschichtlicher Längsschnitte*. Stuttgart: Alfred Kröner Verlag.

Freud, Sigmund. 1989a. "Creative Writers and Day-Dreaming." *Art and Literature*. Ed. Albert Dickson. Harmondsworth: Penguin Books, pp. 129–142.

Freud, Sigmund. 1989b. "The Uncanny." *Art and Literature*. Ed. Albert Dickson. Harmondsworth: Penguin Books, pp. 335–376.

Frost, Graham Nichol. 2007. "Decoding the Code." http://canlit.ca/reviews/decoding_the_code. Accessed 4 September 2020.

Fry, Carrol. 2015. "'Two Musics About the Throne of Ilúvatar': Gnostic and Manichean Dualism in the Silmarillion." *Tolkien Studies*, Volume 12, 77–93.

Frye, Northrop. 1951. "The Archetypes of Literature." *The Kenyon Review*, Winter, Vol. XIII, No. 1. http://www.kenyonreview.org/kr-online-issue/kenyon-review-credos/selections/northrop-frye-656342. Accessed 4 September 2020.

Frye, Northrop. 1967. *Anatomy of Criticism: Four Essays by Northrop Frye*. New York: Atheneum.

Frye, Northrop. 1976. *The Secular Scripture: A Study of the Structure of Romance*. Cambridge: Harvard University Press.

Frye, Northrop. 1990. *Myth and Metaphor: Selected Essays 1974–1988*. Ed. Robert D. Denham. Charlottesville: University Press of Virginia.

Frye, Northrop. 2006. *The Great Code: The Bible and Literature. Collected Works of Northrop Frye. Volume 19*. Ed. Alvin A. Lee. Toronto: University of Toronto Press.

Frye, Northrop. 2007. *Northrop Frye's Notebooks for Anatomy of Criticism. Collected Works of Northrop Frye. Volume 23*. Ed. Alvin A. Lee. Toronto: University of Toronto Press.

Gallant, Richard Z. 2014. "Original Sin in Heorot and Valinor." *Tolkien Studies*, Volume 11, pp. 109–129.

Gamble, Nikki, and Yates, Sally. 2008. *Exploring Children's Literature*. London: Sage.

Gasque, Thomas J. 2000. "Tolkien: The Monsters and the Critters." *J.R.R. Tolkien. Modern Critical Views*. Ed. Harold Bloom. Philadelphia: Chelsea House Publishers, pp. 3–10.

Genette, Gérard. 1980 (1972). *Narrative Discourse*. Trans. Jane E. Lewin. Oxford: Basil Blackwell: Oxford.

Genette, Gérard. 1992 (1979). *The Architext: An Introduction*. Trans. Jane E. Lewin. Berkeley: University of California Press.

Genette, Gérard. 1993 (1991). *Fiction & Diction*. Trans. Catherine Porter. Ithaca: Cornell University Press.

Geppert, Hals Vilmar. 1976. *Der "andere" historiche roman: Theorie und strukturen einer diskontinuierlichen gattung*. Tübingen: Niemeyer.

Godard, Barbara. 1993. "Intertextuality." In: *Encyclopedia of Contemporary Literary Theory: Approaches, Scholars, Terms*. Ed. Irena R. Makaryk. Toronto: University of Toronto Press, pp. 568–571.

Goodman, Nelson. 1976 (1968). *Languages of Art: An Approach to a Theory of Symbols*. Indianapolis: Hackett Publishing Company.

Goodman, Nelson. 1978. *Ways of Worldmaking*. Indianapolis: Hackett Publishing Company.

Works Consulted

Hardin Richard F. 2000. *Love in a Green Shade: Idyllic Romances Ancient to Modern.* Lincoln: University of Nebraska Press.
Harshav, Benjamin. 2007. *Explorations in Poetics.* Stanford: Stanford University Press.
Helms, Randel. 1974. *Tolkien's World.* London: Thames and Hudson.
Heninger, S.K., Jr. 1974. *Touches of Sweet Harmony: Pythagorean Cosmology and Renaissance Poetics.* San Marino: Henry E. Huntington Library and Art Gallery.
Herodotus. 1952. "The History of Herodotus." *Great Books of the Western World: 6. Herodotus, Thucydides.* Ed. Robert Maynard Hutchins. Trans. George Rawlinson. Chicago: Encyclopædia Britannia.
Highlander. 1986. Dir. Russell Mulcahy. 20th Century–Fox.
Holmes, John R. 2005. "Tolkien, Dustsceawung, and the Gnomic Tense: Is Timelessness Medieval or Victorian?" *Tolkien's Modern Middle Ages.* Ed. Jane Chance and Alfred K. Siewers. New York: Palgrave Macmillan, pp. 43–58.
Houghton, John W., and Keesee, Neal K. 2005. "Tolkien, King Alfred, and Boethius: Platonist Views of Evil in the Lord of the Rings." *Tolkien Studies,* Volume 2, pp. 131–159.
Houghton, John William. 2003. "Augustine in the Cottage of Lost Play: The Ainulindalë as Asterisk Cosmogony." *Tolkien the Medievalist.* Ed. Jane Chance. New York: Routledge, pp. 171–182.
Hunter, John. 2005. "The Reanimation of Antiquity and the Resistance to History: Macpherson-Scott-Tolkien." *Tolkien's Modern Middle Ages.* Ed. Jane Chance and Alfred K. Siewers. New York: Palgrave Macmillan, pp. 61–75.
Hutcheon, Linda. 1988. *A Poetics of Postmodernism: History, Theory, Fiction.* New York: Routledge.
Isaacs, Neil D. 2000. "On the Need Writing Tolkien Criticism." *J.R.R. Tolkien: Modern Critical Views.* Ed. Harold Bloom. Philadelphia: Chelsea House Publishers, pp. 113–118.
Jackson, Rosemary. 1981. *Fantasy: The Literature of Subversion.* London: Methuen.
Johnson, Samuel. 2005. *A Journey to the Western Isles of Scotland.* The Project Gutenberg eBook. Transcribed from the 1775 edition with the corrections noted in the 1785 errata by David Prince. www.gutenberg.org/files/2064/2064-h/2064-h.htm. Accessed 4 September 2020.
Jowett, B. 1964. "Introduction." *The Dialogues of Plato, Volume III: Cratylus, Phaedrus, Theaetetus, Sophist, Statesman, Philebus, Timaeus, Critias.* Trans. B. Jowett. 4th edition. London: Oxford University Press.
J.R.R. Tolkien Encyclopedia: Scholarship and Critical Assessment. 2007. Ed. Michael D.C. Drout. New York: Routledge.
Jusdanis, Gregory. 1991. *Belated Modernity and Aesthetic Culture: Inventing National Literature.* Minneapolis: University of Minnesota Press.
Kalevala. 1992. Juva: WSOY.
Kalevala: Or Poems of the Kalevala District. 1975. Ed. Elias Lönnrot. Trans. Francis Peabody Magoun, Jr. Cambridge: Harvard University Press.
Kerry, Paul E. (editor) 2011. *The Ring and the Cross: Christianity and the Lord of the Rings.* Madison: Fairleigh Dickinson University Press.
Kocher, Paul. 1973. *Master of Middle-earth: The Achievement of J.R.R. Tolkien.* London: Thames and Hudson.
Kocher, Paul H. 2000. "Cosmic Order." *J.R.R. Tolkien: Modern Critical Views.* Ed. Harold Bloom. Philadelphia: Chelsea House Publishers, pp. 11–26.
Korpua, Jyrki 2005: *Kristillisplatonisia ja muita mytologisia elementtejä J.R R. Tolkienin teoksessa* Silmarillion. Master's Thesis, Oulu University.
Korpua, Jyrki 2012: "Tutut vieraat hobitit." *Portti* 4/2012, pp. 84–87.

Works Consulted

Korpua, Jyrki. 2014. "Good and Evil in J.R.R. Tolkien's Legendarium: Concerning Dichotomy Between Visible and Invisible." *Fafnir—Nordic Journal of Science Fiction and Fantasy Research*, Volume 1, March. http://journal.finfar.org/articles/korpua. Accessed 4 September 2020.
Korpua, Jyrki. 2015. *Constructive Mythopoetics in J.R.R. Tolkien's Legendarium*. Acta Universitatis Ouluensis. Series B, Humaniora 129. Oulu: Oulu University Press.
Korpua, Jyrki. 2016. *Alussa Oli Sana—Raamattu Ja Kirjallisuus*. Helsinki: Avain.
Korpua, Jyrki. 2018. "The Germ of J.R.R. Tolkien's Fantasy: Elements of Kalevala in Tolkien's Fiction." *Transcultural Encounters 2*. Ed. Kari Alenius et al. Rovaniemi: Pohjois-Suomen historiallinen yhdistys, pp. 175–186.
Kumar, Krishan. 1987. *Utopia and Anti-Utopia in Modern Times*. New York: Basil Blackwell.
Laing, Malcolm. 1974. "Preface." *The Poems of Ossian & C: Containing the Poetical Works of James Macpherson, Esq*. Ed. Malcolm Laing. New York: AMS Press.
Landa, Ishay. 2003. "Slaves of the Ring: Tolkien's Political Unconscious." *Historical Materialism*, Vol. 10, No. 4, January. London: Ebsco Publishing, pp. 113–134.
Lazo, Andrew. 2003. "A Kind of Mid-wife: J.R.R. Tolkien and C.S. Lewis—sharing Influence." *Tolkien the Medievalist*. Ed. Jane Chance. New York: Routledge, pp. 36–49.
Lewis, C.S. 1964. *The Discarded Image: An Introduction to Medieval and Renaissance Literature*. Cambridge: Cambridge University Press.
Lewis, C.S. 1967 (1936). *The Allegory of Love: A Study in Medieval Tradition*. London: Oxford University Press.
Lewis, C.S. 1974 (1956). *The Last Battle: A Story for Children*. Harmondsworth: Puffin Books.
Lewis, Sinclair. 1992. *Main Street & Babbitt*. New York: Library of America.
The Lord of the Rings: The Return of the King. 2003. Dir. Peter Jackson. New Line Cinema.
Lovejoy, Arthur O. 1965. *The Great Chain of Being: A Study of the History of an Idea*. New York: Harper & Row.
Lukács, Georg. 1962. *The Historical Novel*. New York: Penguin Books, 1962.
Macpherson, James. 1974. *The Poems of Ossian & C: Containing the Poetical Works of James Macpherson, Esq*. Ed. Malcolm Laing, Esq. New York: AMS Press.
Maher, Michael W. 2003. "'A land without stain': Medieval Images of Mary and Their Use in the Characterization of Galadriel." *Tolkien the Medievalist*. Ed. Jane Chance. New York: Routledge, pp. 225–236.
Manuel, Frank E., and Manuel, Fritzie P. 1979. *Utopian Thought in the Western World*. Oxford: Basill Blackwell.
Martínez Alfaro, María Jésus. 1996. "Intertextuality: Origins and the Development of the Concept." *Atlantis* XVIII (1–2), pp. 268–285.
Mathews, Richard. 2002. *Fantasy: The Liberation of Imagination*. New York: Routledge.
Maxwell, Richard. 2009. *The Historical Novel in Europe, 1650–1950*. Cambridge: Cambridge University Press.
Mäyrä, Frans Ilkka. 1999. *Demonic Texts and Textual Demons: The Demonic Tradition, the Self, and Popular Fiction*. Tampere: Tampere University Press.
Mazzotta, Giuseppe. 2001. *Cosmopoiesis: The Renaissance Experiment*. Toronto: University of Toronto Press.
McGrath, Alister E. 2011. *Christian Theology: An Introduction*. 5th edition. Chichester: Wiley-Blackwell.
McHale, Brian. 1987. *Postmodernist Fiction*. New York: Methuen.
McHale, Brian. 1992. *Constructing Postmodernism*. London: Routledge.
Melberg, Arne. 1995. *Theories of Mimesis*. Cambridge: Cambridge University Press.

Works Consulted

Mendlesohn, Farah. 2008. *Rhetorics of Fantasy*. Middletown: Wesleyan University Press.

Miéville, China. 2009. "There and Back Again: Five Reasons Why Tolkien Rocks." Guest blog in Omnivocarious-site, June 15. http://www.omnivoracious.com/2009/06/there-and-back-again-five-reasons-tolkien-rocks.html. Accessed 4 September 2020.

Moore, Jeff. 2019. "The Best Selling Books of All Time." Ranker.com. https://www.ranker.com/list/best-selling-books-of-all-time/jeff419?ref=found_on&l=2204773. Accessed 4 September 2020.

Možejko, Edward. 1993. "Constructivism." *Encyclopedia of Contemporary Literary Theory: Approaches, Scholars, Terms*. Ed. Irena R. Makaryk. Toronto: University of Toronto Press, 18–20.

Nagy, Gergely. 2003. "The Great Chain of Reading: (Inter-)textual Relations and the Technique of Mythopoesis in the Túrin Story." *Tolkien the Medievalist*. Ed. Jane Chance. New York: Routledge, 239–258.

Nagy, Gergely. 2004. "Saving the Myths: The Re-creation of Mythology in Plato and Tolkien." *Tolkien and the Invention of Myth*. Ed. Jane Chance. Lexington: University Press of Kentucky, pp. 81–100.

Nagy, Gergely. 2005. "The Medievalist('s) Fiction: Textuality and Historicity as Aspects of Tolkien's Medievalist Cultural Theory in a Postmodernist Context." *Tolkien's Modern Middle Ages*. Ed. Jane Chance and Alfred K. Siewers. New York: Palgrave Macmillan, pp. 29–41.

Das Nibelungenlied. 1959. Ed. Helmut de Boor. Leipzig: Dieterich'sche Verlaugsbuchhandlung.

Nitzsche, Jane Chance. 1979. *Tolkien's Art "A Mythology for England."* London: Macmillan.

Noel, Ruth S. 1977. *The Mythology of Middle-earth*. London: Thames and Hudson.

Oksala, Teivas. 1983. *Eino leinon tie paltamosta roomaan*. Helsinki: Suomalaisen Kirjallisuuden Seura.

O'Neill, Timothy R. 2000. "The Individuated Hobbit." *J.R.R. Tolkien: Modern Critical Views*. Ed. Harold Bloom. Philadelphia: Chelsea House Publishers, pp. 83–92.

The Oxford Companion to English Literature. 2000. Ed. Margaret Drabble. 6th edition. Oxford: Oxford University Press.

Paskow, Alan. 2004. *The Paradoxes of Art: A Phenomenological Investigation*. Cambridge: Cambridge University Press.

Pearce, Joseph. 1999. *Tolkien: Man and Myth*. London: HarperCollins.

Plato. 1964a. *The Dialogues of Plato, Volume II: Republic, Gorgias, Parmenides*. Trans. B. Jowett. Fourth Edition. London: Oxford University Press.

Plato. 1964b. *The Dialogues of Plato, Volume III: Cratylus, Phaedrus, Theaetetus, Sophist, Statesman, Philebus, Timaeus, Critias*. Trans. B. Jowett. Fourth Edition. London: Oxford University Press.

Plato. 2007. *Ion, Or, on the Illiad*. Ed. Albert Rijksbaron. Boston: Brill.

Plotinus. 2005. *The Enneads*. Trans. Stephen Mackenna. London: Penguin Books.

Prickett, Stephen. 1979. *Victorian Fantasy*. Hassocks: The Harvester Press, 1979.

Propp, Vladimir. 1968. *Morphology of the Folk Tale*. Trans. Laurence Scott. Austin: The American Folklore Society and Indiana University.

Roberts, Matthew. 1989. "Poetics Hermeneutics Dialogics: Bakhtin and Paul de Man." In Gary Saul Morson and Caryl Emerson (eds.). *Rethinking Bakhtin: Extensions and Challenges*. Evanston: Northwestern University Press, pp. 115–134.

Russell, Ford. 2000 (1998). *Northrop Frye on Myth*. New York: Routledge.

Ruthven, K.K. 1976. *Myth*. London: Methuen & Co.

Rutledge, Fleming. 2004. *The Battle for Middle-Earth: Tolkien's Divine Design in the Lord of the Rings*. Grand Rapids: William B. Eerdmans Publishing Company.

Works Consulted

Ryan, Marie-Laure. 1991. *Possible Worlds, Artificial Intelligence, and Narrative Theory.* Bloomington: Indiana University Press.

Ryan, Marie-Laure. 2005. "Possible-worlds Theory." *Routledge Encyclopedia of Narrative Theory.* Ed. David Herman, Manfred Jahn and Marie-Laure Ryan. London: Routledge, pp. 446–450.

Scholes, Robert, and Kellogg, Robert. 1966. *The Nature of Narrative.* New York: Oxford University Press.

Schulze, Earl J. 1966. *Shelley's Theory of Poetry: A Reappraisal.* The Hague: Mouton & Co., Printers.

Scoville, Chester N. 2005. "Pastoralia and Perfectability in William Morris and J.R.R. Tolkien." *Tolkien's Modern Middle Ages.* Ed. Jane Chance and Alfred K. Siewers. New York: Palgrave Macmillan, pp. 93–103.

Shippey, Tom. 2001. *J.R.R. Tolkien: Author of the Century.* London: HarperCollins.

Shippey, Tom. 2003. *The Road to Middle-earth: How J.R.R. Tolkien Created a New Mythology.* Revised and Expanded Edition. New York: Houghton Mifflin Company.

Shippey, Tom. 2007. *Roots and Branches: Selected Papers on Tolkien by Tom Shippey.* Zollikofen: Walking Tree Publishers.

Sidney, Sir Philip. 1968. *The Prose Works of Sir Philip Sidney, Volume III: The Defence of Poesie, Political Discourses, Correspondence, Translation.* Ed. Albert Feuillerat. London: Cambridge University Press.

Sly, Debbie. 2000. "Weaving Nets of Gloom: 'Darkness Profound' in Tolkien and Milton." *J.R.R. Tolkien and His Literary Resonances: Views of Middle-earth.* Ed. George Clark and Daniel Timmons. Westport: Greenwood, pp. 109–120.

Stanford Encyclopedia of Philosophy. http://plato.stanford.edu/entries/goodman-aesthetics. Accessed 4 September 2020.

Tambling, Jeremy. 2010. *Allegory.* New York: Routledge.

Testi, Claudio A. 2013. "Tolkien's Work: Is It Christian or Pagan? a Proposal for a 'Synthetic' Approach." *Tolkien Studies*, Volume 10, pp. 1–47.

Thompson, Raymond H. 1982. "Modern Fantasy and Medieval Romance: A Comparative Study." *The Aesthetics of Fantasy Literature and Art.* Ed. Roger C. Schlobin. Notre Dame: University of Notre Dame Press and The Harvester Press, pp. 211–225.

Tigerstedt, E.N. 1969. *Plato's Idea of Poetical Inspiration.* Commentationes Humanarum Litterarum. Societas Scientarum Fennica Vol. 44 Nr. 2. 1969. Helsinki: Suomen Tiedeseura.

Timmons, Daniel. 2000. "Introduction." *J.R.R. Tolkien and His Literary Resonances: Views of Middle-earth.* Ed. George Clark and Daniel Timmons. Westport: Greenwood.

Todorov, Tzvetan. 1975. *The Fantastic: A Structural Approach to a Literary Genre.* Ithaca: Cornell University Press.

Tolkien, J.R.R. 1967. *The Road Goes Ever On.* London: George Allen & Unwin.

Tolkien, J.R.R. 1975. *The Hobbit, or There and Back Again.* New edition. London: George Allen & Unwin.

Tolkien, J.R.R. 1981. *The Letters of J.R.R. Tolkien.* Ed. Humphrey Carpenter. London: George Allen & Unwin.

Tolkien, J.R.R. 1983. *The Monsters and the Critics and Other Essays.* Ed. Christopher Tolkien. London: George Allen & Unwin.

Tolkien, J.R.R. 1988. *Tree and Leaf.* London: HarperCollins.

Tolkien, J.R.R. 1992. *Unfinished Tales of Númenor and Middle-earth.* Ed. Christopher Tolkien. London: George Allen & Unwin.

Tolkien, J.R.R. 1994. *The Lays of Beleriand: The History of Middle-earth, Volume III.* Ed. Christopher Tolkien. New York: Ballantine Books.

Works Consulted

Tolkien, J.R.R. 1995. "Foreword to the Second Edition." J.R.R. Tolkien, *The Lord of the Rings*. London: HarperCollins.

Tolkien, J.R.R. 1999. *The Silmarillion*. Ed. Christopher Tolkien. London: HarperCollins.

Tolkien, J.R.R. 2002a. *The Book of Lost Tales, Part I: The History of Middle-earth, Volume 1*. Ed. Christopher Tolkien. London: HarperCollins.

Tolkien, J.R.R. 2002b. *The Shaping of Middle-earth: The History of Middle-earth, Volume 4*. Ed. Christopher Tolkien. London: HarperCollins.

Tolkien, J.R.R. 2002c. *The Lost Road and Other Writings: Language and Legend Before the Lord of the Rings: The History of Middle-earth, Volume 5*. Ed. Christopher Tolkien. London: HarperCollins.

Tolkien, J.R.R. 2002d. *The Return of the Shadow: The History of the Lord of the Rings, Part 1: The History of Middle-earth, Volume 6*. Ed. Christopher Tolkien. London: HarperCollins.

Tolkien, J.R.R. 2002e. *Morgoth's Ring: The Later Silmarillion, Part One: The Legends of Aman: The History of Middle-earth, Volume 10*. Ed. Christopher Tolkien. London: HarperCollins.

Tolkien, J.R.R. 2002f. *The Peoples of Middle-earth: The History of Middle-earth, Volume 12*. Ed. Christopher Tolkien. London: HarperCollins.

Tolkien, J.R.R. 2007. *The Children of Húrin*. Ed. Christopher Tolkien. London: HarperCollins.

Tolkien, J.R.R. 2008. *The Fellowship of the Ring: Being the First Part of the Lord of the Rings*. London: HarperCollins.

Tolkien, J.R.R. 2009a. *The Two Towers: Being the Second Part of the Lord of the Rings*. London: HarperCollins.

Tolkien, J.R.R. 2009b. *The Two Towers: Being the Third Part of the Lord of the Rings*. London: HarperCollins.

Tolkien, J.R.R. 2009c. "Fate and Free Will." Ed. by Carl F. Hostetter. *Tolkien Studies*, Volume 6, pp. 183–188.

Vainio, Olli-Pekka. 2003. "Philomythus Misomythukselle." *Perusta* 3. Kauniainen: Perussanoma Oy, pp. 124–128.

Vice, Sue. 1997. *Introducing Bakhtin*. Manchester: Manchester University Press.

Vlastos, Gregory. 1975. *Plato's Universe*. London: Oxford University Press.

Walton, Kendall L. 1990. *Mimesis and Make-Believe: On the Foundations of the Representational Arts*. Cambridge: Harvard University Press.

Weinreich, Frank. 2008. "Metaphysics of Myth: The Platonic Ontology of 'Mythopoeia.'" *Tolkien's Shorter Works*. Ed. Margaret Hiley and Frank Weinreich. Bern: Walking Tree Publishers, pp. 325–347.

West, Richard C. 1970. "Contemporary Medieval Authors." *Tolkien Journal* no. 11. Madison: The University of Wisconsin J.R.R. Tolkien Society, pp. 9–10.

Whittingham, Elizabeth. 2008. *The Evolution of Tolkien's Mythology: A Study of the History of Middle-earth*. Jefferson: McFarland.

Wisner, Linell B. 2010. *Archaism, or Textual Literalism in the Historical Novel*. Diss. Knoxville: University of Tennessee.

Wolf, Mark J.P. 2012. *Building Imaginary Worlds: The Theory and History of Subcreation*. London: Routledge.

Wolfe, Gary K. 1982. "The Encounter with Fantasy." *The Aesthetics of Fantasy Literature and Art*. Ed. Roger C. Schlobin. Notre Dame: University of Notre Dame Press and The Harvester Press, pp. 1–15.

Wood, Ralph C. 2003. "Conflict and Convergence on Fundamental Matters in C.S. Lewis and J.R.R. Tolkien." *Renascence: Essays on Values in Literature*, Vol. 55, No. 4. Milwaukee: Marguette University, pp. 315–338.

Works Consulted

Wood, Tanya. 2000. "Is Tolkien a Renaissance Man? Sir Philip Sidney's Defence of Poesy and J.R.R. Tolkien's 'On Fairy-Stories.'" *J.R.R. Tolkien and His Literary Resonances: Views of Middle-earth.* Ed. George Clark and Daniel Timmons. Westport: Greenwood, pp. 95–108.

Index

Aaru 106
Achilleus 34
Ælfwine of England 25
Aers, David 125–127, 172
afterlife 101–109, 118, 137
The Ages of the Sun 89, 133, 149, 173; *see also* The First Age; The Second Age; The Third Age
"Ainulindalë" 14, 25, 37, 57, 60, 62, 134–135
Ajax 34
"Akallabêth" 14, 57, 81, 149, 153–154
Aladdin 162
Albert Magnus 82
Alice in Wonderland 123
allegory 5, 12, 21, 30, 39, 49, 106, 108, 111, 121, 122–135, 159, 172
Allegory of the Cave *see* Simile of the Cave
Almaren 78
Aman 25, 55, 79; *see also* Valinor
Amasis 160
Anárion 142
Anatomy of Criticism 16, 47, 50, 56, 167
Ancalagon the Black 137
Andromeda 172
Andreth 86, 133, 172
Anduin 53, 56
Angband 79
Anglo-Saxon mythology 169, 173; *see also* English mythology
Ankeny, Rebecca 168
"Annals of Aman and Beleriand" 25
apocalypse 7, 13–14, 51–55, 79, 118, 121, 165
Apollo 138
An Apology for Poetry see *The Defence of Poesie*
Aquarius 172
Aquila 172

Aragorn 27, 35, 51–52, 54, 70, 74, 76–77, 101, 108–109, 123–124, 132–133, 154, 169, 172
Aramis 34
Arcadia 42
archetype 3, 36, 50–56, 73, 99
Arda 1, 8, 14–15, 58–60, 66, 77–81, 84–89, 121, 132–134, 164–165, 168, 172
Argo 172
Argonauts 172
Aristotle 30–31, 63, 82–83, 94, 101, 103
Arnor 52, 149
Arthur, King of the British: character 21, 106, 147; adaptations 21, 42, 44; Arthur's departure 147–148; mythology 21, 106, 111, 138
Arwen 108–109, 141, 169
Ashbaugh, Anne Freire 85
Aslan 106, 132
Athos 34
Atlantis 5–6, 8, 34, 94, 104, 132, 141–142, 148–153
Attebery, Brian 4
Augustine of Hippo 2, 87
Aulë 59, 88–89
Avalon 106
Awntyrs off Arthure 44
Azog 170

Bacon, Francis 150
Baggins, Bilbo 22–24, 27, 68, 73, 112, 120, 131, 135–136, 154–155, 157, 164, 170
Baggins, Frodo 19, 23, 27, 46, 49, 51–52, 72–77, 89–90, 103, 106–107, 120, 131–132, 135–136, 139, 141, 154, 157, 163, 169–170, 172
Bakhtin, Mikhail 26–28
Baldr 111, 138

Index

Balrog 53, 55, 70–71, 74, 132
Barad-dûr 173
Barfield, Owen 11–12, 92, 96–97, 102, 110, 112
Barthes, Roland 92–93
The Battle for Middle-earth. Tolkien's Divine Design in The Lord of the Rings 134
Battle of Camlann 106
Beleg 38, 144
Beleriand 25, 81, 173
Benardete, Seth 41
Beowulf 9–11, 139, 143, 145
"Beowulf: The Monsters and the Critics" 10
Beren 35, 136, 145–147
The Bible 5, 14, 24, 37, 41, 49, 52, 62, 64–65, 125–127, 130–131, 135, 138–141, 172
Bilbo; Bilbo Baggins *see* Baggins, Bilbo
Bilbo's Last Song 164
Biographia Literaria 5, 94, 96, 99
The Black Book of Carmarthen 23
Black Númenoreans 173; *see also* Faithful Men; Númenor
Black Riders *see* Nazgûl
Black sword *see* Gurthang
Blake, William 9
Bloom, Harold 41, 168
Boethius 15, 65, 68–69
Bolg 170
Bombadil, Tom 48–49, 75, 107, 128, 169
The Book of Aneirin 23
"The Book of Chronicles" 41
"The Book of Exodus" 49
The Book of Lost Tales 35, 84
"The Book of Revelation" 139, 172
The Book of Taliesin 23
Border Ballads 30
Boromir 27, 108, 132, 169
The Bow and the Lyre: A Platonic Reading of the Odyssey 41
Bratt, Edith 43
Bree 53
Bregolas 172
Brljak, Vladimir 167
Brooke-Rose, Christine 168
Brothers Grimm *see* Grimm, Jacob; Grimm, Wilhelm
Brunhild 162
Brynhildr *see* Brunhild
Bulgaria 169
Burgess, Anthony 35

Calaquendi *see* High Elves
The Cambridge Companion to Utopian Literature 150
Campanella, Tomaso 150
Campbell, John Francis 39
Campbell, Joseph 169
Carey, John 150
Carpenter, Humphrey 17, 21, 31, 43, 88, 92, 110–112, 125–126, 142–143
Carroll, Lewis 9, 48, 123
Carter, Lin 8, 42, 47, 99, 171
Cassiopeia 172
Celeborn 117
Celtic mythology 20, 79
chain of being 82–90, 168
Chalcidus 86
Chance, Jane 9–10, 167
Chandler, Daniel 93, 167
Charmides 86
Chatterton, Thomas 28–30; *see also* Rowley, Thomas
Chaucer, Geoffrey 65
Cherubim 53
The Children of Húrin 28, 36–37, 42–43, 143
Chuch Fathers 2; *see also* Augustine of Hippo; Origen of Alexandria; St. Jerome
Cicero 159
Cilli, Orozo 62
La Citta del Sole see The City of the Sun
The City of the Sun 150
Clayes, Gregory 150
Clifford, Gay 127–128
A Clockwork Orange 35
Clute, John 23
Coalbiters *see* Kolbítar
Cole, G.D.H. 43
Coleridge, Samuel Taylor 5, 12, 94–99, 122–124
Conan-series 4
constructive poetics 4–6, 18, 39, 100
constructivism 167, 169
Coulter, James A. 1, 125
Council of Elrond 26–27, 75, 117, 120, 162; *see also* Elrond
"Counting of Years" 25
Cratylus 51
Critias 34, 149–152
Cuiviénen 53, 79

Dahl, Roald 123
Dáin I Ironfoot 170

186

Index

Dante 41, 56, 65, 130
Darwin, Charles 9
Dasent, Sir George 20
De Anima 101
De Animalibus 82
De Docta ignorantia see *On Learned Ignorance*
De instituione musica 15
De Officiis 159
De Oratore 124
The Defence of Poesie 5, 94, 167
De Man, Paul 27–28
Demiurge 64, 83, 85, 91; *see also* Prime Mover
Denethor 52–54, 1051–106, 129
Denham, Robert D. 52–53
Denis the Carthusian 127
De Saint-Exupéry, Antoine 123
de Troyes, Chrétien 42
Diderot, Dennis 32
Dillon, John 101, 114–115
Dionysus 111
Dior 146
Discworld series 173
The Divine Comedy 41, 56
Doctorow, Cory 168
Dol Guldur 171
Doležel, Lubomír 5, 19
Don Quixote 169
Dracula 45
Drout, Michael 11
DuBois, Nancy 37
Dumas, Alexander père 33–34, 162
Dúnedain *see* Faithful Men
Dunharrow 77
Dunsany, Lord 41–42
dwarves 71, 88–90, 114–115, 120, 130, 136, 155 170

Eärendil 15, 137–138, 146–147, 152, 172
Earthsea series 172
Eco, Umberto 20, 33–34, 62–63, 66, 69
Edda(s) 80, 106, 162, 171
Eddison, E.R. 42
Eden, Bradford Lee 15, 115, 172
Egypt 2, 34, 153
Eldar *see* High Elves
Elendil 142, 154
Elendili *see* Faithful Men
Elrond 26–27, 76, 117–118, 120–121, 128, 145, 162; *see also* Council of Elrond
Elros 152, 172
Elwe Thingol 152
Elwing 146
Elysium 106
Emmaus 133
The Encyclopedia of Science Fiction 23
England 8, 10, 17, 20–21, 25, 32, 36, 109–110, 142
English mythology 11, 17, 20–21, 44, 79; *see also* Anglo-Saxon mythology
The Enneads 2, 82, 101
Éomer 169
Éowyn 75, 154
Eriador 89
Eriol *see* Ælfwine of England
Eriugene, John Scotus 69
Eru 2, 13–15, 37, 51–52, 57–69, 72, 79, 83–89, 97, 115, 133–134, 139, 141, 148–149, 153
eschatology 118–119, 133
Esty, Jed 9, 109–110
eucatastrophe 59, 109, 117, 119, 121, 126, 131, 165, 170
Evans, Jonathan 168
Evil 4, 7–8, 14, 50, 55, 57–59, 62–64, 70, 73–75, 79, 118, 121, 129, 131–133, 139–143, 147, 151, 158, 163, 170, 173
Explorations in Poetics 18

Faërie 79, 91
The Faerie Queene 41, 122
Fairbairns 23
fairy-stories 33, 54, 156, 169
Faithful Men 81–82, 131, 133, 141–142, 149, 152, 172; *see also* Númenor
The Fall of Arthur 21
The Fantastic: A Structural Approach to a Literary Genre 169
fantasy (as a genre) 3–4, 45–47, 148; *see also* fantasy novel; genre
fantasy novel 4, 11, 41; *see also* fantasy (as a genre); novel
Fantasy: The Liberation of Imagination 41
Faramir 105–106, 154
Farmer Giles of Ham 168
The Father Christmas Letters 168
Fëanor 80–81, 141, 145–147, 172
Ficino, Marsilio 2, 66
Field of Cormallen 170
Fimi, Dimitra viii, 12, 167–168
Finarfin 172

Index

Finder, Jan Howard vii
Finnish mythology 5, 17, 20–21, 138, 142, 169, 171
Finrod 85–86, 116, 133–134
Finwë 80, 141, 147, 172
Fionwë 118
The First Age (of the Sun) 78, 81, 133, 140, 149, 173; *see also* The Ages of the Sun
Flame Imperishable *see* Imperishable Flame
Flaubert, Gustave 162
Flieger, Verlyn viii, 9–11, 15, 17, 21–23, 30, 40, 65–66, 68, 83, 110, 112–113, 136, 142, 145, 169, 171–172
Ford, Patrick 169
Forster, L.W. 43–44
Foucault, Michel 19
France 32, 44
Freud, Sigmund 9
Frodo; Frodo Baggins *see* Baggins, Frodo
Frye, Northrop 4, 7–9, 16, 24, 28, 34–37, 40, 42–43, 47–56, 63–64, 91, 119–120, 128, 139, 161, 167–168, 170

Galadriel 52–53, 56, 70, 74, 107, 117, 121, 133, 141, 171–172
Galdor 27
Galen 63
Gamble, Nikki 99
Gamgee, Sam 23, 35–36, 56, 76, 131–132, 136, 154, 163, 169–170
Gandalf 27, 38, 48, 51–56, 70–78, 105–107, 111, 115–116, 120, 123, 129, 132–133, 136, 139–141, 154–155, 162, 169–170
Ganymedes 172
Gantz, Jeffrey 169
Gasque, Thomas J. 36
Gautier, Théophile 159
Genesis 62, 65, 127, 135, 139
Genette, Gérard 19
genre 3–4, 6, 10–11, 16, 19–20, 28, 33, 36–56, 118, 136, 148, 150, 168–169; *see also* fantasy (as a genre)
Saint George 138
Geppert, Hals Vilmar 35
German(ic) mythology 5, 17, 20–21, 125, 139, 142, 156
Giant Spiders 52, 54
Gide, André 159
Gil-Estel 137
Gimlé 106

Gimli 74, 111, 133, 169
Glaurung 37–38, 143
Glóin 26–27
Glorfindel 27, 52, 54, 76–77, 162
goblins 120, 136, 155, 170; *see also* orcs
Godard, Barbara 19
Goethe, Johann Wolfgang 32
Goldberry 49
Golden Fleece 172
golem 171
Gollum 68, 90, 121, 131, 157, 169
Gondolin 25, 117, 152, 173
Gondor 27, 52–55, 105, 129–131, 141–142, 149, 154, 170
Good 4, 7–8, 14, 50, 55, 59, 6, 62–64, 70, 73, 120–121, 128, 131–132, 155, 158
Goodman, Nelson 171
Gorthaur the Cruel *see* Sauron
Gospel of Saint John 113
Götz von Berlichingen 32
The Great Code. The Bible and Literature 37
Great Eagles 52, 54, 120, 137, 170
The Great Ring 7–8, 27, 71–76, 89–90, 120–121, 131–132, 136, 141, 148, 154–163, 170; *see also* ring motif; Ring of Gyges; Ring of Polycrates
The Great War *see* World War I
Greek mythology 17, 20, 34, 72, 106, 128, 138, 151–152, 171–172
Grima 75
Grimm, Jacob 28, 30, 39
Grimm, Wilhelm 28, 30, 39
Gurthang 38, 118, 144

Hades 72, 171
The Halls of Mandos 87, 108, 118
harmony 50, 59, 62–63, 65–66, 85–86, 97, 113
Harrison, M. John 46
Harshav, Benjamin 4–6, 18–19
Hastings, Peter 49, 171
Hebbel, Friedrich 159
Hecateus the historian 153
Hel 171
Helms, Randel 72
Heninger, S.K., Jr. 91
Heraclitus 72, 104
The Heralds of Valdemar series 173
The Hero with Thousand Faces 169
Herodotus 30, 153, 159–162
Hesiod 106, 151

Index

heteroglossia 26–28
Higgins, Melissa 11
High Elves 75–77, 80–82, 148, 170; *see also* Noldor; Teleri; Vanyar
high fantasy 11, 16, 28, 99, 136, 163
Historia Animalium 82
The Historical Novel (book) 32
historical novel (genre) 6, 9, 20, 31–35, 162; *see also* novel
The History (by Herodotus) 160
History and Antiquities of Bristol 29
The History of the Middle-earth 8, 12, 14–15, 22, 25, 35, 45, 71, 77, 104, 133, 145, 149
Hobbiton 135; *see also* The Shire
Holmes, John R. 169
Homer 41
The House of Bëor 133, 172
The House of Finwë 141
The House of the Wolfings 44
Howard, Robert E. 42
Hrushovski, Benjamin *see* Harshav, Benjamin
Huan 52, 54
Hume, David 150
Hunter, John 15
Húrin 36, 118, 143, 172
Hutcheon, Linda 92

The Idea of a Perfect Commonwealth 150
Idril 152
Iliad 15, 41
Illuin 78; *see also* The Lamps of Valinor
Ilmarinen 145
Ilmatar 148
Ilúvatar *see* Eru
Imperishable Fire *see* Imperishable Flame
Imperishable Flame 53, 55, 58, 67
Indis 172
The Inklings (book) 126
The Inklings (literary group) 3, 102, 106, 109–116, 126
Interrupted Music: The Making of Tolkien's Mythology 11
intertextuality 4, 12, 19–20, 26, 62, 93, 121, 138, 147–148, 150, 159–160, 164, 167–168, 172–173; *see also* intratextuality
intratextuality 4–6, 12, 18–19, 22–23, 26, 35–36, 56, 90, 133, 138, 145, 162–164, 167, 172; *see also* intertextuality
Introduction à la littérature fantastique *see* *The Fantastic: A Structural Approach to a Literary Genre*
The Invisible Man 156
Ion 31
Ireland 25
Irmo 170
Isengard 50, 52, 54, 123
Ishtar 111
Isildur 27, 142
Islandia 23
Istari 38, 73, 120, 133, 136, 139–140, 154
Ivanhoe 35

Jackson, Peter 107
Jackson, Rosemary 96
James and the Giant Peach 123
Jason 138
St. Jerome 24
Jerusalem 53
Johnson, Samuel 29, 169
Jones, Gwynn 169
Jones, Thomas 169
Joseph 34
A Journey to the Western Islands of Scotland 169
Jowett, B. 86, 173
Joyce, James 9, 35
J.R.R. Tolkien: Author of the Century 11
J.R.R. Tolkien Encyclopedia. Scholarship and Critical Assessment 11
Judas Iscariot 132

Kalevala 5, 15, 17, 30, 43, 69, 116, 138, 142–148, 169, 171–173
Kay, Guy Gavriel viii
Kellogg, Robert 39, 167
Kerry, Paul E. 172
Khazad-Dûm *see* Moria
King Arthur *see* Arthur, King of the British
The King of the Elflands's Daughter 42
Kipling, Rudyard 41
Kocher, Paul 68, 74–75, 85, 102, 168
Kolbítar 110
Kristeva, Julia 169
Kullervo 43, 138, 142–145
Kumar, Krishan 150–151

Lackey, Mercedes 173
Lafontaine, Jean de 159
Laing, Malcolm 29
Laketown 53

Index

Lalaith 36
Lampe, G.W.H. 127
The Lamps of Valinor 78–79, 81; see also Illuin; Ormal
Landino, Christophoro 91
Languages of Art: An Approach to a Theory of Symbols and Ways of Worldmaking 171
The Last Battle (concept) 15, 118, 145, 168, 172
The Last Battle (book) 106, 123; see also Narnia series
Laurelin 79; see also The Trees of Valinor
Le Guin, Ursula K. 172
Le Roi Candaule (drama) 159
"Le Roi Candaule" (short story) 159
Le Roi Candaule et me maître en droit 159
"Leaf by Niggle" 92, 122
Lean, Edward Tangya 110
Legolas 74, 77, 133, 169
Lessing, Gotthold Ephraim 32
The Letters of J.R.R. Tolkien 43; see also letters written by J.R.R. Tolkien
letters written by J.R.R. Tolkien 17, 20, 39, 41, 43–44, 49, 64, 67, 69, 82, 99, 104, 109, 119, 125, 128, 130, 141–142, 161, 171; see also *The Letters of J.R.R. Tolkien*
Lévi-Strauss, Claude 93
Lewis, C.S. 3, 41, 68–69, 83–87, 92, 102–106, 110–112, 122–123, 125, 132, 153, 171
Lewis, Matthew Gregory 42
The Little Prince 123
Locus amoenus (mythical place) 52, 106
long defeat 14, 117–122
Lönnrot, Elias 28, 30, 39, 169
The Lord of the Rings: The Return of the King (movie) 107
Lórien 53, 55, 70, 73, 117, 141, 170–171
The Lost Road (concept) 53, 55
"The Lost Road" (story) 103
Lothlórien see Lórien
Lovejoy, Arthur O. 83
Lukács, Georg 20, 32–33
Luonnotar see Ilmatar
Lúthien 35, 116, 136, 145–147, 152
Lyrical Ballads 99

The Mabinogion 23, 169
Macbeth 173
MacDonald, George 9, 41, 123
Macpherson, James 9, 28–30

Macrobius 153
Maedhros 146–147; see also Sons of Fëanor
Maglor 146–147; see also Sons of Fëanor
Maher, Michael W. 172
The Man and the Beasts see *De Animalibus*
Mandos 80, 87, 108, 118
Manwë 58–59, 61, 73, 80–81, 140, 153
Martínez Alfaro, María Jésus 168–169
Marx, Karl 9, 32
Mary, mother of Jesus 141, 172
Mathews, Richard 29, 41, 171
Maxwell, Richard 31–33, 162
Mäyrä, Frans Ilkka 165
Mazzotta, Giuseppe 66, 91
McGrath, Alister E. 62, 109, 118
Melian 146, 152
Melkor see Morgoth
Mendlesohn, Farah 45–47, 103
Meriadoc Brandybuck see Merry
Merry 72, 76, 90
Miéville, China 168
Milton, John 9, 41, 52, 129
Mimesis as Make-Believe: On the Foundations of the Representational Arts 171
Minas Tirith 24, 53, 55, 105, 154
Míriel 172
Mirkwood 53, 55, 77
Mitchison, Naomi 49
Mithrandir see Gandalf
Moby Dick 53
Modern Critical View: J.R.R. Tolkien 168
modernism 9, 50; see also postmodernism
The Monk 42
Moore, Jeff 11
Mordor 27, 36, 53–55, 70, 141, 160, 170, 172
More, Thomas 150
Morgoth 15, 38, 49, 52, 54, 57–61, 63, 66–67, 70–71, 77–82, 86, 116–118, 131, 133, 137, 139, 143, 146–147, 149, 170
Morgoth's Ring 77, 117, 133, 168
Moria 26, 55, 70–71, 111, 115, 130, 140
The Morphology of the Folk Tale 169
Morris, William 9, 35, 42–44
Mount Doom 89–90, 131, 163
Mouth of Sauron 173
Murray, Robert 109, 119
Music of the Ainur 8, 13–17, 57–63, 65, 87, 97, 172
Myth and Metaphor 167
"Mythopoeia" (poem) 16

Index

"Die Nacket Königin aus Lydia" 159
Nagy, Gergely 3, 10, 13
The Name of Rose 20, 34
names 19, 25, 36, 49, 54, 83, 169; of the Creator 13, 83, 148; of Dwarves 114; of Elves 114; of Ents 113; of Hobbits 113; of Númenoreans 108; of Rohirrim 28; power of names 109–116
Napoleon 32
Narnia series 106, 111, 122, 125, 132; see also *The Last Battle*
The Nature of Narrative 167
Nazgûl 71–72, 74–77, 155, 158; see also Witch King of Angmar
The New Atlantis 150
"The New Shadow" 45
New Testament 14
New Weird 168
Das Nibelungenlied 125, 162
Nicolas of Cusa 82
Nicolaus of Damascus 159
Nietzsche, Friedrich 9
The Night Angel series 173
Nile Delta 106
Nilfheim 171
The Nine see Nazgûl
Noah 141–142
Noel, Ruth S. x
Noldor 80–81, 172; see also High Elves; Noldor; Teleri
Il nome della rosa see *The Name of Rose*
Norse mythology see Scandinavian mythology
novel 4, 6, 9, 20, 26–28, 32–35, 41–42, 44, 150, 169; see also fantasy novel; historical novel; science fiction novel
Númenor 8, 49, 52–55, 57, 69, 73, 81–82, 84–85, 104–105, 108–109, 130–132, 140–142, 149–154, 170, 173; see also Black Númenoreans; Faithful Men

Odyssey 41
Oedipus 138, 143–145
"Of the Rings of Power and the Third Age" 57, 82, 89
"Of Túrin Turambar" 35, 105, 142
The One Ring see The Great Ring
Oksala, Teivas 159
Old Forest 53, 55
Old Testament 14, 24, 135, 140
Olórin see Gandalf

On Animals see *De Animalibus*
"On Fairy-Stories" 5, 39, 73, 91–95, 98, 100, 113, 128
On Learned Ignorance 82
The Once and Future King 44
Orcs 50, 115, 124, 129, 157, 170; see also goblins
Origen of Alexandria 2, 87, 125
Ormal 78; see also The Lamps of Valinor
Orodruin see Mount Doom
Oromë 54
The Oxford Companion to English Literature 3
Oxford University 3, 15, 109–110

palantír 169–170
The Palm-Wine Drinkard 35
Panza, Sancho 169
Paradise Lost 41, 129
The Paradoxes of Art: A Phenomenological Investigation 171
Paskow, Alan 171
Pearce, Joseph 40
Pearl 9, 122
Pêcheux, Michel 19
Pengoloð the Sage 25
Peregrin Took see Pippin
Phaedo 104
Phaedrus 86
Philo 125
Philodemus of Gadara 124–125
Piers Plowman and Christian Allegory 125
Pippin 76, 90, 106–107, 170
Plotinus 1–2, 66, 82, 101
Plutarch 106, 159
The Poems of Ossian 29, 169
Poetic Diction 97, 112
Poetics (by Aristotle) 30–31
Pohjola 146
Polyclitus 63
Polycrates 160–162
Porthos 34
postmodernism, 10–11, 92, 167; see also modernism
post-structuralism 92
Pratchett, Terry 173
The pre–Raphaelites 9
Prickett, Stephen 96
primary world 4, 98, 100, 139; see also sub-creating; sub-creator
Prime Mover 83–84; see also Demiurge

Index

Princess and the Goblin 123
Prometheus 53
Propp, Vladimir 169
Puluclitus 63
Pythagoras 63, 97, 173

Quennar Onótimo 25
"Quenta Silmarillion" 14, 57, 78, 81, 121, 137, 146–147, 152
A Question of Time: J.R.R. Tolkien's Road to Faerie 11
The Quran 172

Radagast 27
Ragnarök 118, 172
Rauros 53
realism 15–16, 18, 29, 32–34, 48, 51–56, 60, 95, 99–100
The Red Book of Hergest 23
The Red Book of Westmarch 22–25
The Republic 6, 30–31, 51, 82, 95, 100, 104, 150, 156–159
The Return of the Shadow 75, 121
A Rhetoric of the Unreal: Studies in Narrative and Structure, Especially the Fantastic 168
Rhetorics of Fantasy 45–47
Riders of Rohan 15, 26, 28
The Ring and the Cross: Christianity and The Lord of the Rings 172
Der Ring des Nibelungen 161
Ring motif 5, 117, 154–163; *see also* The Great Ring; Ring of Gyges; Ring of Polycrates
Ring of Gyges 6, 162; *see also* The Great Ring; ring motif; Ring of Polycrates
Ring of Polycrates 160–162; *see also* The Great Ring; ring motif; Ring of Gyges
Ringwraiths *see* Nazgûl
The Road Goes Ever On (book) 85
"The Road Goes Ever On" (poem) 166
The Road to Middle-earth: How J.R.R. Tolkien Created a New Mythology 11, 135
Roberts, Matthew 28
Rohan 15, 26, 124, 130
Rohirrim *see* Riders of Rohan
role-playing games 4
Roman mythology 17, 20–21, 104, 106
romance 16, 28, 35, 41–48, 52, 54–55, 110, 169
Romances of Alexander 44

romanticism 35, 51–56, 108, 136, 149, 169; romantic fairy-tale 16, 45; Romantic period 95, 99, 159
The Roots of the Mountains 44
Rosebudy, Brian 135
Rowley, Thomas 29; *see also* Chatterton, Thomas
Rúmil of Tuna 25
Russell, Ford 167
Rutledge, Fleming 134

Sach, Hans 159
Sam; Sam Gamgee *see* Gamgee, Sam
Samos 160
Sampo 145–147, 173
Saruman 27, 38, 50, 54, 74–75, 124, 128–129, 131, 133, 136, 140
Sauron 15, 27, 48–49, 70–75, 78, 82, 89, 116, 139–142, 149, 153–155, 158, 163, 169–171, 173
scala naturæ *see* chain of being
Scandinavian mythology 5, 17, 20–21, 80, 111–112, 118, 128, 139, 142, 156, 171–172
Scholes, Robert 39, 167
Schulze, Earl J. 95
science fiction 23, 42–43, 46, 110–111
science fiction novel 111; *see also* novel
Scott, Walter 9, 20, 30–32, 35, 41
Scoville, Chester N. 27
The Second Age (of the Sun) 81–82, 149, 154, 163, 170; *see also* The Ages of the Sun
Second World War *see* World War II
secondary world 18, 21, 23, 32–33, 46, 91, 94–98, 103, 113, 123, 134; *see also* sub-creating; sub-creator
The Secular Scripture 167
"Septuagint" 24
Seraphim 53
Shakespeare, William 173
The Shaping of Middle-earth 168
Shelley, Mary 9
Shelley, Percy Bysshe 95
Shippey, Tom viii, 9–11, 23, 28, 30, 41–42, 44, 48–50, 70, 122, 129–130, 135, 147, 161, 168–170, 172–173
The Shire 32, 47, 52, 54–55, 120, 131, 135–136; *see also* Hobbiton
Sidney, Sir Philip 5, 94–95, 167
Siegfried 162
Siewers, Alfred K. 9–10
Sigurd 138, 143–144

Index

Silmarils 53, 56–57, 78, 80–81, 145–147, 171, 173
Simile of the Cave 159
Sindar 54, 173
Sir Gawain and the Green Knight 9
Sly, Debbie 41
Smaug 112, 120
Smith of the Wootton Major 168
Socrates 62, 92, 104, 173
Solon 34, 94
The Song of the Ainur *see* The Music of the Ainur
The Sons of Elendil 154
The Sons of Fëanor 146–147; *see also* Maedhros; Maglor
Sophist 51, 101
Sophocles 143
speculative fiction 25–26, 29–31, 33
Spenser, Edmund 9, 41, 122
Splintered Light: Logos and Language in Tolkien's World 11
Stanford Encyclopedia of Philosophy 171
Stevenson, Robert Louis 41
Stoker, Bram 45
"The Story of Kullervo" 43, 142
sub-creator; sub-creating 1, 4–5, 20, 40, 64, 90–91, 98, 100, 112–113, 164
suicide 104–106, 143–145
Swift, Jonathan 32
Szentmihaly, Peter Szabo 41, 99

"Tale of Years" 25
Tambling, Jeremy 124, 128, 130
Têlecles 161
Teleri 80; *see also* High Elves; Noldor; Vanyar
Telperion 79; *see also* The Trees of Valinor
Tennyson, Alfred Lord 9
Thames 53
Thangorodrim 137
Thebes 153
Théoden 123–124, 161
Theodore, son of Têlecles 161
The Third Age (of the Sun) 19, 36, 55, 57, 82, 89, 141, 154, 170, 172; *see also* The Ages of the Sun
Thompson, Raymond H. 44
Thorondor 137
Thórr 128
Thranduil 77
The Three Musketeers 33–34, 162

Tigerstedt, E.N. 91
Timaeus 6, 34, 62, 64–67, 82, 84, 86, 91–92, 149–153, 173
The Timeless Halls 57, 59–60, 67, 69, 84, 137
Timmons, Daniel 138
Todorov, Tzvetan 46, 169
Tol Eressëa 25
Tolkien, Christopher 7, 12, 24, 28, 42, 45, 149, 168
Tolkien, Edith *see* Bratt, Edith
Tolkien Encyclopedia: Scholarship and Critical Assessment 11
Tolkien's Library. An Annotated Checklist 62
Tolkien's Modern Middle Ages 9
Tom Bombadil *see* Bombadil, Tom
Treebeard 50, 90, 113, 129
The Trees of Valinor 53, 55, 79, 171; *see also* Laurelin; Telperion
Les Trois Mousquataires see *The Three Musketeers*
Tulkas 118
Tuonela 171
Tuor 172
"Turambar and the Foalóke" 35
Túrin Turambar 35–38, 43, 105, 118, 130, 138, 142–145, 167, 172
Two Trees *see* The Trees of Valinor

Udûn 70; *see also* Utumno
Ulmo 53, 55, 59
Ulysses 35
Undying Lands *see* Valinor
The Unfinished Tales 35, 73, 140, 149, 170
Ungoliant 52, 54, 80–81
Urwen *see* Lalaith
Utopia (book) 150
Utopia (mythical place) 149–150
Utopia literature 106, 149–151
Utumno 79

Väinämöinen 69, 116, 146–148
Vainio, Olli-Pekka 172
"Valaquenta" 14, 37, 57, 78
Valaraukar *see* Balrog
Valinor 51, 53, 55, 69, 73, 75, 77, 79–81, 84, 107, 114, 118, 131, 136–137, 140–141, 146–147, 152–153, 170, 172; *see also* Aman
Vanyar 80; *see also* High Elves; Noldor; Teleri

Index

Varda 79
Vice, Sue 26–28
Vico, Giambattista 37
video games 4
Vingilot 137, 146
Virgil 106
Virgin Mary *see* Mary, mother of Jesus
Vlastos, Gregory 64
Volsunga Saga 138, 162
Voltaire 32
Völuspá 106
"The Voyage of Eärendel" 15
"Vulgate" 24

Wagner, Richard 9, 125, 161
Waldman, Milton 17, 20, 39, 64, 67, 69, 82, 128, 142
Walton, Kendall L. 171–172
Watcher in the Water 53, 55
Weeks, Brent 173
Weinreich, Frank 3
Wells, H.G. 156
West, Richard C. 41
What Coleridge Thought 97

White, T.H. 41, 44
The White Book of Rhydderch 23
Whittingham, Elizabeth viii, 17, 22, 40, 66, 119, 135, 172
Williams, Charles 3, 110–112
Wisner, Linell B. 167
Witch King of Angmar 74; *see also* Nazgûl
The Wizards *see* Istari
Wolf, Mark J.P. viii, 3, 7, 12, 98
Wolfe, Gary K. 98–99
Wood, Ralph C. 103, 132
Wood, Tanya 94
World War I 21, 44
World War II 44, 123
Works and Days 151
The Worm Ouroboros 42
Wright, Austin Tappan 23
Wynne, Hilary 11

Yates, Sally 99
Yavanna 79

Zeus 149, 152

www.ingramcontent.com/pod-product-compliance
Ingram Content Group UK Ltd.
Pitfield, Milton Keynes, MK11 3LW, UK
UKHW042010140426
5217IPUK00015B/1088